Michaela Judy & Wolfgang Knopf (Ed.)

In the Mirror of Competences
Im Spiegel der Kompetenzen

Supervision and Coaching in Europe
Supervision und Coaching in Europa

Concepts and Competences
Konzepte und Kompetenzen

D1728775

„Band 4 der Reihe „Supervision – Coaching – Organisationsberatung"
der ÖVS – Österreichische Vereinigung für Supervision und Coaching
des bso – Berufsverband für Coaching, Supervision und Organisationsberatung Schweiz
der DGSv – Deutsche Gesellschaft für Supervision

in Kooperation mit ANSE – Association of National Organisation for
Supervision in Europe (Vienna) und EUROCADRES – Council of European
Professional and Managerial Staff (Brussels)

Bibliografische Information Der Deutschen Nationalbibliothek

Die Deutsche Nationalbibliothek verzeichnet diese Publikation in der
Deutschen Nationalbibliografie; detaillierte bibliografische Daten sind im Internet über
http://dnb.d-nb.de abrufbar.
Alle Angaben in diesem Fachbuch erfolgen trotz sorgfältiger Bearbeitung ohne Gewähr,
eine Haftung der Herausgeber, der Autoren oder des Verlages ist ausgeschlossen.
Alle Rechte, insbesondere das Recht der Vervielfältigung und der Verbreitung sowie der
Übersetzung, sind vorbehalten.

1. Auflage 2016
Copyright © 2016 Facultas Verlags- und Buchhandels AG
Facultas Universitätsverlag, 1050 Wien, Österreich
Übersetzung aus dem Englischen: Michaela Judy
Korrektorat: Sabine Sauerzapf
Satz: Wandl Multimedia
Covergestaltung: Norbert Novak, Wien
Druck: finidr
Printed in the E.U.
ISBN 978-3-7089-1480-0

Michaela Judy & Wolfgang Knopf (Ed.)

In the Mirror of Competences
Im Spiegel der Kompetenzen

Supervision and Coaching in Europe
Supervision und Coaching in Europa

Concepts and Competences
Konzepte und Kompetenzen

facultas

Content Overview

Inhaltsverzeichnis

**ECVision. A European Competence Framework
of Supervision and Coaching** 184
*Marina Ajdukovic, Lilja Cajvert, Michaela Judy, Wolfgang Knopf,
Hubert Kuhn, Krisztina Madai, Mieke Voogd*

**Validating Competences. The ECVision Reference Table
ECTS-ECVET** 224
Marina Ajdukovic, Lilja Cajvert, Michaela Judy, Hubert Kuhn

**An Overview of Supervision and Coaching in Austria,
Croatia, Germany, Hungary, Sweden, The Netherlands
and Europe** 258
*Wolfgang Knopf, Marina Ajdukovic, Hubert Kuhn, Krisztina Madal,
Mieke Voogd, Lilja Cajvert*

ECVision. Ein Europäisches Kompetenzprofil für Supervision und Coaching

Introduction and Enforcement

Sijtze de Roos
Martin Jefflén
Michaela Judy

Vorworte und Einführung

Sijtze de Roos

Martin Jefflén

Michaela Judy

Foreword of the editors

The present Volume 4 is part of the series "Supervision – Coaching – Organisational Consulting" that has been published since 2009 by professional associations in German-speaking countries, and provides a further contribution to the professionalisation of these counselling formats.

Professionalisation is based on comprehensible and structured procedures and processes, standardised training and continuous development within the framework of professional organisations and associations.

In the last twenty years these developments were characterised by rapid changes in the work environment and an increased acceptance of supervision and coaching as supportive and accompanying measures, as well as by rapid changes of the comprehension of concepts in this process.

The comparability of the increasing scientific research on effectiveness and efficiency turned out to be difficult, due to the fact that a requisite common basis – for the purpose of clarifying the varying applied conceptual frameworks – was only marginally present. In particular, it lacked the European context; language and national developments defined the respective concepts and their use.

The autonomous theoretical conceptualisation of supervision and its practical dissemination as well as education emanated initially mainly from institutions in the German-speaking countries and the Netherlands. Via "coaching" the concepts from the Anglo-American world gained increasing importance – especially in the non-German speaking countries – where university departments in particular began to get involved in this field of research.

Thus began a long-overlooked – yet alarming – development: The international language of science is English. The possibilities to integrate findings from German-speaking countries in a common European development of theory and practice, failed due to the lack of existing English translations.

This mutual European development and professional policy is the goal of ANSE (Association of National Organisations for Supervision in Europe), which – for the first time – made possible the EU-funded project "ECVision",

Vorwort der HerausgeberInnen

Der vorliegende Band 4 der Reihe „Supervision – Coaching – Organisationsberatung", die seit 2009 von den deutschsprachigen Berufsverbänden herausgegeben wird, bietet einen weiteren Beitrag zur Professionalisierung dieser Beratungsformate.

Professionalisierung basiert auf nachvollziehbaren und strukturierten Verfahren und Prozessen, standardisierter Aus- und Weiterbildung sowie kontinuierlicher Weiterentwicklung im Rahmen von Berufsorganisationen.

Diese Entwicklungen waren in den letzten zwanzig Jahren gekennzeichnet von rasanten Veränderungen in der Arbeitswelt und erhöhter Akzeptanz von Supervision und Coaching als unterstützende und begleitende Maßnahmen, aber auch von schnellen Veränderungen der Begriffsverständnisse in diesem Prozess.

Die Vergleichbarkeit der zunehmenden wissenschaftlichen (Be-)Forschung zu Wirksamkeit und Effizienz stellte sich als schwierig heraus, da eine dafür notwendige allgemeine Basis – im Sinne einer Klärung der hier in den unterschiedlichsten Konzepten angewandten Begrifflichkeiten – nur marginal vorhanden war. Insbesondere fehlte der europäische Kontext, Sprache und nationale Entwicklungen bestimmten die jeweiligen Konzepte und deren Nutzung.

Die eigenständige theoretische Konzeptualisierung von Supervision und ihre praktische Verbreitung sowie Ausbildung ging zunächst hauptsächlich von deutschsprachigen und niederländischen Einrichtungen aus. Über „Coaching" bekamen Konzepte aus dem angloamerikanischen Raum vor allem in den nicht deutschsprachigen Ländern zunehmende Bedeutung, wo sich insbesondere Universitätsinstitute in diesem Bereich zu engagieren begannen.

Damit begann auch eine lange übersehene, bedenkliche Entwicklung: Die internationale Sprache der Wissenschaft ist Englisch. Die Möglichkeiten, Erkenntnisse aus den deutschsprachigen Ländern in eine gemeinsame europäische Weiterentwicklung von Theorie und Praxis zu integrieren, scheitern an dem Mangel vorhandener englischer Übersetzungen.

to assign a European team of experts to compile an overview of the different concepts and definitions as well as a basic description of the competence of supervisors and coaches.

The bilingual publication of the project results at hand – merely the historical outlines at the end of the book are only in English – is not be understood as a final framework of definitions, but as a basis for professional discussion, which enables a continuous European development of theory and practice of supervision and coaching.

As might be expected with such a large project, gratitude is owed to many: The European Commission, as sponsor, the Wiener Volkshochschulen as coordinating institution, our partners ANSE, EUROCADRES, TOPS Munich-Berlin e.V., the University of Gothenburg, the University of Zagreb, as well as CoachKwadraat, and of course all of the colleagues involved. Furthermore, we thank all associations and board members who supported this project in many ways, and finally our thanks go to the publisher Facultas and its editorial office.

Vienna, 2016

Diese gemeinsame europäische Weiterentwicklung und Berufspolitik ist das Ziel der ANSE (Association of National Organisations for Supervision in Europe), der das EU-geförderte Projekt „*ECVision*" zum ersten Mal ermöglichte, ein europäisches ExpertInnenteam damit zu beauftragen, einen Überblick über die unterschiedlichen Konzepte und Definitionen sowie eine grundlegende Beschreibung der Kompetenz von SupervisorInnen und Coaches zu erarbeiten.

Die hier vorliegende zweisprachige Publikation der Projektergebnisse – lediglich die historischen Abrisse am Buchende gibt es nur in Englisch – versteht sich nicht als letztgültige Definitionsfolie, sondern als Grundlage einer Fachdiskussion, die eine kontinuierliche europäische Weiterentwicklung von Theorie und Praxis für Supervision und Coaching ermöglicht.

Dank gebührt, wie bei einem so großen Projekt nicht anders zu erwarten, Vielen: Der europäischen Kommission als Fördergeber, den Wiener Volkshochschulen als koordinierender Einrichtung, den Partnern ANSE, EURO-CADRES, TOPS München-Berlin e.V., Universität Göteborg, Universität Zagreb, sowie CoachKwadraat, und natürlich den beteiligten Kolleginnen und Kollegen. Weiters allen Verbänden und Vorständen, die dies in mannigfaltiger Weise unterstützt haben, und schlussendlich dem Verlag Facultas und seinem Lektorat.

Wien, 2016

ANSE – Professional Development on a European Footing

On behalf of the ANSE community, I feel privileged to present the results of four years hard work on the "ECVision Glossary of Supervision and Coaching in Europe" and the "European Competence Framework of Supervision and Coaching".

ECVision Project Team, management and steering committee present us with the fruits of their fine efforts, which really deserve our full and critical attention. For ANSE, this ECVision Project is no doubt the most important project we ever embarked upon, and certainly the most complex and comprehensive. The outcomes, I expect, will put our further professional development on a European footing, enhance cross-border exchange and help us to understand each other better.

For the first time in ANSE history, the glossary will allow us to base discussion and discourse on a mutually acceptable and clarified terminology of supervision and coaching, without infringing on the diversity that is one of the main strengths of the European supervision and coaching community. I am sure the results of this beautiful project will enhance our professional identity, and strengthen our commitment to further develop our services.

The competence framework enables us to clearly focus on validation of theories, practices and training. What used to seem an unattainable fantasy – cross-border exchange of trainers and educators, and our students graduating on composite courses, consisting of training programmes in, say, Amsterdam, Riga, Vienna or Berlin – has at least now attained the status of a feasible idea. In any case, the framework will, I am sure, be of great service to the professional exchange of practices and theory according to shared standards. And this, in turn will enhance our value to clients, wherever in Europe they live and work.

With presenting and discussing these outcomes at the last project conference in Vienna we move on to the next stage: the dissemination of glossary and framework, and having it put into practice. There is much to be done!

Sijtze de Roos – ANSE President

ANSE – Professionsentwicklung auf europäischer Grundlage

Als Vertreter der ANSE-Fachgemeinsacht ist es mir eine Ehre, die Ergebnisse von vier Jahren harter Arbeit am „ECVision Glossar für Supervision und Coaching in Europa" und dem „Europäischen Kompetenzprofil für Supervision und Coaching" zu präsentieren.

Das ECVision Projektteam und das Steuerungskomitee präsentieren uns die Früchte ihrer Arbeit, die unsere volle und kritische Aufmerksamkeit verdient. Für die ANSE ist ECVision zweifellos das wichtigste, komplexeste und umfassendste Projekt, das wir je unternommen haben. Ich erwarte zuversichtlich, dass die Ergebnisse uns ermöglichen werden, unsere weitere berufliche Entwicklung auf eine europäische Grundlage zu stellen, grenzüberschreitenden Austausch zu fördern und einander besser zu verstehen.

Erstmals in der Geschichte der ANSE wird uns das Glossar ermöglichen, auf Basis einer akzeptablen und geklärten Terminologie Diskussionen und Diskurse über Supervision und Coaching zu führen, ohne die Vielfalt – eine der wichtigsten Stärken der europäischen Supervisions- und Coaching-Fachwelt – zu vernachlässigen. Ich bin zuversichtlich, dass die Ergebnisse dieses Projekts unsere berufliche Identität verbessern und unser Engagement stärken werden, um unsere Dienstleistungen weiterzuentwickeln.

Das Kompetenzprofil ermöglicht es, uns klar auf die Validierung von Theorien, Praktiken und Ausbildungen zu konzentrieren. Was früher eine unerreichbare Fantasie schien – grenzüberschreitender Austausch von AusbildnerInnen, und Studierende, die auf Basis von Trainingsprogrammen graduieren, die in, sagen wir, Amsterdam, Riga, Wien oder Berlin absolviert wurden – all dies hat jetzt zumindest den Status einer machbaren Idee!

In jedem Fall wird das Kompetenzprofil von großem Nutzen für den professionellen Austausch von Praktiken und Theorie auf Basis gemeinsamer Standards sein. Und dies wiederum wird auch für unsere KlientInnen von Nutzen sein, wo auch immer in Europa sie leben und arbeiten.

Nach Präsentation und Diskussion dieser Ergebnisse bei der letzten Projektkonferenz in Wien geht es weiter in die nächste Phase: die Verbreitung von Glossar und Kompetenzprofil, und deren Umsetzung in die Praxis. Es gibt viel zu tun!

Sijtze de Roos – ANSE Präsident

Eurocadres – A Message of European Cohesion

Despite tension at political level and tendencies of anti-EU backlash, European integration and cohesion move forward. This takes place in economy, education, science, and culture with various impacts on the systems of professional standards, Europe-wide recognition of diplomas and the real opportunities and perspectives of free movement of employed or self-employed professionals within an open European labour market.

Eurocadres, the Council of European Professional and Managerial Staff, recognised European social partner, has always valued facilitating the professional rights and opportunities of its more than five million members in European countries with all of its professional and managerial levels. In particular, Eurocadres' focus has been on efforts to take down barriers for Europe-wide cross-border professional careers and self-determined free movement.

One of the key questions is to develop and guarantee trust in the quality of professional work. Given a large variety of levels, curricula, paths of qualification and innumerable certificates, the challenge is to work for a Europe with more transparency, comparability, fair recognition and – in a longer perspective – better harmonisation within the qualification and certification systems at high standards.

Eurocadres therefore cooperates with several European professional organisations, amongst them ANSE, the Association of National Organisations of Supervision in Europe.

ANSE's proposal to Eurocadres for a joint project for a European Competence Framework of Supervision and Coaching fit well into Eurocadres' political strategy, and therefore it was a clear choice to join and support the project as an active partner, including hosting the first European conference in early 2014 where the project regarding the ECVision Glossary for supervision and coaching in accordance with the European Qualification Framework was presented.

Now the project team, supported by additional experts, is presenting the detailed European Competence Framework Matrix of Supervision and

Eurocadres – Eine Botschaft europäischen Zusammenhalts

Trotz Spannungen auf politischer Ebene und Anti-EU-Tendenzen schreiten europäische Integration und Zusammenhalt voran. Dies geschieht in Wirtschaft, Bildung, Wissenschaft und Kultur mit vielfältigen Auswirkungen auf die Systeme der beruflichen Standards, auf europaweite Anerkennung von Diplomen und die realen Möglichkeiten und Perspektiven der Mobilität von ArbeitnehmerInnen oder Selbstständigen innerhalb eines offenen europäischen Arbeitsmarkts.

Eurocadres, der Rat der Europäischen Fach- und Führungskräfte, anerkannter europäischer Sozialpartner, hat stets darauf Wert gelegt, die beruflichen Rechte und Möglichkeiten seiner mehr als fünf Millionen Mitglieder in den europäischen Ländern auf allen Fach- und Führungsebenen zu unterstützen. Insbesondere hat Eurocadres den Fokus auf die Bemühungen gelegt, Hindernisse für europaweite grenzüberschreitende berufliche Mobilität zu beseitigen.

Eine Schlüsselfrage betrifft die Entwicklung und Sicherung des Vertrauens in die Qualität professioneller Arbeit. Angesichts einer Vielzahl von Niveaus, Lehrplänen, Qualifizierungswegen und unzähligen Zeugnissen, besteht die europäische Herausforderung darin, mehr Transparenz, Vergleichbarkeit, faire wechselseitige Anerkennung und – auf längere Sicht – bessere Harmonisierung innerhalb der Qualifizierungs- und Zertifizierungssysteme auf hohem Niveau zu schaffen. Eurocadres kooperiert daher mit mehreren europäischen Berufsverbänden, darunter die ANSE.

Die Einladung der ANSE, an einem gemeinsamen Projekt zur Entwicklung eines europäischen Kompetenzprofils für Supervision und Coaching teilzunehmen, passte daher gut in die politische Strategie von Eurocadres. Deshalb war es eine klare Entscheidung, das Projekt als aktiver Partner zu unterstützen, u. a. auch als Gastgeber der ersten Konferenz Anfang 2014, wo das ECVision Glossar für Supervision und Coaching vorgestellt wurde.

In Wien präsentierte das Projekt-Team, unterstützt durch ExpertInnen, das detaillierte europäische Kompetenzprofil für Supervision und Coaching, und setzte damit europaweit vergleichbare Standards und Definitionen. Dies

Coaching, thus setting Europe-wide comparable standards and definitions. This will be a strong basis for next steps towards establishing recognised European professional cards that clearly show the professional standards of their holders. Eurocadres continues to play an active role and to support the idea of a professional card for supervision and coaching, an evident proof of quality standards within the professional community and vis-à-vis the clients, a signal of trademark and a message of European cohesion.

Martin Jefflén
President of Eurocadres

wird eine solide Grundlage für die nächsten Schritte zu einer anerkannten europäischen „Professional Card" bieten, die nachvollziehbar die professionellen Standards ihrer InhaberInnen darstellt. Eurocadres wird weiterhin aktiv die Idee einer „Professional Card" für Supervision und Coaching unterstützen, als Nachweis der Qualitätsstandards in der Fachwelt wie auch gegenüber KundInnen, ein Signal und eine Botschaft des europäischen Zusammenhalts!

Martin Jefflén
Präsident von Eurocadres

ECVision. Supervision and Coaching in Europe: Concepts and Competences
An Introduction

Michaela Judy

This manual provides the key products of the Project *ECVision. A European System of Comparability and Validation of Supervisory Competences,* funded by Leonardo – Development of Innovation.

Those key products are:
- A Glossary: ECVision. A European Glossary of Supervision and Coaching
- A Competence Framework: ECVision. A European Competence Framework of Supervision and Coaching
- An ECTS-ECVET Reference: Validating Competences. The ECVision Reference Table ECTS-ECVET

Furthermore, the esteemed reader will be offered three scientific articles.

Wolfgang Knopf questions both the policy aspects and the sustainability of the ECVision outcomes.

Heidi Möller analyses the relationship between scientific theory and occupational practice, taking into account the differing priorities of both fields. Based on ECVision she finally gives an outlook on the necessity of further research.

Based on a case example *Erik de Haan* looks at how three professions (leadership, coaching & supervision) can work together to mitigate and balance the risks of leadership.

The last chapter gives an overview of the Austrian, Croatian, Dutch, German, Hungarian, Swedish, and European history of supervision and coaching.

ECVision. Supervision und Coaching in Europa: Konzepte und Kompetenzen
Eine Einführung

Michaela Judy

Dieses Handbuch enthält die wichtigsten Ergebnisse des Projekts *ECVision. Ein Europäisches System der Vergleichbarkeit und Validierung supervisorischer Kompetenzen*, gefördert im Rahmen des EU-Programms LEONARDO.

Die Hauptergebnisse sind:

- Ein Glossar: ECVision. Ein Europäisches Glossar für Supervision und Coaching
- Ein Kompetenzprofil: ECVision. Ein Europäisches Kompetenzprofil für Supervision und Coaching
- Eine ECTS-ECVET Referenztabelle: Kompetenzen validieren.

Darüber hinaus laden wir die LeserInnen zu drei wissenschaftlichen Artikeln ein.

Wolfgang Knopf behandelt sowohl berufspolitische Aspekte wie auch jene der Nachhaltigkeit der ECVision-Ergebnisse.

Heidi Möller analysiert *die Beziehung zwischen* wissenschaftlicher Theorie und Beratungspraxis unter Berücksichtigung der verschiedenen Prioritäten beider Felder. Basierend auf ECVision schließt sie mit einem Ausblick auf die Notwendigkeit zukünftiger Forschungserfordernisse.

Erik de Haan verdeutlicht mit Fallbeispielen, wie Führung, Coaching und Supervision im Zusammenspiel die Risiken von Führung reduzieren können.

ECVision Philosophy

ECVision was dedicated to provide instruments in order to assure the comparability of supervisory and coaching competences.

The basic methodological assumptions are referring to the development of a European common ground by:

- Creating comparability,
- Using the existing EQF principles and to the two validation systems ECTS and ECVET,
- Providing a sound grounding for developing comparable formal outcomes of different validation processes.

The ECVision Philosophy is based on three principles:

- Generic approach
- Focus on the interaction of persons, professional tasks and organisations
- Connection with the professional community

Generic Approach

ECVision does not aim at the harmonisation of the various prevalent definitions and approaches. It does aim at the transparency and comparability of different considerations, tasks and responsibilities and of professional standards.

There is a strong need for the latter due to a higher degree of professional mobility and activities, which nowadays go beyond borders of countries and mother tongues.

ECVision does not refer to specific counselling theories, tools or techniques. Instead, we decided on a classification of characteristics common to counselling processes that are referring to the interaction of persons, professional tasks and organisations.

To do so, we described generic key words and competences based upon the core literature used in European professional discourses. We discovered those generic groundings being more consistent than expected. Actually, differences show up according to theories, professional background, environment, and the working fields they are applied to.

Comparability within the ECVision products emerges from having identified generic key words and competences showing up in nearly all European professional discourses.

Die ECVision-Philosophie

Deklariertes Ziel von ECVision war es, Instrumente zu entwickeln und zur Verfügung zu stellen, die der Vergleichbarkeit supervisorischer Kompetenzen dienen.

Für deren Entwicklung gingen wir von folgenden methodologischen Annahmen aus:
- Kriterien für Vergleichbarkeit entwickeln;
- Die bereits etablierten EQR-Prinzipien sowie die beiden Validierungssysteme ECTS und ECVET nutzen;
- Eine solide Basis zur Entwicklung vergleichbarer formaler Lernergebnisse – auch unterschiedlicher Validierungsprozesse – zu schaffen.

Die ECVision Philosophie basiert auf drei Prinzipien:
- Generische Prinzipien
- Fokus auf die Interaktion von Personen, beruflichen Aufgaben und Organisationen
- Anbindung an die Fachwelt

Generische Prinzipien

ECVision zielt nicht auf eine Harmonisierung der verschiedenen gängigen Definitionen und Ansätze ab. Vielmehr geht es um die Schaffung von Transparenz und Vergleichbarkeit in Bezug auf verschiedene Konzepte, Aufgaben und Verantwortlichkeiten sowie von professionellen Standards. Dies ist umso wichtiger, weil berufliche Mobilität heute über die Grenzen von Ländern und Muttersprachen hinausgeht.

ECVision bezieht sich nicht auf spezielle Beratungstheorien, -instrumente oder -techniken. Stattdessen entschieden wir uns für eine Klassifizierung von Eigenschaften, die in jenen Beratungsprozessen relevant werden, die das Zusammenwirken von Personen, beruflichen Aufgaben und Organisationen im Fokus haben. Zu diesem Zweck haben wir generische Schlüsselwörter und Kompetenzen beschrieben, auf der Grundlage der Basisliteratur in europäischen professionellen Diskursen.

Wir entdeckten, dass sich diese generischen Grundprinzipien konsistenter darstellten als erwartet. Tatsächlich zeigen sich Unterschiede v. a. in Bezug auf Theorien, Umwelten, sowie Berufs- und Arbeitsfelder.

Vergleichbarkeit ergibt sich bei den ECVision Ergebnissen folgerichtig aus der Identifizierung generischer Schlüsselwörter und Kompetenzen, wie sie in fast allen europäischen professionellen Diskursen aufscheinen.

Focus on the interaction of persons, professional tasks and organisations

Supervision and coaching intervene at the point of intersection, where human beings interact in their specific functional and social roles and their working environments.

Supervision and coaching aim at facilitating individual and organisational changes or at releasing tension or conflicts in daily job situations. To do so, supervision and coaching refer to different theoretical orientations. Supervisors and coaches mainly follow humanistic, psychodynamic and systemic approaches, by creatively integrating methods and core qualities of professional counselling.

The terms supervision and coaching indicate formats of counselling to serve the professional development of persons, teams, and organisations.

The different approaches and methods often overlap; sometimes, they are even identical. The terminology used is fluid and often changes or shifts.

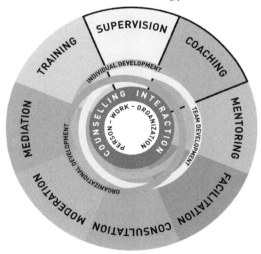

The decision to use the term supervision or coaching refers to both different histories of development and key aspects of activities in the field. It may also relate to different "schools" which have been training supervisors or even relate to long-term national or institutional traditions.

The following chart shows how supervision and coaching are embedded in the bigger picture of counselling and consulting.

The ECVision products do not provide an outline of the very many formats of coun-

Fig. 1: Embedding of Supervision and Coaching

selling, consulting, and training. They focus entirely on supervision and coaching.

Connection with the professional community

The markets for counselling in the professional and organisational context of a company are manifold, yet there is little common basis of terminology.

Fokus auf die Interaktion von Person, beruflichen Aufgaben und Organisation

Supervision und Coaching intervenieren, wo Menschen in ihren spezifischen funktionalen und sozialen Rollen in ihren Arbeitsumgebungen in Interaktion treten. Supervision und Coaching zielen auf die Unterstützung individueller und organisatorischer Veränderungen oder auf die Lösung von Spannungen und Konflikten in der täglichen Arbeit ab.

Dazu beziehen sich SupervisorInnen/Coaches auf unterschiedliche Theoriemodelle. SupervisorInnen und Coaches folgen hauptsächlich humanistischen, psychodynamischen und systemischen Konzepten, und integrieren kreativ Methoden und Kernqualitäten professioneller Beratung.

Die Begriffe Supervision und Coaching verweisen auf Beratungsformate, die der beruflichen Entwicklung von Personen, Teams und Organisationen dienen.

Konzepte und Methoden hingegen überschneiden sich häufig, manchmal sind sie sogar identisch. Die Terminologie verschwimmt, ändert oder verschiebt sich. Die Entscheidung, den Begriff Supervision oder Coaching zu verwenden, resultiert aus unterschiedlichen Entwicklungsgeschichten und Kernaktivitäten. Ebenso kann sie sich auf verschiedene „Schulen" in Supervisionsausbildungen oder auf nationale oder institutionelle Traditionen beziehen.

Die nebenstehende Grafik zeigt, wie Supervision und Coaching in das Gesamtbild der Beratung im beruflichen Kontext eingebettet sind. Die ECVision Ergebnisse geben keinen Überblick über die vielfältigen Formate von Beratung und Training, sie konzentrieren sich ganz auf Supervision und Coaching.

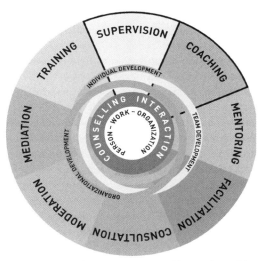

Abb. 1: Einbettung von Supervision und Coaching

Until now, supervision and coaching – mainly freelance professions – have lacked a common and consistent way of describing skills and competences on a European level.

There are national and European professional counselling associations such as:

- the Association of National Organisations for Supervision in Europe (ANSE; *http://www.anse.eu*)
- the European Association for Supervision and Coaching in Europe (EASC; *http://www.easc-online.eu/*),
- the International Coach Federation (ICF; *http://www.coachfederation.at/*),
- the European Mentoring and Coaching Council (EMCC; *http://www.emccouncil.org/*).

These associations have set standards for vocational education and training of supervisors and/or coaches. Their standards define the minimal formal criteria of how to become a supervisor or coach. The regulations for membership and accreditation provide orientation although they differ in focus and scope.

To provide a short insight into different approaches and their origin, the esteemed reader will find historical outlines of the developments of the two professions in the project countries at the end of this manual.

Though ECVision relates mainly to ANSE policies and ANSE member associations, we were able to establish contact with the other big European professional counselling associations as well. Two conferences gave the opportunity for discussing the outcomes thoroughly within the professional community and for getting input for further development of our professions.

The ECVision products are going to bridge the more or less separated ways of describing standards differently, and therefore bring the professional community nearer to the goal of adopting a collective frame of comparability for supervision and coaching.

ECVision Quality Assurance

The ECVision project team created and compiled the products of ECVision:

- Marina Ajdukovic (Croatia)
- Lilja Cajvert (Sweden)
- Michaela Judy (Austria)
- Wolfgang Knopf (EU/Austria)
- Hubert Kuhn (Germany)

Anbindung an die Fachwelt

Die Märkte für Supervision, Coaching und andere Beratungsformate in der Arbeitswelt sind vielfältig, doch es fehlte den freien Berufen Supervision und Coaching bislang eine gemeinsame und konsistente Beschreibung auf europäischer Ebene.

Sicher gibt es nationale wie europäische Berufsverbände:

- „Association of National Organisations for Supervision in Europe" (ANSE; http://www.anse.eu),
- „European Association for Supervision and Coaching in Europe" (EASC; http://www.easc-online.eu/),
- „International Coach Federation" (ICF; http://www.coachfederation.at/),
- „European Mentoring and Coaching Council" (EMCC; http://www.emccouncil.org/).

Diese Verbände haben Standards für die berufliche Aus- und Weiterbildung erstellt. Sie definieren die minimalen formalen Kriterien, um SupervisorIn oder Coach zu werden. Die Regelungen für die Mitgliedschaft und Akkreditierung geben Orientierung, obwohl sie sich im Fokus und im Umfang oft beträchtlich unterscheiden.

Obwohl sich ECVision vor allem auf ANSE Berufspolitik und ANSE Mitgliedsverbände bezieht, waren wir in der Lage, professionelle Kontakte mit den beiden großen europäischen Berufsverbänden für Coaching zu etablieren.

Zwei Konferenzen gaben Gelegenheit zur gründlichen Diskussion der Ergebnisse in der Fachwelt und vermittelten Inputs für die Weiterentwicklung unserer Berufe.

Die ECVision Ergebnisse tragen damit erfolgreich zur einer Überbrückung unterschiedlicher Beschreibungslogiken von Standards bei und bringen so die Fachwelt dem Ziel eines gemeinsam akzeptierten Rahmens für Vergleichbarkeit von Supervision und Coaching näher.

ECVision Qualitätssicherung

Entwickelt und ausgearbeitet wurden die Ergebnisse vom Projektteam des LEONARDO-Projekts ECVision: Marina Ajdukovic (Kroatien), Lilja Cajvert (Schweden), Michaela Judy (Österreich), Wolfgang Knopf (EU/Österreich),

- Krisztina Madai (Hungary)
- Mieke Voogd (The Netherlands).

The project team represents a purposeful sample of competent members, chosen according to the criteria of experience as a supervisor/coach and their research work and publications concerning these issues; their institutional integration into European and national professional politics and policy was also an important factor. The team consists of representatives of two private and two university training providers for Supervision, and they are representatives of methodological and societal diversity.

Furthermore, ten experts provided professional feedback on the glossary:

- Guido Baumgartner (Switzerland)
- Hans Björkman (Sweden)
- Elisabeth Brugger (Austria)
- Susanne Ehmer (Germany/Austria)
- Erik de Haan (United Kingdom/The Netherlands)
- Tone Haugs (Norway)
- Louis van Kessel (The Netherlands)
- Helga Messel (Sweden)
- Heidi Möller (Germany)
- Heidemarie Müller-Riedlhuber (Austria)

These experts supported the glossary by critical reading and a wider range of perspectives.

The steering committee provided the all-important external perspective on processes and therefore contributed indispensably to the quality assurance of ECVision.

Sincere thanks to:

- Barbara Gogala (Slovenia)
- Eva Nemes (Hungary)
- Gerald Musger (Austria/Belgium)
- Andreas Paula (Austria)

The ECVision Products

ECVision Glossary

The ECVision glossary aims at providing orientation and a mainstream description of how today's professional discourses in Europe use both terms.

Hubert Kuhn (Deutschland), Krisztina Madai (Ungarn) und Mieke Voogd (Niederlande).

Die Mitglieder des Projektteams wurden gezielt nach den folgenden Kriterien ausgewählt: Erfahrung als SupervisorIn/Coach sowie Forschungsarbeiten und Publikationen zu diesen Themen; ihre institutionelle Integration in die europäischen und nationalen Berufspolitiken war ebenfalls ein wichtiger Faktor.

Das Team besteht aus VertreterInnen von zwei privaten und zwei universitären Ausbildungsanbietern für Supervision; darüber hinaus repräsentieren die Mitglieder des Projektteams methodische und gesellschaftliche Vielfalt.

Zusätzlich stellten zehn ExpertInnen dem Glossar ihr professionelles Feedback zur Verfügung:

- Guido Baumgartner (CH),
- Hans Björkman (SE),
- Elisabeth Brugger (AT),
- Susanne Ehmer (DE/AT),
- Erik de Haan (UK),
- Tone Haugs (NO),
- Louis van Kessel (NL),
- Helga Messel (SE),
- Heidi Möller (DE),
- Heidemarie Müller-Riedlhuber (AT).

Die ExpertInnen unterstützen die Ergebnisse durch kritisches Lesen und erweiterte Perspektiven.

Das Steuerungskomitee – Barbara Gogala, Eva Nemes, Gerald Musger, Andreas Paula – sorgte für die unverzichtbare Außenperspektive und damit für die Qualitätskontrolle des Projekts.

Die ECVision Ergebnisse

Das ECVision Glossar

Das vorliegende Glossar versteht sich als Orientierung und Beschreibung, wie der Mainstream der aktuellen professionellen Diskurse in Europa diese beiden Begriffe verwendet.

Darüber hinaus bietet es Beschreibungen verwandter Begriffe und erläutert die verschiedenen Formen des Verständnisses und die Perspektiven, die auf diesem Gebiet zur Verfügung standen.

In addition, it offers descriptions of related terms and explains the different forms of comprehension and the perspectives that were available in the field.

It provides a structure that is to be continued as permanent work in progress: structured enough to serve as a basis for a common terminology and flexible enough to be adapted to new conditions within the fast changing of our field that has been investigated and researched.

Methodology

To create the glossary, the project team first of all defined the domain of the glossary: "counselling the interaction between individuals, work and organisation".

Within this domain, we focussed on supervision and coaching. The glossary is not only a dictionary but also an outline of the European diversity of supervision and coaching. The main goal of the glossary is to step forward in the development of a competence profile for supervision and coaching.

Initially, we based the contents of this glossary on a research of the literature available concerning supervision and coaching in Sweden, Germany, Austria, Hungary, Croatia, and the Netherlands. Each project team member focussed on relevant books, articles, and research reports used in the participating institutions and at those universities and colleges in the countries providing training in supervision and/or coaching. We also collected relevant terms that are characteristic for supervision and coaching. Some listed terms we excluded after discussing them because they did not seem appropriate according to our domain.

We discussed and agreed upon the following main categories to describe supervision and coaching:
• Stakeholders
• Core qualities
• Types
• Settings
• Methods
• Outcomes

Finally we agreed to describe in more detail the selected terms by using the previously identified main literature in its respective countries. If a concept or term was not defined, it was left open for further discussion.

The completed glossary draft was then sent to the experts of the project to be reflected and commented. After that, the project coordinator compiled

Es bietet eine Struktur, die als „work in progress" dauerhaft fortgesetzt werden kann: strukturiert genug, um als Grundlage für eine gemeinsame Terminologie zu dienen, und flexibel genug, um neuen Bedingungen innerhalb des sich schnell ändernden Feldes, das wir untersucht und erforscht haben, angepasst werden zu können.

Methodologie

Um das Glossar zu erstellen, definierte das Projektteam zunächst die Domäne des Glossars:„Beratung der Interaktion von Personen, beruflichen Aufgaben und Organisationen". Innerhalb dieser Domäne konzentrierten wir uns auf Supervision und Coaching. Das Glossar ist nicht nur ein Wörterbuch, sondern auch eine Übersicht der europäischen Vielfalt von Supervision und Coaching. Das Glossar ist darüber hinaus ein unverzichtbarer Schritt hin zur Entwicklung eines Kompetenzprofils für Supervision und Coaching.

Zunächst bauten wir den Inhalt des Glossars auf Recherchen der verfügbaren Literatur über Supervision und Coaching in Schweden, Deutschland, Österreich, Ungarn, Kroatien und den Niederlanden auf. Jedes Mitglied des Projektteams fokussierte auf relevante Bücher, Artikel und Forschungsberichte, die in den beteiligten Institutionen und Universitäten zum Einsatz kamen. Wir haben auch relevante Begriffe, die charakteristisch für Supervision und Coaching sind, gesammelt. Einige Begriffe schlossen wir nach eingehender Diskussion wieder aus, wenn sie nicht genau in unsere Domäne passten.

Wir einigten uns auf die folgenden Hauptkategorien:
- Akteure
- Kernqualitäten
- Arten
- Settings
- Methoden
- Ergebnisse

Schließlich haben wir uns darauf geeinigt, die ausgewählten Begriffe mithilfe der Literatur detaillierter zu beschreiben. Wurde ein Konzept oder ein Begriff nicht definiert, blieb es/er zunächst offen und wurde gemeinsam weiter definiert.

Der fertige Glossar-Entwurf wurde dann an die ExpertInnen des Projekts ausgeschickt, um reflektiert und kommentiert zu werden. Die Projektkoordinatorin kompilierte nach neuerlicher Diskussion im Projektteam alles in ein einziges Dokument, das der Fachwelt im Februar 2014 während der

everything in one single document which was considered and negotiated with the professional community in February 2014 during the two-day conference "Getting involved! A Common Terminology for Supervision and Coaching in Europe", organised by our project partner EUROCADRES, the Council of European Professional and Managerial Staff.

The ECVision Competence Framework

A description of learning competence outcomes in supervision and coaching presents specific challenges, which are briefly outlined below.

Almost all relevant research on supervision and coaching refers to the working relationship as the main active factor. Therefore, we did not merely have to characterise personal skills, but also those characterising relationship in the case of supervision and coaching. We are referring to relationship intervening at the point of intersection, where individuals interact in their specific functional and social roles in their working environments.

The Glossary and the Competence Framework are linked inseparably; the competence framework is based on the key terms we have already defined. Consequently, the methodology of their development applied closely intertwined.

Methodology

We decided on three approaches and/or concepts as methodological guidelines:
• The ECVision Glossary
• Bloom's Taxonomy and
• The European Qualification Framework.

The impacts of these concepts on the Competence Framework are explained below.

The ECVision Glossary for Supervision and Coaching

We took the core qualities and methods of the glossary as a starting point. Therefore, corresponding definitions for all the required competencies can be found in the Glossary.

zweitägigen Konferenz „Eine gemeinsame Terminologie für Supervision und Coaching in Europa" vorgestellt wurde, organisiert von unserem Projektpartner EUROCADRES.

Das ECVision Kompetenzprofil

Lernergebnisorientierte Beschreibung steht in Bezug auf Beratungsberufe vor besonderen Herausforderungen, die im Folgenden kurz umrissen werden sollen.

Fast alle relevanten Forschungsarbeiten zu Supervision & Coaching beschreiben die Arbeitsbeziehung als hauptsächlichen Wirkfaktor. Wie in allen Berufen die an und mit Beziehung arbeiten, kommt der professionellen Haltung von SupervisorInnen/Coaches besondere Bedeutung zu.

So ist es nicht damit getan, die persönlichen Fähigkeiten von SupervisorInnen/Coaches zu beschreiben, es geht in hohem Maße darum, diese Beziehungen zu charakterisieren. Im Falle von Supervision und Coaching geht es um Beziehungen, die an den Schnittstellen intervenieren, wo Menschen in ihren spezifischen funktionalen und sozialen Rollen und ihren Arbeitsfeldern sichtbar werden.

Das Glossar und das Kompetenzprofil sind ohne einander nicht denkbar, das Kompetenzprofil wäre kaum so möglich gewesen, hätten wir die Schlüsselbegriffe nicht bereits definiert.

Damit war auch die Methodologie ihrer Entwicklung aufs Engste verknüpft.

Methodologie

Für das Kompetenzprofil haben wir drei Konzepte als methodologische Richtlinien gewählt:
• Das ECVision Glossar
• Die Taxonomie von Bloom
• Den Europäischen Qualifikationsrahmen

Die Einflüsse dieser Konzepte auf das Kompetenzprofil seien im Folgenden kurz umrissen.

Bloom's Taxonomy

We used and adapted – according to European standards – Bloom's Taxonomy to describe learning outcomes and competences of the supervisor/coach. (Cf. Kennedy, Hyland, Ryan: Writing and Using Learning Outcomes)

Both Bloom's cognitive and emotional taxonomy are in some ways applicable to the tasks supervisors/coaches have to fulfil. We took both taxonomies, allowing for the fact that the required skills generally aim to open new scopes of action for others – the supervisees/coachees.

The taxonomy we used and the related behaviour are:

- Applying: apply, adopt, identify, keep, set, use.
- Analysing: distinguish, differ, differentiate, link, review.
- Evaluating: assess, challenge, choose, clarify, confront, connect, estimate, explore.
- Facilitating: address, articulate, communicate, contain, contribute, discuss, encourage, explain, express, facilitate, foster, gain, meta-communicate, observe, offer, present, process, provide, question, realise, recognise, refer, reflect, respond, stand, stimulate, supply, support, take into account, verbalise.
- Creating: adapt, adjust, anticipate, build, co-create, create, demonstrate, design, deal with, decide, focus on, handle, integrate, intervene, lead, maintain, master, model, monitor.

The European Qualification Framework

We referred to the EQF structure to describe knowledge, skills and performance relating to the different competences:

"Competence" means the indispensable, fundamental characteristics of supervision and coaching.

"Knowledge" describes facts, principles, theories and practical knowledge that any supervisory work is based on.

"Skills" describe the cognitive and practical ability to apply this knowledge in order to counsel effectively.

The core of the Competence Framework is the description of **"Performance"**. Without a comprehensible description of related behaviour, we do not consider competence descriptions as meaningful. With the focus on performance criteria, we have formulated learning outcomes that should be observable in the distinct behaviours of supervisors/coaches. That goes as well for expected learning outcomes of trainees of qualified training for supervision and coaching.

Das ECVision Glossar für Supervision und Coaching

Wir haben die Kernqualitäten und Methoden des Glossars als Ausgangspunkt genommen. Daher findet sich zu allen Kompetenzen auch eine ent-
sprechende Definition.

Die Taxonomie von Bloom

Wir haben – europäischen Standards entsprechend – die Taxonomie von
Bloom genutzt, sie jedoch den Erfordernissen einer Beschreibung von Lernergebnissen und Kompetenzen von SupervisorInnen/Coaches angepasst.
(Vgl. Kennedy/Hyland/Ryan: Writing and Using Learning Outcomes).
Tatsächlich sind sowohl Blooms kognitive wie auch emotionale Taxonomie
in gewisser Weise anwendbar für die Aufgaben, die SupervisorInnen/Coa-
ches zu erfüllen haben.

Wir haben beide Taxonomien unter Berücksichtigung der Tatsache verwendet, dass die erforderlichen Fähigkeiten in der Regel auf die Erschlie-
ßung neuer Handlungsspielräume für andere abzielen – für die Supervisan-
dInnen/Coachees.

Die Taxonomie, mit der wir gearbeitet haben, und die damit verbundenen
Verhaltensweisen sind daher:

- Anwenden: abgleichen, beobachten, einnehmen, einsetzen, nutzen,
  kommunizieren, pflegen, reagieren, verwenden, leisten.
- Analysieren: artikulieren, bearbeiten, erforschen, erkennen, Erkenntnisse
  gewinnen, studieren.
- Evaluieren: beurteilen, beziehen, einschätzen, entscheiden, festlegen, fokussieren, klären, identifizieren, in Zusammenhang bringen, infrage stellen, integrieren, meta-kommunizieren, reflektieren, überprüfen, unterscheiden, untersuchen, verdeutlichen, vermitteln, verstärken, wählen.
- Ermöglichen: ansprechen, anbieten, anpassen, behandeln, beziehen, einbeziehen, eingehen, erleichtern, ermutigen, fördern, fordern, fungieren,
  Kontakt/Spannung halten, stimulieren, teilnehmen, unterstützen, wah-
  ren.
- Erschaffen: co-kreieren, beherrschen, entwickeln, führen, generieren,
  gestalten, handhaben, kreieren, intervenieren, Lösungen finden, realisie-
  ren, schaffen.

Der Europäische Qualifikationsrahmen

Die Beschreibungslogik folgt den Deskriptoren des EQR in der Beschreibung supervisorischer Kompetenz über Kenntnisse, Fertigkeiten und Performance.

Thus, the ECVision performance criteria correspond with the CEDEFOP definition of assessment criteria based on learning outcomes statements:

"Typically the assessment criteria will contain more detail about the context in which the learner is expected to be able to do something or the level of autonomy expected." (CEDEFOP: USING LEARNING OUTCOMES; European Qualifications Framework Series: Note 4; www.cedefop.europa.eu%2Ffiles%2FUsing_learning_outcomes.pdf9; p.16.)

The dedicated focus on the description of observable behaviour allows a much better definition of learning outcomes. It serves as a guideline, providing transparent communication of both self-assessment and assessment by qualified others.

The Competence Framework sets a standard by setting it apart from the prevailing confusion of terms in the European professional communities of supervision and coaching:

It can considerably better be determined now whether someone meets the performance criteria: whether he/she is within the range of expertise of the Competence Framework – regardless of calling himself/herself coach or supervisor.

We have focused on formulating the new Competence Framework by cutting across the various schools and approaches.

Undoubtedly, the methodological implementation of skills may differ; undoubtedly, schools and training providers set their own priorities, which often exceed our present descriptions.

Nevertheless, one might "use her/his own bias" when observing interactions, or she/he might be "working with transference and countertransference" – the competence within both approaches lies in the meaningful and theory-based use of the process of relationship.

At this point – and this has been our major concern – it is now possible to define the attitudes, qualities, and tools a supervisor/coach has to demonstrate when he/she works professionally.

We have avoided engaging in detailed descriptions of tools but negotiated how to ascertain that supervisors/coaches have a clear and reflected understanding and sound tools at their disposal – as we have laid out in the Glossary.

It allows both clear criteria of observation for assessing supervisory competences to be applied and a wide and diverse scope for practical implementation.

We are quite clear about the borders of our achievements: Using competence and learning outcome orientation meaningfully requires an ongoing critical as well as professional dialogue.

Die **„Kompetenz"** bezeichnet jeweils jene unverzichtbaren fundamentalen Charakteristika professioneller Beratung in Supervision und Coaching.

Die **„Kenntnisse"** beschreiben Fakten, Grundsätze, Theorien und Praxiswissen, die supervisorischem Arbeiten zugrunde liegen müssen.

Unter **„Fertigkeiten"** beschreiben wir die kognitiven wie praktischen Fähigkeiten, diese Kenntnisse anzuwenden um effektiv beratend tätig werden zu können.

Das Herzstück des Kompetenzprofils ist die Beschreibung der **Performance**. Ohne die Nachvollziehbarkeit, wie genau Kompetenz wahrnehmbar wird, halten wir Kompetenzbeschreibungen für wenig sinnvoll.

Mit dem Fokus auf Performance-Kriterien haben wir darüber hinaus bereits Lernergebnisse formuliert, die am Ende einer qualifizierten Ausbildung zu Supervision und Coaching im Verhalten der AusbildungskandidatInnen beobachtbar sein sollten.

Die ECVision Performance-Kriterien entsprechen also auch der CEDEFOP Definition von Bewertungskriterien auf Basis von Lernergebnis-Aussagen.

„Typischerweise beinhalten Bewertungskriterien Einzelheiten über den Kontext, in dem Lernende voraussichtlich in der Lage sein werden, etwas zu tun, oder den Grad der erwarteten Autonomie" (vgl. CEDEFOP: Using Learning Outcomes, S. 16).

Der dezidierte Fokus auf die Beschreibung beobachtbaren Verhaltens ermöglicht eine echte Lernergebnisorientierung, er dient als Richtschnur, die Fremd- wie Selbsteinschätzung kommunizierbar und damit transparent macht.

Das Kompetenzprofil setzt einen Standard, indem es sich von der herrschenden Begriffsverwirrung in den europäischen Berufsgemeinschaften der Supervision und Coaching abhebt: nun kann weitaus klarer bestimmt werden, ob jemand die Performance-Kriterien erfüllt, unabhängig davon, ob er/sie sich SupervisorIn, resp. Coach nennt.

Wir haben uns darauf konzentriert, die Kompetenzen des neuen Kompetenzprofils quer über die verschiedenen Schulen und Ansätze hinweg zu formulieren.

Zweifellos variiert die methodische Umsetzung der Kompetenzen, zweifellos setzen Schulen und Ausbildungsanbieter eigene Akzente, die vielfach über das von uns Beschriebene hinausgehen.

Dennoch: ob jemand die eigene „Voreingenommenheit" zur Beobachtung von Wechselwirkungen nutzt, oder mit dem psychoanalytischen Konzept von Übertragung und Gegenübertragung arbeitet – die Kompetenz besteht in beiden Konzepten darin, dem Prozess der Beziehungsgestaltung theoriegeleitet Sinn zu verleihen und ihn damit überprüfbar zu gestalten.

This task we hand over to the professional community whose critical attention and creative use will decide about the sustainability of our products.

ECVision Reference Table between ECTS-ECVET

Training programmes in supervision and coaching in Europe are provided by universities (which refer to the ECTS) as well as by private companies and job-oriented adult education centres (which until now have no consented validation instruments). The reference table is dedicated to provide a model for accreditation and validation of learning outcomes in education and training of supervision and coaching in Europe.

Methodology

For introducing the ECVision competence framework as a practicable validation instrument it took four steps:

1. First of all, we decided upon using the two European credit systems ECTS and ECVET for our task.

"ECTS is a learner-centred system for credit accumulation and transfer based on the transparency of learning outcomes and learning processes. It aims to facilitate planning, delivery, evaluation, recognition and validation of qualifications and units of learning as well as student mobility.

Credit (ECTS): Quantifying refers to Learning Activities, the volume of learning based on the workload students need in order to achieve the expected learning outcomes of a learning process at a specified level.

ECVET is a technical framework for the transfer, recognition and, where appropriate, accumulation of individuals' learning outcomes with a view to achieving a qualification.

ECVET is intended to facilitate the recognition of learning outcomes in accordance with national legislation, in the framework of mobility, for the purpose of achieving a qualification.

"Credit for learning outcomes" (credit) means a set of learning outcomes of an individual which have been assessed and which can be accumulated towards a qualification or transferred to other learning programmes or qualifications.

http://www.ecvet-info.at/de/node/2)

ECVET points mean a numerical representation of the overall weight of learning outcomes in a qualification and of the relative weight of units in relation to the qualification." (Be-TWIN: ECvet-ECTS: Building Bridges and Overcoming Differ-

Auf dieser Ebene – das war uns ein zentrales Anliegen – wird es möglich zu definieren, welches die Haltungen, Qualitäten und das Handwerkszeug sind, die ein/e SupervisorIn/Coach braucht, um professionell zu arbeiten.

Wir haben uns nicht auf methodisches Handwerkszeug im Detail eingelassen, sondern stets danach gefragt, woran man merken kann, dass ein/e SupervisorIn/Coach über ein klares und reflektiertes Verständnis und ein solides Handwerkszeug verfügt.

Das ermöglicht sowohl klare Beobachtungskriterien zur Bewertung supervisorischer Kompetenz als auch weite und vielfältige Spielräume in der konkreten Umsetzung.

Wir sind uns der Grenzen unseres Unterfangens bewusst: um Kompetenz- und Lernergebnisorientierung sinnvoll zu nutzen, braucht es einen ständigen kritischen wie auch fachlichen Dialog.

Diese Aufgabe übergeben wir der professionellen Gemeinschaft, deren kritische Aufmerksamkeit und kreative Nutzung über die Nachhaltigkeit unserer Ergebnisse entscheiden wird.

Die ECVision Referenztabelle ECTS-ECVET

Ausbildungen für Supervision und Coaching in Europa werden von Universitäten (die sich auf ECTS beziehen) als auch von Privatanbietern (die bisher über keine übergreifenden Validierungsinstrumente verfügen) angeboten. Die Referenztabelle dient als Modell für die Akkreditierung und Validierung von Lernergebnissen in der Ausbildung von Supervision und Coaching in Europa über ECTS und ECVET.

Methodologie

Für die Einführung des ECVision Kompetenzrahmens als praxisorientiertes Validierungsinstrument brauchte es vier Schritte:

1. Zunächst einmal haben wir uns für die beiden europäischen Leistungspunktesysteme ECTS und ECVET entschieden.

„ECVET ist ein System zur Ansammlung, Übertragung und Anrechnung von Leistungspunkten in der beruflichen Aus- und Weiterbildung. … Kenntnisse, Fertigkeiten und Kompetenzen, die Lernende in einem Bereich der beruflichen Bildung erworben haben, sollen auch in einem anderen Bildungskontext anerkannt werden können. Die Kernelemente von ECVET sind:

ences. A Methodological Guide Produced in the Framework of the Be-Twin Project, p. 18)

2. Secondly, the VET curricula for supervision of the consortium members TOPS, Univ. of Gothenburg, Univ. of Zagreb and ASYS (Partner of VHS GmbH) were described using the Competence Framework. Managing our inner diversity was one of our core values in doing that. We not only accepted, but also embraced the autonomy and specificity of each training provider involved. This meant respecting the different ways of using the Competence Framework and presenting it in our curricula.

3. Both the TOPS and ASYS curriculum were exemplarily assigned to the learning units according to the Competence Framework, and to ECVET. A separate reference table between the two training programmes gives a first impression of how learning units based upon the ECVision Competence Framework could be used for a memorandum of understanding between VET providers for supervision and coaching.

4. We related the TOPS curriculum to that of the University of Zagreb, which was already accredited in ECTS. For doing so, we used the Be-TWIN-Matrix (Be-TWIN, p. 27) to provide valid correspondence between academic and private VET for supervision basing on the curricula of TOPS (ECVET) and University of Zagreb (ECTS). *"The methodology proposed by Be-TWIN strives to be instrumental for "a dialogue" between two important instruments in higher education (HE) and vocational education and training (VET) – the ECTS and ECVET credit systems. … Be-TWIN suggests a model which rests on transparency and readability of learning outcomes and learning activities."* (Be-TWIN, p. 5)

The reference table between TOPS (ECVET) and University of Zagreb (ECTS) finally shows how learning outcomes of both credit systems are easily comparable by using the ECVision competence framework.

ECVision Outlooks

The authors of this work want to place practice and theory transparently and comparably at the disposal of the professional community of supervisors and coaches and give a new momentum to the improvement of theory and practice in the field.

In the long run the ECVision products will:

• Contribute profoundly to a European terminology of supervision and coaching.

Einheiten von Lernergebnissen: ECVET basiert auf der strukturierten Beschreibung einer Qualifikation in so genannten Einheiten von Lernergebnissen:

- Lernergebnisse bezeichnen unabhängig von Lernort, Lernkontext und Lerndauer, was Lernende wissen, verstehen und in der Lage sind zu tun, nachdem ein Lernprozess abgeschlossen ist.
- Einheiten sind Teile einer Qualifikation, die aus zusammengehörigen Lernergebnissen bestehen („Bündel von Lernergebnissen").

ECVET-Punkte: ECVET-Punkte liefern zusätzliche Informationen und beschreiben in numerischer Form das „Gesamtvolumen" einer beruflichen Qualifikation sowie die Bedeutung der einzelnen Einheiten von Lernergebnissen in Relation zur gesamten Qualifikation.

- ECVET-Punkte werden zunächst der gesamten Qualifikation zugeordnet. Die Gesamtsumme wird dann auf die Einheiten entsprechend ihrem relativen Gewicht in Relation zur Qualifikation aufgeteilt.
- Bei der Kalkulation von ECVET-Punkten ist folgende…Übereinkunft zu beachten: Für die Kenntnisse, Fertigkeiten und Kompetenzen, die in einem Jahr in einer formalen Vollzeit-Berufsausbildung erworben werden, können 60 Punkte vergeben werden.
- ECVET-Punkte sind immer im Zusammenhang mit den Lernergebnisbeschreibungen zu betrachten."
  (siehe http://www.ecvet-info.at/de/node/2)

2. Zum Zweiten wurden die Curricula der Supervisions-Lehrgänge der Konsortiumspartner TOPS, Univ. Göteborg, Univ. Zagreb und ASYS (Partner von VHS GmbH) unter Verwendung des Kompetenzprofils beschrieben. Unsere eigene innere Vielfalt sorgsam zu handhaben war dabei ein fundamentaler Wert. Dies bedeutete, die Unterschiedlichkeit der Nutzung des Kompetenzprofils und seiner Darstellung in unseren Lehrplänen zu respektieren.

3. Die Curricula sowohl von TOPS als auch ASYS wurden exemplarisch Einheiten von Lernergebnissen nach dem Kompetenzprofil sowie ECVET-Punkten zugeordnet. Eine separate Referenztabelle zwischen den beiden Schulungsprogrammen vermittelt einen ersten Eindruck davon, wie Einheiten von Lernergebnissen auf der Grundlage des ECVision Kompetenzprofils für eine Partnerschaftsvereinbarung zwischen Ausbildungsanbietern für Supervision und Coaching eingesetzt werden könnten.

4. Wir setzten das ECVET-akkreditierte TOPS-Curriculum in Beziehung zu jenem der Universität Zagreb, das bereits in ECTS akkreditiert war. Dazu verwendeten wir die Be-TWIN-Matrix (Be-TWIN, S. 27), um eine valide

- Contribute profoundly to the implementation of the European approach to learning outcomes into the professional community of supervision and coaching.
- Facilitate bilateral agreements on the programme level, module level and course level of Training for supervision and coaching according to the National legal frameworks.
- Serve as an analytic tool for generic skills of supervisors and coaches.

None of the ECVision products represent a "biblical canon", but they are an important European contribution in a rapidly changing world of work. They provide the further development of the theory and practice of supervision and coaching in Europe by making its issues and outcomes more transparent and comparable.

Entsprechung zwischen einer privaten (TOPS/ECVET) und einer akademischen (Universität Zagreb/ECTS) Ausbildung für Supervision zu schaffen.

„Die von Be-TWIN vorgeschlagene Methodologie möchte instrumental sein für einen „Dialog" zwischen zwei wichtigen Instrumenten in der Hochschulbildung (HE) und der beruflichen Bildung (VET) – ECTS und ECVET Akkreditierungssysteme. ... Be-TWIN schlägt ein Modell vor, das auf Transparenz und Lesbarkeit der Lernergebnisse und Lernaktivitäten beruht." (Be-TWIN, S. 5)

Die Referenztabelle zwischen TOPS (ECVET) und der Universität Zagreb (ECTS) zeigt schließlich, wie leicht vergleichbar die Lernergebnisse beider Kreditsysteme werden, wenn man dazu das ECVision Kompetenzprofil nutzt.

ECVision Ausblicke

Die AutorInnen dieses Handbuchs wollen Praxis und Theorie von Supervision und Coaching der Fachwelt transparent und vergleichbar zur Verfügung stellen, sowie neue Impulse für die Weiterentwicklung von Theorie und Praxis auf diesem Gebiet geben.

Auf lange Sicht werden die ECVision Ergebnisse:

* Zu einer europäischen Terminologie von Supervision und Coaching tiefgreifend beitragen.
* Zur Umsetzung des Europäischen Ansatzes der Lernergebnisorientierung in der Fachwelt von Supervision und Coaching tiefgreifend beitragen.
* Bilaterale Partnerschaftsvereinbarungen zwischen Ausbildungsanbietern für Supervision und Coaching – im Rahmen der nationalen Gesetze – ermöglichen, auf der Ebene von Programmen, Modulen und Kursniveau.
* Als analytisches Werkzeug zur Feststellung generischer Kompetenzen von SupervisorInnen und Coaches dienen.

Die ECVision Ergebnisse sind kein „Kanon" für alle Zeiten, weit mehr ein Work-in-Progress-Projekt in Zeiten raschen Wandels.

Wenn sie jedoch Theorie und Praxis von Supervision und Coaching in Europa transparenter und vergleichbarer machen, und damit Impulse für deren Weiterentwicklung setzen, haben sie ihr Ziel erreicht!

ECVision
Research and Outlooks
A European Glossary

Wolfgang Knopf
Heidi Möller
Erik de Haan

ECVision
Forschungsperspektiven

Ein europäisches Glossar

Wolfgang Knopf
Heidi Möller
Erik de Haan

Continuing Quality Development: ECVision – An Important Step Forward in the Professionalisation of Supervision and Coaching

Wolfgang Knopf

Recent decades can be seen as a success story for supervision and – in latter years – for coaching as well. Tackling the interaction between "Person – Work – Organisation" supervision and coaching have taken an important and relevant role in a world of rapid changes and developments in the workplace, offering reflection with task orientation.

Since the founding of ANSE (Association of National Organisations for Supervision in Europe) in 1997, the promotion of quality is one of its main objectives. ANSE represents more than 8,000 qualified supervisors and coaches in the field of consulting in 22 European countries and more than 80 training institutions. While ANSE takes care of professional interests on a supranational level, there has been a need to develop common standards on a European level. This was done in the very beginning by defining so-called "minimal standards" to be seen on ANSE's homepage (www.anse.eu). A lot of discussions have been necessary to overcome the disparities which arose from different theoretical approaches and historical roots and to at least establish the initial basis for a professional understanding of supervision. These standards have to be met to become a full member of ANSE. However, this has been and still is simply a useful consensus at a minimal level, but it represents the first important definition of quality criteria.

For further quality development, this definition was too narrow for ANSE. From the 80s on, the gap between science and consulting has gradually diminished, thus leading to a broader definition of supervision and coaching:

Permanente Qualitätsentwicklung: ECVision – ein wichtiger Schritt in der Professionalisierung von Supervision und Coaching

Wolfgang Knopf

Die vergangenen Jahrzehnte können als Erfolgsgeschichte für Supervision und – in späteren Jahren – auch für Coaching gesehen werden. An den Schnittstellen der Interaktion zwischen „Person – Arbeit – Organisation" nehmen Supervision und Coaching mit ihren Angeboten von Reflexion und Aufgabenorientierung eine wichtige und relevante Rolle ein in einer Welt der schnellen Veränderungen und Entwicklungen am Arbeitsplatz.

Seit der Gründung der ANSE (Verband der Nationalen Organisationen für Supervision in Europa) im Jahr 1997, ist die Förderung der Qualität eines ihrer Hauptziele. Die ANSE vertritt mehr als 8.000 qualifizierte Supervisor-Innen und Coaches auf dem Beratungsmarkt in 22 europäischen Ländern und in mehr als 80 Ausbildungseinrichtungen. Die ANSE kümmert sich um berufspolitische Interessen auf supranationaler Ebene, woraus eine besondere Notwendigkeit erwächst, gemeinsame Standards auf europäischer Ebene zu entwickeln. Dies wurde in den Anfängen durch die Definition von sogenannten „Mindeststandards", publiziert auf der ANSE Homepage (www.anse.eu), getan. Viele Diskussionen wurden notwendig, um Differenzen, die aus unterschiedlichen theoretischen Ansätzen und historischen Wurzeln entstehen, zu überwinden und zumindest eine Ausgangsbasis für ein professionelles Supervisions-Verständnis zu etablieren. Diese Standards müssen erfüllt sein, um ein vollwertiges Mitglied der ANSE zu werden.

Diese waren zunächst ein nützlicher Konsens auf einem minimalen Niveau, nichtsdestoweniger repräsentieren sie die erste wichtige Definition von Qualitätskriterien.

Für eine weitreichendere Qualitätsentwicklung der ANSE war diese Definition zu wenig. Ab den 80er Jahren verringerte sich die Kluft zwischen Wissenschaft und Beratung nach und nach, was zu einer breiteren Definition

Table 1: Members of ANSE (www.anse.eu)

Members of ANSE	Associate members of ANSE	Members of the ANSE Network
Austria	Slovakia	Czech Republic
Bosnia and Herzegovina	Ukraine	Finland
Croatia		Great Britain
Estonia		Greece
Germany		Iceland
Hungary		Poland
Ireland		Romania
Italy		Sweden
Latvia		
Lithuania		
Netherlands		
Norway		
Slovenia		
Spain		
Switzerland		

Mutual agreement on recognition with ASCCANZ (Australia + New Zealand)
Agreement with EUROCADRES (www.eurocadres.eu)

Tabelle 1: Mitglieder der ANSE (ww.anse.eu)

Mitglieder von ANSE	Verbindungs- mitglied von ANSE	Mitglied von ANSE-Netzwerk
Österreich	Slowakien	Tschechische Republik
Bosnien und Herzegovina	Ukraine	Finnland
Kroatien		Großbritannien
Estland		Griechenland
Deutschland		Island
Ungarn		Polen
Irland		Rumänien
Italien		Schweden
Lettland		
Litauen		
Niederlande		
Norwegen		
Slowenien		
Spanien		
Schweiz		

Gegenseitiges Alleinvertriebsabkommen mit ASCCANZ (Australia + New Zealand)

Vereinbarung mit EUROCADRES (www.eurocadres.eu)

"Supervision/Coaching was now seen as a scientifically based, practically orientated and ethically linked concept of individual and organisational consulting activities within the working world."[1]

Consequently, supervisors and coaches additionally need specific socio-scientific knowledge. This is:

- standard knowledge regarding organisations including types and concepts, organisational development phases and changing processes;
- a specific handling of knowledge to be able to analyse formal phenomena and interior structures within organisations;
- schemata for the diagnosis of the relationship between environment and organisation, conflict management, efficiency of decision processes, avoidance of wasting human resources, development of creativity and increase of commitment. And minimum knowledge of the development of "the learning organisation" is a requirement.

These needs lead us to the conclusion that integration of different knowledge is a main aim of supervision and coaching.

In order to follow these developments as a professional body, ANSE had to support a basic understanding on a European level. A clear and – as far as possible – evidence-based description of terms, concepts and competencies was missing. This was mentioned at several conferences run by ANSE, and also seen in the experience within ANSE's "International Intervision Groups", where supervisors and coaches from different countries and with different theoretical approaches came together and, first of all, had to clarify definitions. Dealing with diversity within their own profession was a demanding task. This experience was the focus of the 2010 Grundtvig project "Counselling in a Multicultural Europe". The result of this project is a module which can be used in training programmes for supervisors and coaches and also in further education. A further small step was made in the method of clarification applied, but it did not go far enough. On the one hand, a lot was learned about the difficulties of comparing the different approaches to supervision and coaching in the participating countries, on the other hand, it was only possible to explore those superficially. The need to dig deeper and find a consistent way of describing supervisory skills and competences was obvious. Therefore, a further project had to be developed and presented as a proposal to Brussels. In 2012, the LEONARDO-Project ECVision was selected

---

[1]   Möller, H./Kotte, S. (2015): Supervision: Past-Present-Future. In: PiD Psychotherapie im Dialog 1/2015, 16–25.

von Supervision und Coaching führte: „Supervision/Coaching wurde nun als ein wissenschaftlich fundiertes, praxisorientiertes und ethisch angebundenes Konzept individueller und organisationaler Beratungstätigkeit in der Arbeitswelt gesehen."[1]

Folglich müssen SupervisorInnen und Coaches zusätzlich über sozialwissenschaftliches Wissen verfügen, konkret bedeutet das:

- Standardwissen über Organisationen, einschließlich Typen und Konzepte, Organisationsentwicklung, Phasen und Veränderungsprozesse;
- Ein spezifischer Einsatz von Wissen um formale Phänomene sowie Innenstrukturen von Organisationen zu analysieren; Schemata für die Diagnose der Beziehung zwischen Umwelt und Organisation, zu Konfliktmanagement, Effizienz von Entscheidungsprozessen, mit dem Ziel, Humanressourcen gezielt einzusetzen, Kreativität zu entwickeln und das Engagement zu erhöhen.
- Minimale Kenntnisse über die Entwicklung von „lernenden Organisationen" ist ebenfalls eine Voraussetzung.

Diese Anforderungen führen uns zu dem Schluss, dass die Integration von differenziertem Wissen ein Hauptziel von Supervision und Coaching darstellt.

Um diesen Entwicklungen als Berufsverband einen Rahmen zu geben, musste die ANSE ein grundlegendes Verständnis auf europäischer Ebene unterstützen. Eine klare und – soweit möglich – evidenzbasierte Beschreibung der Begriffe, Konzepte und Kompetenzen fehlte. Dies wurde auf mehreren Konferenzen der ANSE laufend erwähnt, und auch die Erfahrungen in den ANSE „Internationalen Intervisionsgruppen", in denen die SupervisorInnen und Coaches aus verschiedenen Ländern und mit unterschiedlichen theoretischen Ansätzen zusammen an professionsrelevanten Themen arbeiten, und zu Beginn stets Definitionen klären mussten. Umgang mit Vielfalt im eigenen Beruf erwies sich als anspruchsvolle Aufgabe.

Diese Erfahrung war der Fokus des Grundtvig-Projekts „Beratung in einem multikulturellen Europa" 2009–10. Das Ergebnis des Projekts ist ein Handbuch mit Modulen, das in Ausbildungsprogrammen für SupervisorInnen und Coaches wie auch in der Weiterbildung genutzt werden kann.

Ein weiterer kleiner Schritt betraf die Methode, mit der eine Klärung vorangetrieben werden konnte, aber sie ging nicht weit genug. Einerseits lern-

---

[1]   Möller, H./Kotte, S. (2015). Supervision: Past-Present-Future. In: PiD Psychotherapie im Dialog 1/2015, 16–25.

by the European Commission to develop a European System of Comparability and Validation of Supervisory Competences.

In my view, this project is a very important step for ANSE and for the community of supervisors and coaches. Two main results are found in this manual:

- a **glossary** to guarantee comparability of terms, definitions and legal frameworks, and
- a **competence framework** to guarantee comparability of supervisory competences and qualifications by describing them in terms of learning outcomes.

These outcomes should not be seen as 'the sole truth' of supervision and coaching devices and practices. The idea is to see it as an orientation, as a basis for fruitful discussions and further developments.

The **glossary** is an attempt to collect all important terms in use within supervision and coaching, and it offers descriptions and definitions. This compilation should be useful for consultants but also for organisations and clients assigning/recommending or undertaking supervision or coaching. The glossary should be seen as a basic resource for disambiguation for providers of training programmes in supervision and coaching. Ultimately, it should be beneficial for everyone concerned. In addition to being a clarification tool, it is an initial step towards establishing a professional identity for supervisors and coaches on a European level.

Within the **competence framework,** you will find competences described, on different levels, covering all activities of supervisors and coaches regarding their profession: as a supervisor/coach or as a trainer/educator for supervision/coaching or as a meta-supervisor/meta-coach. This means:

- the competence framework is of great importance for providers of training programmes in supervision and coaching, using it to describe curricula in terms of learning outcomes. It can be used to ascertain the competences of their trainers and meta-supervisors and to guarantee, as far as possible, the quality of the staff.
- Supervisors and coachees can use the competence framework for self-assessment and further education.
- Human resource managers can use the competence framework as a checklist when dealing with consultants and their proposals.
- National organisations for supervision and coaching can use the competence framework to adjust standards and for quality management. The use at national policy level for all discussions regarding the EQF (Eu-

ten wir viel über die verschiedenen Zugänge und Ansätze zu Supervision und Coaching in den beteiligten Ländern, andererseits fehlten die Ressourcen, um diese mehr als oberflächlich zu erkunden.

Die Notwendigkeit, tiefgreifender zu arbeiten und eine konsistente Form zu finden, um supervisorische Fähigkeiten und Kompetenzen zu beschreiben, war offensichtlich.

Aus diesem Bedarf heraus wurde ein weiteres Projekt entwickelt und der Europäischen Kommission zur Förderung vorgelegt.

Im Jahr 2012 wurde das LEONARDO-Projekt *„ECVision. Ein Europäisches System der Vergleichbarkeit und Validierung supervisorischer Kompetenzen"* von der Europäischen Kommission ausgewählt.

Aus meiner Sicht ist dieses Projekt ein sehr wichtiger Schritt für die ANSE und für die Fachwelt der SupervisorInnen und Coaches.

Zwei Hauptergebnisse, die auch in diesem Handbuch nachzulesen sind, dienen diesem Zweck besonders:

- ein **Glossar**, um die Vergleichbarkeit der Begriffe, Definitionen und rechtlichen Rahmenbedingungen zu gewährleisten und
- ein **Kompetenzprofil**, um die Vergleichbarkeit der Kompetenzen und Qualifikationen von SupervisorInnen und Coaches zu gewährleisten, indem es sie lernergebnisorientiert beschreibt.

Diese Ergebnisse stellen selbstverständlich nicht „die einzige Wahrheit" dar, wie Fertigkeiten und Praktiken von Supervision und Coaching beschrieben werden können. Die Idee ist, sie als Orientierung zu sehen, als Grundlage für fruchtbare Diskussionen und Weiterentwicklungen.

Das **Glossar** ist ein Versuch, alle wichtigen Begriffe, die aktuell in den Diskursen von Supervision und Coaching in Verwendung sind, zu sammeln und Beschreibungen und Definitionen dazu anzubieten. Diese Zusammenstellung soll nicht nur für BeraterInnen nutzbar sein, sondern auch für Unternehmen und KundInnen, die Supervision und Coaching zuweisen, empfehlen oder anwenden. Das Glossar soll weiters als grundlegende Ressource zur Begriffsklärung für Ausbildungsanbieter von Supervision und Coaching dienen. Letztlich soll es von Vorteil für alle Beteiligten sein, nicht zuletzt als erster Schritt hin zur Schaffung einer Berufsidentität für SupervisorInnen und Coaches auf europäischer Ebene.

Innerhalb des **Kompetenzprofils** finden sich die beschriebenen Kompetenzen wieder und decken auf verschiedenen Ebenen die Aktivitäten von SupervisorInnen und Coaches ab, sei es in Bezug auf ihren Beruf: als Super-

ropean Qualification Framework) and the NQF (National Qualification Framework) is desirable.
- The scientific community can use ECVision outcomes as a starting point for research and further systematics.
- ANSE will promote and support the use and further development of the glossary and competence framework and the critical discussion of these issues.

Finally, a critical reflection of the materials should be enhanced. As already mentioned before, these ECVision outcomes offer a starting point. When dealing with competences and learning outcomes it is always dangerous to focus solely on visibly measured results. Supervisors and coaches need to have a wide range of attitudes, behaviour, and professional competence which cannot be described operationally or measured.

To put it in a nutshell, use the manual and give us feedback.

visorIn/Coach oder als AusbilderIn für Supervision/Coaching oder als Lehr-SupervisorIn, bzw. Lehr-Coach.

Das heißt im Weiteren:

- Das Kompetenzprofil ist von großer Bedeutung für Ausbildungsanbieter von Supervision und Coaching, die es nutzen können, um die Lehrpläne in Lernergebnissen zu beschreiben. Es kann genutzt werden, um die Kompetenzen ihrer AusbilderInnen und Lehr-SupervisorInnen zu ermitteln und, so weit wie möglich, die Qualität des Personals zu gewährleisten.
- SupervisorInnen und Coaches können das Kompetenzprofil zur Selbsteinschätzung und Weiterbildung verwenden.
- PersonalleiterInnen können das Kompetenzprofil als Checkliste beim Umgang mit SupervisorInnen und Coaches und deren Vorschlägen verwenden.
- Nationale Verbände für Supervision und Coaching können das Kompetenzprofil nutzen, um Standards anzupassen und das Qualitätsmanagement zu adjustieren. Der Einsatz auf nationaler politischer Ebene für alle Diskussionen über den EQR (Europäischer Qualifikationsrahmen) und den NQR (Nationaler Qualifikationsrahmen) ist wünschenswert.
- Die wissenschaftliche Fachwelt kann die ECVision Ergebnisse als Ausgangspunkt für die Forschung und die Weiterentwicklung von Systematiken verwenden.
- Die ANSE wird proaktiv die Nutzung und Weiterentwicklung des Glossars und des Kompetenzprofils sowie die kritische Diskussion über diese Fragen fördern und unterstützen.

Schließlich sollte eine kritische Reflexion der Materialien angeregt werden. Wie bereits erwähnt, bieten diese ECVision Ergebnisse einen Ausgangspunkt für diese kritische Reflexion. Beim Umgang mit Kompetenzen und Lernergebnissen ist es immer gefährlich, sich nur auf sichtbare Messergebnisse zu konzentrieren. SupervisorInnen und Coaches brauchen eine breite Palette von Einstellungen und Verhalten – professionelle Kompetenz, die nicht operationalisiert beschrieben und gemessen werden kann.

Um es auf den Punkt zu bringen: Verwenden Sie dieses Handbuch und geben Sie uns Feedback!

Research on Supervision and Coaching Skills
Past – Present – Future

Heidi Möller

Introduction: On the relationship between scientific theory and occupational practice

Researchers and practitioners in the field of supervision and coaching are constantly affirming the significance and relevance of their respective subject areas. In publications and at conferences, occupational practice and scientific theory emerge as an interdependent duality: Practitioners emphasise the importance of scientifically safeguarding and professionalising the coaching process, while at the same time making an active contribution to the quality of its form. Scientists, on the other hand, insist on the valuable and indispensable nature of dialogue with practitioners. Nevertheless, mutual accusations still abound: Practitioners allege that scientific theory does not support counsellors (Möller, Kotte & Oellerich, 2013). Scientists claim that supervision and coaching practitioners, in spite of lacking empirical evidence, uphold "unambiguous coaching concepts" (Scherf, 2010, S. 11), close their minds to research – particularly to anything that goes beyond post-hoc surveys, and are not really interested in or curious about research outcomes, being chiefly concerned about demonstrating the legitimacy of their own craft (Haubl, 2009).

These differing perspectives are related to the differing priorities of both fields. While supervision and coaching seek to make clients capable of functioning, "organised scepticism" (Kieser, 2005) is the hallmark of a scientific outlook. In the field of counselling, insecurity must be blotted out, sometimes even through the use of really simple models. Complexity enhancement and receptiveness to different perspectives is usually just a passing phase in the transition from a wide-reaching perspective to the selective functional options of a counselling situation. One of the supervisor's and coach's func-

Forschung zu Supervision und Coaching-Kompetenz
Vergangenheit – Gegenwart – Zukunft

Heidi Möller

Einleitung: Zum Verhältnis von Wissenschaft und Praxis

ForscherInnen und PraktikerInnen im Feld von Supervision und Coaching versichern sich häufig ihrer wechselseitigen Bedeutsamkeit und Relevanz. Praxis und Wissenschaft unterstreichen in Publikationen, auf Kongressen und in ihren jeweiligen Vorträgen ein Komplementärverhältnis: Es sei wichtig, das beraterische Vorgehen wissenschaftlich abzusichern, zu professionalisieren und einen aktiven Beitrag zur Qualitätssicherung des Formats zu leisten, so die PraktikerInnen. Die WissenschaftlerInnen wiederum betonen, dass der Dialog mit PraxisexpertInnen wertvoll und unverzichtbar sei. Dennoch trifft man auch auf wechselseitige Vorwürfe: Die Wissenschaft unterstütze die Beratungspraxis nicht, so der Vorwurf von Praxisseite (Möller, Kotte & Oellerich, 2013). Die Supervisions- und CoachingpraktikerInnen verträten trotz fehlender empirischer Absicherung „vor Eindeutigkeit strotzende Beratungskonzepte" (Scherf, 2010, S. 11), verschlössen sich vor der Forschung, insbesondere vor allem, was über Post-hoc-Befragungen hinausginge, und seien nicht wirklich interessiert und lernbereit gegenüber Forschungsergebnissen, sondern vor allem daran, das eigene Tun legitimiert zu wissen (Haubl, 2009) – so die Wissenschaftsperspektive.

Diese unterschiedlichen Blickachsen haben mit den unterschiedlichen primären Aufgaben der beiden Felder zu tun. Während Supervision und Coaching darauf abzielen, die KlientInnen handlungsfähig zu machen, ist der „organisierte Skeptizismus" (Kieser, 2005) Wesensmerkmal einer wissenschaftlichen Haltung. In der Beratung muss Unsicherheit absorbiert werden, zuweilen auch durch Rückgriff auf recht einfache Modelle. Komplexitätserweiterung, ein Öffnen des Blicks auf unterschiedliche Perspektiven, ist in der Regel nur ein vorübergehendes Stadium, um vor dem Hintergrund

tions is that of "insecurity buffer" – which can also imply that "coaches must firmly assert their council." (Kieser, 2005, S. 12). Conversely, the function of scientists is to sustain an outlook of ignorance, criticism, challenge and uncertainty in the face of seemingly undeniable facts, while continuing to raise new and specific questions, thus enhancing differentiation and complexity. It is precisely through these specific means of dealing with complexity that both fields earn their keep – retaining and winning over clients, or raising research funds.

Closed shop versus observation and monitoring

Supervision and coaching, especially in individual settings, are more of a closed shop than any other form of counselling. Gaining confidence is essential, while the development of a sustainable working relationship is a crucial success factor. By comparison with other counselling and personal development programmes like training or team building, clients appreciate the coaching format's intimate and protected space in which they can discuss their concerns and problems "face to face" (Looss, 2006), without being witnessed by a third party. However, research in the field of coaching and supervision requires the most direct possible access to counselling processes. In addition to questionnaires, audiovisual recordings are the medium of choice for gaining unhindered access to whatever happens in the coaching and supervision black box (Ianiro & Kauffeld, 2011). This is so important, as we are dealing with role-specific biased perceptions of successful counselling outcomes: self-reports by clients and coaches on the effects of coaching are for instance more positive than the assessment of third parties, e.g. personnel managers (Böning & Fritschle, 2005; De Meuse et al., 2009; Haubl 2009; Kotte & Möller, 2013). For this very reason, research inevitably penetrates the intimate space between counsellor and client, potentially disrupting it – an apprehension that many coaches and supervisors cite as a pretext for not participating in research (Kotte, Schubert & Möller, draft).

Supervision research landscape

A review of primarily qualitative studies in the area of supervision reveals that these studies are seldom systematically associated with other studies or preparatory work, dealing instead with individual and often specific subject matter. This challenges us to seek workable ways of linking scientifically val-

einer umfassenderen Sicht auf eine Beratungssituation reflektierter Handlungsoptionen auswählen und umsetzen zu können. Eine Funktion von SupervisorInnen und Coaches ist die des „Unsicherheitsabsorbierers" – das kann auch implizieren: „Berater müssen ihren Rat mit Bestimmtheit vertreten." (Kieser, 2005, S. 12).

Die Aufgabe von WissenschaftlerInnen ist es dagegen, in einer Haltung des Nichtwissens, des Kritisierens, Hinterfragens und Anzweifelns scheinbar fester Tatsachen zu verbleiben, immer neue, spezifischere Fragen aufzuwerfen und damit Differenzierung und Komplexität zu erhöhen. Und auf diese je spezifischen Weisen des Umgangs mit Komplexität verdienen die beiden Bereiche ihr Geld – halten und gewinnen KlientInnen bzw. werben Forschungsgelder ein.

Closed Shop versus Beobachtung und Messung

Supervision und Coaching, insbesondere im Einzelsetting, sind mehr noch als andere Beratungsformate ein „Closed Shop". Vertrauensarbeit ist zentral, der Aufbau einer tragfähigen Arbeitsbeziehung von wesentlicher Bedeutung für den Erfolg. KlientInnen schätzen an dem Format Coaching in Abgrenzung zu anderen Beratungs- und Entwicklungsangeboten wie Trainings oder Teamentwicklungen gerade den intimen, geschützten Raum, in dem sie „unter vier Augen" (Looss, 2006) über ihre Anliegen und Probleme sprechen können, ohne dass Dritte mithören. Coaching- und Supervisionsforschung braucht dagegen einen möglichst direkten Zugang zu Beratungsprozessen. Video- oder Audioaufnahmen sind neben Fragebögen *das* Mittel der Wahl um einen unverstellten Zugang zu dem, was in der „Black Box" Coaching und Supervision (Ianiro & Kauffeld, 2011) passiert, zu bekommen. Das ist deshalb so wichtig, weil wir es mit rollenspezifischen Wahrnehmungsverzerrungen auf den Beratungserfolg zu tun haben: Self-Reports von KlientInnen und Coaches zu den Wirkungen von Coaching fallen z. B. positiver aus als die Beurteilung von Dritten, z. B. PersonalerInnen (Böning & Fritschle, 2005; De Meuse et al., 2009; Haubl 2009; Kotte & Möller, 2013;). Damit dringt Forschung aber notwendigerweise in den intimen Raum zwischen BeraterInnen und KlientInnen ein und stört diesen möglicherweise – eine Befürchtung, die von vielen Coaches und SupervisorInnen als Hinderungsgrund für die Teilnahme an Forschung benannt wird (Kotte, Schubert & Möller, in Vorber.).

id research models and methods with approaches that appeal to practitioners. There is now an unprecedented need to develop consistent and modular research programmes and to implement these over the long term, instead of continuing to produce a multitude of individual qualifying theses.

The field of supervision research is generally predominated by the voluntary disclosure of information by supervisees and supervisors, either through surveys or interviews – notably with regard to the supervision process and its effectiveness. Generally speaking, supervision and coaching research shows very high levels of satisfaction with this form of counselling. Admittedly, postgraduate research findings (e.g. Arthur, Bennett, Edens & Bell, 2003) suggest that satisfaction is only tenuously linked to truly relevant success criteria on which practitioners base their assessments, e.g. improved self-efficacy, enhanced responsiveness or behavioural changes. In addition to the voluntary disclosure of information, qualitative case studies using different methods (e.g. content analysis, depth hermeneutics) based on supervision transcripts constitute another approach to research. There are however very few studies which examine factual interaction through participative observation or audiovisual recordings. We rarely find longitudinal or randomised control group models from which conclusions may be drawn about the causal effects of supervision based on a wide range of samples.

Status of coaching research

The emerging field of coaching research is gaining ground and has currently surpassed the status of supervision research. Both nationally and internationally, an increasing number of academic "islands" are being established to study coaching as a specific counselling form. The number of scientific research articles published on the subject of coaching has increased rapidly in recent years.

In addition to individual papers, general overviews are also being published. These include reviews, which collate research results in a descriptive format while also outlining and evaluating study content (Carey et al., 2011; De Haan & Duckworth, 2012; Ely et al., 2010; Grant, 2010; Greif, 2013). Additionally, two meta-analyses have been published on the effectiveness of coaching (De Meuse et al., 2009; Theeboom et al., 2014). Meta-analyses bring together a number of results from different studies.

Greif (2013) distinguishes here between general and specific effects, focusing on the general effects of coaching on clients, such as general effectiveness assessments and satisfaction with coaching as well as achievement of

Die Forschungslandschaft Supervision

Bei der Sichtung der vor allem qualitativen Studien in der Supervision fällt auf, dass diese Studien selten systematisch an andere Studien oder Vorarbeiten anknüpfen, sondern eher einzelne, oft spezifische Themen behandeln. Dies fordert uns auf, nach praktikablen Lösungen zu suchen, wie wissenschaftlich valide Forschungsdesigns und -methoden mit für PraktikerInnen attraktiven Herangehensweisen verknüpft werden können.

Viel stärker als bisher geht es auch darum, systematische Forschungsprogramme, die aufeinander aufbauen, zu entwickeln und langfristig umzusetzen, statt weiterhin nur eine Vielzahl vereinzelter Qualifizierungsarbeiten zu produzieren.

In der Supervisionsforschung insgesamt überwiegen Selbstauskünfte von SupervisandInnen und SupervisorInnen, sei es durch Fragebogenuntersuchungen oder Interviews – und zwar sowohl im Hinblick auf Prozessverläufe als auch Erfolgsmaße von Supervision. Insgesamt finden sich in der Supervisions- und Coachingforschung generell sehr hohe Zufriedenheitswerte mit diesem Beratungsformat. Allerdings legen Befunde aus der Weiterbildungsforschung (u. a. Arthur, Bennett, Edens & Bell, 2003) nahe, dass Zufriedenheit nur sehr schwach mit den „eigentlichen", für die Berufspraxis relevanten Erfolgsmaßen wie: verbesserte Selbstwirksamkeit, erhöhte Reflexivität oder Verhaltensänderungen zusammenhängt. Neben Selbstauskünften sind qualitative Fallanalysen unterschiedlicher methodischer Ausrichtung (z. B. Inhaltsanalyse, Tiefenhermeneutik), auf der Grundlage von Supervisionstranskripten ein weiterer Forschungszugang. Sehr selten aber sind Studien, in denen die tatsächliche Interaktion – mittels teilnehmender Beobachtung oder Audio- und Videoaufzeichnungen – untersucht wird. Kaum finden wir Längsschnitt- oder randomisierte Kontrollgruppendesigns, die an großen Stichproben tatsächlich kausale Rückschlüsse auf die Effekte von Supervision zulassen.

Stand der Coachingforschung

Das junge Forschungsfeld Coachingforschung befindet sich auf dem Vormarsch und ist der Supervisionsforschung z. Z. überlegen. Sowohl national als auch international bilden sich immer mehr universitäre „Inseln" heraus, die das Format Coaching untersuchen. Die Zahl der wissenschaftlichen Artikel, die zum Thema Coaching erschienen sind, ist in den letzten Jahren rasant angestiegen.

goals, reporting high results in a large proportion of studies (Grafe & Kronig, 2011; Linley et al., 2010). But are these results any more than a "friendly thank you" (Greif, 2008, S. 219; Kauffeld, 2010)? In a seminar context, meta-analyses show that high levels of satisfaction and success do not necessarily correlate closely with learning outcomes (Arthur et al., 2003; Ely & Zaccaro, 2011).

Further studies on general coaching outcomes show the following:

- A reduction of negative effects such as stress, and an increase in general wellbeing through coaching (Grant et al., 2010; Theeboom et al., 2014)
- Significantly positive changes in resilience and self-awareness (Sherlock-Storey et al., 2013)
- An increase in career satisfaction (Bozer & Sarros, 2012).

For example, a study by Leonard-Cross (2010) shows that coaching participants compared with a control group subsequent to a two-year coaching course, performed better in terms of self-awareness beliefs. Other positive effects were also highlighted:

- Specific, physically observable changes in the client's behaviour or performance with respect to coaching purposes and goals
- More effective leadership
- Improved interpersonal relationships, team work and communication abilities
- Changes in dealing with conflict, changes in self-awareness, self-acceptance
- Personality development

These effects can be identified in various studies (Curtis & Kelly, 2013; De Haan et al., 2013; De Meuse, 2009; Ellam-Dyson & Palmer, 2011; Kines et al., 2010; Kochanowski et al., 2010; Theeboom et al., 2014). The results of qualitative studies show that coaching, besides bringing about improvements in personnel management with respect to individual self-awareness and especially with respect to conflict resolution, is perceived as being effective (Cerni et al., 2010; Kühl, 2014) and that coaching raises the client's awareness over their own counter-productive professional behaviour, thus positively influencing individual motivation and performance (Cox & Patrick, 2012).

Primary studies also examine the negative effects of coaching and their causes, from the coach's and client's perspective (De Meuse, 2009; Schermuly et al., 2014; Seiger & Künzli, 2011). Results show that coaching can indeed also have negative effects, both for the client and the coach.

Neben Einzelstudien werden auch Überblicksarbeiten veröffentlicht. Zum einen sind dies Reviews, die eher in beschreibender Form die Forschungsergebnisse zusammentragen und die Studienlage skizzieren und bewerten (Carey et al., 2011; De Haan & Duckworth, 2012; Ely et al., 2010; Grant, 2010; Greif, 2013). Des Weiteren existieren bis heute zwei Metaanalysen zur Wirksamkeit von Coaching (De Meuse et al., 2009; Theeboom et al., 2014). In Metaanalysen werden mehrere Studien quantifizierend zu Metadaten zusammengefasst.

Greif (2013) unterscheidet hier zwischen allgemeinen und spezifischen Wirkungen. Über die allgemeinen Wirkungen von Coaching auf die KlientInnen, die allgemeine Erfolgseinschätzung und die Zufriedenheit mit dem Coaching sowie die Zielerreichung, berichtet ein Großteil der Studien hohe Werte (Grafe & Kronig, 2011; Linley et al., 2010). Aber bedeuten diese Ergebnisse mehr als ein „freundliches Dankeschön" (Greif, 2008, S. 219; Kauffeld, 2010)? Metaanalysen im Seminarkontext zeigen, dass hohe Zufriedenheits- und Erfolgseinschätzungen nicht unbedingt stark mit den Lernergebnissen korrelieren (Arthur et al., 2003; Ely & Zaccaro, 2011).

Weitere Studien zu den allgemeinen Ergebnissen von Coaching berichten:
- die Reduktion negativer Affekte, wie etwa Stressbelastung bzw. die Steigerung des allgemeinen Wohlbefindens durch Coaching (Grant et al., 2010; Theeboom et al., 2014)
- signifikant positive Veränderungen der Resilienz und des Selbstbewusstseins (Sherlock-Storey et al., 2013)
- Steigerung der Karriere-Zufriedenheit (Bozer & Sarros, 2012).

So zeigt beispielsweise eine Studie von Leonard-Cross (2010), dass Coaching-TeilnehmerInnen im Vergleich zu einer Kontrollgruppe im Anschluss an ein zweijähriges Coaching höhere Werte in Bezug auf ihre Selbstwirksamkeitsüberzeugungen zeigten. Weitere positive Effekte konnten gezeigt werden:
- spezifische, konkret beobachtbare Verhaltens- oder Leistungsveränderungen bei den KlientInnen im Hinblick auf die Anlässe und Ziele der Coachings,
- effektivere Führung,
- Verbesserung der interpersonalen Beziehungen, der Zusammenarbeit und Kommunikationsfähigkeit,
- veränderter Umgang mit Konflikten, Selbstreflexion, Selbstakzeptanz
- Persönlichkeitsentwicklung.

Diese Effekte lassen sich in verschiedenen Studien ausmachen (Curtis & Kelly, 2013; De Haan et al., 2013; De Meuse, 2009; Ellam-Dyson & Palmer,

A number of assessments on the effectiveness of leadership development programmes with integrated coaching modules have shown that training and coaching, when jointly delivered, are more effective than training alone (Ladyshewsky, 2007; Kochanowski et al., 2010; Kotte & Möller, 2013; Wallis, 2010). Furthermore, a few qualitative studies have highlighted the specific added benefits of coaching, including more realistic self-appraisal and enhanced self-efficacy (e.g. Spencer, 2011).

Organisational considerations could be factored into the assessment of coaching's effectiveness through the use of 360°-feedback as a measuring instrument. In this respect, various studies have shown that coaching processes and the attendant changes observed in the client have been positively and successfully assessed by the client's superiors and colleagues (Kaufel et al., 2006; Scherm & Scherer, 2011). In most of these studies however, the extent to which these effects have actually been achieved through the medium of coaching still remains an open question.

Möller & Kotte (2011) conclude that a number of coaching studies are indeed based on client self-assessments, that they often relate to student populations, and that the diversity of coaches (professional experience, theoretical background, primary occupation) makes comparison difficult.

What can we do as a group?

At European level, the ECVision Competence Framework for Supervision and Coaching has primarily succeeded in summarising the concepts of this form of counselling, while also producing a common glossary. Secondly, the project group – with the support of international experts – has defined a set of counselling skills specifically for supervision and coaching: the demonstration of knowledge, capability and performance, central to the practice of supervision and coaching: competencies that should be imparted through further education in the field of supervision and coaching.

In this regard, a systematic supervision and coaching research programme could help to place both forms of counselling on scientifically solid ground. However, this cannot be achieved without a sustainable working relationship between occupational practice and scientific theory. Practitioners expect transparency with respect to research goals and methods, as well as technical and organisational support where collaborative work is concerned. They expect research to be manageable and not overly time-consuming. Above all, they expect equal measures of cooperation. While supervisors and coaches have a genuine and substantial interest in research, they want to be involved

2011; Kines et al., 2010; Kochanowski et al., 2010; Theeboom et al., 2014). Die Ergebnisse von qualitativen Studien zeigen, dass Coaching neben einer Verbesserung in der Personalführung im Hinblick auf die individuelle Selbstreflexion und vor allem die Konfliktbewältigung als wirksam erlebt wird (Cerni et al., 2010; Kühl, 2014) und dass Coaching das Bewusstsein der KlientInnen über ihr eigenes kontraproduktives Arbeitsverhalten steigert und dies die individuelle Motivation und Arbeitsleistung positiv beeinflusst (Cox & Patrick, 2012).

Erste Studien fragen nun auch nach negativen Effekten von Coaching und ihren Ursachen aus der Perspektive von KlientInnen und Coaches (De Meuse, 2009; Schermuly et al., 2014; Seiger & Künzli, 2011). Die Studienergebnisse zeigen, dass Coaching durchaus auch negative Wirkungen sowohl für KlientInnen als auch für den Coach haben kann.

Eine Vielzahl von Evaluationen zur Wirksamkeit von Führungsentwicklungsprogrammen mit integrierten Coaching-Bausteinen zeigt, dass Training und Coaching gemeinsam wirksamer sind als reines Training (Ladyshewsky, 2007; Kochanowski et al., 2010; Kotte & Möller, 2013; Wallis, 2010). Einige qualitative Studien verdeutlichen darüber hinaus den spezifischen Zusatznutzen von Coaching, zum Beispiel eine realistischere Selbsteinschätzung und erhöhte Selbstwirksamkeit (u. a. Spencer, 2011).

Eine Möglichkeit des Einbezugs des organisationalen Kontexts in die Untersuchung der Wirksamkeit von Coaching stellt der Einsatz von 360°-Feedbacks als Messinstrument zur Erfassung der Wirksamkeit dar.

Hier zeigen verschiedene Studien, dass Coachingprozesse und die damit einhergehenden Veränderungen der KlientInnen von Vorgesetzten und MitarbeiterInnen als positiv und erfolgreich eingeschätzt werden (Kaufel et al., 2006; Scherm & Scherer, 2011). Allerdings bleibt in den meisten der genannten Studien die Frage offen, inwieweit die Effekte tatsächlich durch das Coaching erzielt wurden.

Möller & Kotte (2011) fassen zusammen, dass eine Vielzahl der Coachingstudien allerdings auf Selbsteinschätzungen der KlientInnen basieren, oft an Studierendenpopulationen erhoben wurden und durch die Heterogenität der Coaches (Berufserfahrung, theoretischer Hintergrund, Primärprofession) schwer vergleichbar sind.

in the definition of "relevant" questions (see Möller, Oellerich, Schubert & Kotte, 2014). They also expect elaborated research models that are compatible with the respective types of counselling. They want feedback on results and last but not least, expect the benefits of research to be reflected in everyday life. Under no circumstances do they wish to serve as guinea pigs for bachelor and master students, who do not really understand much about coaching and supervision.

As far as scientific theory is concerned, a change of thinking is required when it comes to self-definition: The role of researchers is also to provide practitioners with a service, i.e. they must endeavour to identify the latter's needs and respond to them.

Research in further education

The ECVision project provides an excellent basis for further education in supervision and coaching! Thanks to its intelligent design, the candidates' skills development process – beyond the *Happy Sheets* (satisfaction surveys) stage – is underpinned by hard facts: the acquisition and transfer of learning. Kirkpatrick (1998) distinguishes four levels of outcome with respect to further education:
• Participant satisfaction (reaction)
• Learning
• Behaviour
• Results

Möller and Drexler (2007, 2009, 2010, 2011, 2012) established the basic concepts, which, with the help of ECVision inputs, could prepare the ground for further supervision and coaching training research on a broad international scale. Catering to the needs of further education institutes, we could jointly develop a range of different research models. Earlier preparatory work could serve as an example. In a **preliminary assessment** (Scharmer's sculpture principle), the participants' motivation to undergo further training was evaluated. Interestingly, this did not seek to distinguish between motivation with regard to coaching or supervision. Further education candidates were subsequently presented with a leadership problem which they were asked to explore with the help of guiding questions, to propose a diagnosis, and to come up with some initial ideas on the counselling process. External evaluators (experienced coaches) were asked to process the same scenario in the same way, for purposes of comparison. Working on the premise that

Was können wir gemeinsam tun?

Mit dem ECVision Kompetenzprofil für Supervision und Coaching ist es auf europäischer Ebene gelungen, zunächst einmal die Begrifflichkeiten dieser Beratungsformate zu synchronisieren und ein konsensfähiges Glossar zu erarbeiten. In einem zweiten Schritt erreichte die Projektgruppe mithilfe von internationalen ExpertInnen, beraterische Kompetenzen für die Supervision und das Coaching zu formulieren: Kenntnisse, Fähigkeiten und Performance auszuweisen, die für die Supervisions- und Coachingpraxis zentral sind und in Supervisions- und Coachingweiterbildungen vermittelt werden sollten.

Hier könnte eine systematische Supervisions- und Coachingforschung ansetzen, um die beiden Beratungsformate auf wissenschaftlich solide Füße zu stellen. Dies geht allerdings nicht ohne eine tragfähige Arbeitsbeziehung zwischen Praxis und Wissenschaft. PraktikerInnen erwarten Transparenz in Hinblick auf die Forschungsziele und -methoden, technisch organisatorische Unterstützung bei der Mitarbeit, dass die Forschung für sie handhabbar und nicht zu zeitaufwendig ist und vor allem eine Kooperation auf Augenhöhe.

SupervisorInnen und Coaches haben ein genuines, inhaltliches Interesse an Forschung, wollen aber mitdefinieren, was „relevante" Fragestellungen sind (vgl. Möller, Oellerich, Schubert & Kotte, 2014). Sie erwarten zudem elaborierte Forschungsdesigns, die mit der jeweiligen Beratungspraxis kompatibel sind. Sie wollen die Rückmeldung der Ergebnisse und letztlich einen Benefit aus der Forschung, der in ihrer Alltagspraxis spürbar ist. Auf keinen Fall wollen sie Versuchskaninchen für Bachelor- und Masterstudierende sein, die von Coaching und Supervision nicht wirklich etwas verstehen.

Mit Blick auf die Wissenschaft ist ein Umdenken in der Selbstdefinition erforderlich: ForscherInnen sind auch DienstleisterInnen für die PraktikerInnen, d. h. sie müssen sich bemühen, deren Bedarfe zu identifizieren und darauf zu reagieren.

Weiterbildungsforschung

Für den Weiterbildungsbereich Supervision und Coaching ist das ECVision Projekt eine hervorragende Grundlage. Mit Hilfe von intelligenten Designs lässt sich der Kompetenzentwicklungsprozess der KandidatInnen jenseits der *Happy Sheets* (Zufriedenheitsmessungen) auf einer Hard-Fact-Ebene durch Messung von Lernerfolg und Lerntransfer begleiten.

further training in the field of supervision and coaching also supports informal learning, such as the basic concepts of business economics without this subject matter being specifically included in the curriculum or defined as a learning goal, the candidates took part in a knowledge test. The following instruments were used for personality assessment, self-management competence and attachment patterns:

- BIP – Business Inventory of Personality (Hossiep & Paschen, 2003)
- MES – Meta-Emotion Scale (Mitmansgruber, 2005)
- MAAS – Mindful Attention and Awareness (Brown & Ryan, 2003)
- AAQ – Questionnaire on "experiental avoidance" (Hayes et al., 2004)
- FEE – Questionnaire on remembered parenting styles (Schumacher et al., 2000)
- AAS – Attachment and relationship questionnaire (Schmidt et al., 2004)

For purposes of assessing empathy skills development, candidates took part in two emotional intelligence tests: FEEL (Kessler et al., 2002) and CATS (Forming, Levy & Ekman, 2000).

While undergoing further education (**accompanying research**), participants evaluate their own learning progress using questionnaires while the respective lecturers do the same, so that we are able to compare self-image and public image. **The post-assessment** covered the following dimensions: problem-solving skills, diagnostic skills, conversational skills (role-play), interpersonal skills and knowledge.

Research on training programmes for coaching

Table 2: Training programmes for Coaching

Start of the training programme	Survey after each workshop	End of the training programme
Instruments: Sculpting Case examples Test of knowledge Exploration of affects Questionnaire	*Instruments:* Test of self-evaluation and the estimation of others according to the learning progress	*Instruments:* Case examples Test of knowledge Exploration of affects Questionnaire

Kirkpatrick (1998) unterscheidet vier unterschiedliche Ebenen von Weiterbildungszielen:

- Zufriedenheit der TeilnehmerInnen (reaction)
- Lernerfolg (learning)
- Transfererfolg (behaviour)
- Unternehmenserfolg (results)

Möller und Drexler (2007, 2009, 2010, 2011, 2012) haben erste Konzepte vorgelegt, die durch die ECVision Arbeitsergebnisse eine Weiterbildungsforschung auf breiter internationaler Ebene anstoßen könnten. Den Bedarfen der Weiterbildungsinstitute angepasst, könnten wir gemeinsam differenzierte Forschungsdesigns entwickeln. Zur Veranschaulichung sei an dieser Stelle die bisherige Vorarbeit illustriert.

In einer **Prämessung** (Skulpturarbeit nach Scharmer) wurde die Weiterbildungsmotivation der TeilnehmerInnen erhoben, die sich interessanterweise nicht von der Motivation, ein Coaching oder eine Supervision aufzusuchen, unterschied. In einem weiteren Schritt wurde den WeiterbildungskandidatInnen ein Führungsproblem als Arbeitsprobe vorgelegt, das sie anhand von Leitfragen explorieren, anschließend eine Problemdiagnose erstellen und erste Ideen zum beraterischen Vorgehen entwickeln sollten. Externe Rater – langjährig erfahrene Coaches – wurden gebeten, zum Vergleich dasselbe Fallbeispiel analog zu bearbeiten. Da wir davon ausgehen, dass Weiterbildungen in Supervision und Coaching auch informelles Lernen ermöglichen, so zum Beispiel eine Menge Grundlagenwissen im Bereich der Betriebswirtschaft vermitteln, ohne dass dies im Curriculum ausgewiesen ist oder als Lernziel formuliert ist, nahmen die KandidatInnen an einem Wissenstest teil. Zu Persönlichkeitsdiagnostik, Selbstmanagementkompetenz und Bindungsmustern wurden folgende Instrumente eingesetzt:

- BIP – Bochumer Inventar zur berufsbezogenen Persönlichkeitsbeschreibung (Hossiep & Paschen, 2003)
- MES – Meta-Emotion Scale (Mitmansgruber, 2005)
- MAAS – Mindful Attention and Awareness Scale (Brown & Ryan, 2003)
- AAQ – Fragebogen zu „experiental avoidance" (Hayes et al., 2004)
- FEE – Fragebogen zum erinnerten elterlichen Erziehungsverhalten (Schumacher et al., 2000)
- AAS – Fragebogen zur Art der Bindung oder Beziehung (Schmidt et al., 2004)

European research on supervision and coaching

As a basic rule, supervision and coaching research needs to be systematic. It must take account of the coach, the supervisor, the clients, their professional relationships and organisational considerations (e. g. triangular contracts, the organisation's coaching culture). Firstly, the competence framework of European supervisors and coaches could be broadly examined using ECVision as a basis. Secondly, there is a need for differentiated counselling research, which empirically examines the counselling process as well as supervision and coaching outcomes.

On the first point regarding the examination of European coach and supervisor competence frameworks, ECVision provides an excellent basis for implementing supervisory and coaching skills and gaining access to a broad sample of supervisors and coaches across Europe. This would provide an effective means of studying the similarities and differences in the competence frameworks of counsellors working in different sectors (non-profit, public, private), branches and countries, or of those preferring the definition of coach and/or supervisor. At the same time, additional factors such as age, professional experience, gender, primary education and cultural influences, etc. could be considered.

On the second point regarding differentiated counselling research, the counselling process as well as coaching and supervision outcomes are essential. In this respect, research could take both a qualitative and quantitative approach.

Supervision and coaching research must be theory-driven and may systematically draw on existing theories and findings in the fields of clinical, personal and social psychology, as well as in the fields of business economics, management research and sociology, in order to develop research hypotheses.

In order for comparable results to be delivered, consistent, standardised, reliable and validated, measuring processes must be applied to large sample groups, with a systematic assessment of client, supervisor/coach and contextual variables, as well as performance criteria. In this regard, we can also build upon ECVision's results: Coach and supervisor competences can be incorporated as supervisor/coach-related variables into comprehensive process outcome models. This can be used to determine, for example, their influence on the emergence of a stable work relationship between coach and coachee.

In the future, coaching and supervision should also undergo a more rigorous comparison with other current initiatives such as training or mentoring programmes, instead of with „weak" control groups, in order to gain insights into the differential indication of different development forms.

Um die Kompetenzentwicklung im Bereich der Empathie zu messen, nahmen die KandidatInnen an zwei Emotionserkennungstests teil: FEEL (Kessler et al., 2002) und CATS (Forming, Levy & Ekman, 2000).

Während der Weiterbildung (**Begleitforschung**) schätzten die TeilnehmerInnen ihren eigenen Lernfortschritt per Fragebogen ein und die jeweiligen DozentInnen taten das gleiche, so dass wir Selbstbild und Fremdbild vergleichen konnten. Die **Postmessung** erfolgte in den Dimensionen: Problemlösekompetenz, diagnostische Kompetenz, Gesprächsführungskompetenz (im Rollenspiel), Beziehungsfähigkeit und Wissen.

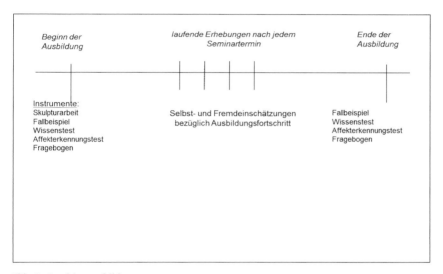

Abb. 2: Coachingausbildung

Europäische Supervisions- und Coachingforschung

Grundsätzlich muss Supervisions- und Coachingforschung systematischer angelegt werden und Coach, SupervisorIn, KlientInnen und ihre Arbeitsbeziehung und den organisationalen Kontext berücksichtigen (z. B. Dreieckskontrakte, Coachingkultur der Organisation). Zum einen können auf der Grundlage von ECVision die Kompetenzprofile europäischer SupervisorInnen und Coaches umfassend untersucht werden. Zum anderen ist eine differenzierte Beratungsforschung nötig, die sowohl den Beratungsprozess als auch die Outcomes von Supervision und Coaching empirisch untersucht.

Tools of choice would include longitudinal investigations, with several survey dates and catamnestic records for determining long-term „sleeper" effects, particularly inherent in organisational performance criteria (Ely et al. 2010).

ECVision ensures that the set of competences lends itself to comparison. The following research questions are of particular relevance and should be examined using multiple methods (large sample size and breadth as well as differentiated and process-analytical in-depth investigations):

Coach-client relationship as a central performance factor: This specifically entails a precise description of coach/customer/interaction variables, in order to define what constitutes a "good", i.e. helpful relationship. Which facets define the quality of the coach/supervisor-client relationship (rapport, esteem, trust, etc.)? Which supervisor/coach and client-related variables, which process-related variables and which organisational factors influence the quality of the relationship? In this regard, the aforementioned ECVision competences could be validated as predictors for relationship quality. What is the right match between coach/supervisor and client? To what extent can non-verbal, mimetic interactions function as predictors for coaching outcomes (Benecke und Krause 2005)? In addition to standardised questionnaires and process reviews, systematic transcript and video analyses using qualitative as well as quantitative approaches, are particularly promising (e.g. B. Ianiro and Kauffeld 2011).

Process research on what generally occurs in the coaching/supervision process: How does a working relationship develop between the coach/supervisor and client (and where applicable between the employer and client organisation) via the counselling process? What fulfilment and emotional control processes take place through coaching? What models, schools and methods do coaches and supervisors claim to work by, and do they actually put these into practice (allegiance, adherence)? How do clients react to different initiatives (responsiveness)? Methodical process reviews (e.g. working bond with reference to Grawe, client self-efficacy or supervisor/coach countertransference with reference to analytical process reviews) or even intersessional reviews focusing on the period between sessions and thus incorporating work routines, would be useful.

Not without diagnosis

As far as the outlined research questions are concerned, practitioners must overcome their aversion, reserve or even denial with regard to diagnosis: Re-

Zum ersten Punkt, der Untersuchung der Kompetenzprofile europäischer SupervisorInnen und Coaches: Hier bietet ECVision eine hervorragende Grundlage, um supervisorische Kompetenzen zu operationalisieren und in einer großen Stichprobe von SupervisorInnen europaweit zu erfassen.

Auf diese Weise können Ähnlichkeiten und Unterschiede in den Kompetenzprofilen von BeraterInnen, die u. a. in verschiedenen Sektoren (Nonprofit-Sektor, öffentlicher Sektor, Privatwirtschaft) oder Branchen tätig sind, in verschiedenen Ländern arbeiten oder sich eher als Coaches und/oder SupervisorInnen definieren, ermittelt werden. Gleichzeitig können weitere Einflussfaktoren wie Alter, Berufserfahrung, Geschlecht, Primärausbildung und kulturelle Einflussfaktoren etc. berücksichtigt werden.

Was den zweiten Punkt, eine differenzierte Beratungsforschung, betrifft, sind sowohl der Beratungsprozess als auch die Outcomes von Supervision und Coaching zentral. Dabei kann die Forschung sowohl qualitative als auch quantitative Zugänge umfassen.

Die Supervisions- und Coachingforschung muss theoriegeleitet erfolgen und kann vorhandene Theorien und Befunde aus klinischer, Persönlichkeits-, Sozialpsychologie, aber auch Betriebswirtschaftslehre, Managementforschung und Soziologie systematisch zur Hypothesenbildung nutzen.

Um Ergebnisse vergleichbar zu machen, müssen einheitliche, standardisierte, reliable und validierte Messverfahren an großen Stichproben eingesetzt werden, über die KlientInnen-, SupervisorIn/Coach- und Kontextvariablen sowie Ergebniskriterien systematisch erhoben werden. Auch hier können wir auf den Ergebnissen von ECVision aufbauen: Die für Coaches und SupervisorInnen definierten Kompetenzen können als Variablen auf Coach-Seite in umfassendere Prozess-Outcome-Modelle aufgenommen werden. So kann zum Beispiel ihr Einfluss auf die Entstehung einer stabilen Arbeitsbeziehung zwischen Coach und Coachee ermittelt werden.

Zukünftig müssen Coaching und Supervision auch härteren Vergleichen mit anderen gängigen Interventionen, also z. B. mit Trainings- oder Mentoring-Programmen statt mit „schwachen" Kontrollgruppen unterzogen werden, auch um Hinweise auf die differentielle Indikation unterschiedlicher „Entwicklungsformate" zu erhalten.

Wünschenswert wären auch längsschnittliche Untersuchungen mit mehreren Erhebungszeitpunkten bzw. Katamnesen zur Ermittlung von Langzeit- bzw. „Sleeper"-Effekten, wie sie insbesondere bei organisationalen Ergebnismaßen naheliegen (Ely et al. 2010).

ECVision sichert die Vergleichbarkeit der erfassten Kompetenzen. Konkret sind folgende Forschungsfragen von besonderer Relevanz und sollten

search of effectiveness cannot be conducted without comparable input data! Coach and customer variables and their influence on the supervision or coaching process and its outcomes must be systematically assessed. To date, client attributes (attitude, personality, gender, receptiveness to coaching or supervision, etc.) as well as coach/supervisor attributes (professional experience, theoretical/conceptual orientation, etc.) have barely been investigated.

Meaningful research of effectiveness cannot take place without a differentiated assessment of the client's attributes, of the team dynamics surrounding her and of the organisational coaching parameters. The term "diagnosis" derives from the Greek verb "diagignóskein", encompassing the different facets of perception and information processing and spanning the stages of cognition through to resolution. The verb means "to learn about something/someone in detail", "to decide" or "to resolve" (see. Möller & Kotte, 2014). In taking a differentiated approach towards "diagnosis" or scrutiny, the observer's "diagnostic" spectacles must be adjusted to the narrowest possible viewing angle. Similarly, a consistent diagnostic approach is the bedrock of professional counselling practices, as opposed to an approach based solely on personal preferences and assumptions. The systematic gathering and processing of information for the purpose of substantiating, monitoring and optimising programmes and initiatives, should be considered a "good" routine counselling practice. The challenge is to scientifically structure and systematise the investigative and exploratory endeavours that are integral to coaching and supervision, channelling these efforts into the establishment of counselling best practices.

Appeal to supervisors and coaches

As practitioners, you are urged to leave your comfort zone, to refrain from avoidance tactics, and to provide researchers with access to your supervision processes. This also entails acceptance of the critical question as to what extent the protection of the counselling environment for the sake of the client is really a priority. Or rather, is it not a welcome excuse for avoiding observation and possible judgement by a third party (researchers), thereby escaping the attendant fears of supervisor and coach? The role of science is to establish an equitable and balanced cooperative relationship which supports constructive dialogue with practitioners. It is our hope that the latter will provide researchers with their own perspectives, ideas and expectations. This may be helped along by growing external pressures, calling for stricter

multimethodal (über große Fallzahlen in die Breite, aber auch differenzierte, prozessanalytische Untersuchungen in die Tiefe) untersucht werden:

Coach-KlientInnen-Beziehung als zentraler Wirkfaktor: Dabei geht es insbesondere um eine genaue Beschreibung von Coach-, KlientInnen- und Interaktionsvariablen, um zu definieren, was eine „gute", d. h. hilfreiche Beziehung ausmacht. Welche Facetten definieren die Qualität der Coach/SupervisorIn-KlientInnen-Beziehung (Rapport, Wertschätzung, Vertrauen usw.)? Welche Variablen auf SupervisorIn/Coach- und KlientInnenseite, welche Prozessvariablen und welche organisationalen Kontextfaktoren beeinflussen die Beziehungsqualität? Hier könnten z. B. die ECVision Kompetenzen wie oben beschrieben als Prädiktoren für Beziehungsqualität überprüft werden. Was ist eine gute Passung zwischen Coach/SupervisorIn und KlientIn? Inwieweit können u. a. nonverbale, mimische Interaktionen als Prädiktoren für den Coachingerfolg fungieren (Benecke und Krause 2005)? Neben standardisierten Fragebögen sowie Prozessskalen nach jeder Sitzung sind hier insbesondere systematische Transkript- und Videoanalysen sowohl qualitativer Art wie auch mittels standardisiert-quantitativer Beobachtungsverfahren erfolgversprechend (z. B. Ianiro und Kauffeld 2011).

Prozessforschung zur Frage, was im Coaching oder der Supervision überhaupt passiert: Wie gestaltet sich das Arbeitsbündnis zwischen Coach/SupervisorIn und KlientIn (und ggf. Auftraggeber bzw. KlientInnenorganisation) über den Beratungsprozess? Welche Zielfindungs- und Emotionsregulationsprozesse finden im Coaching statt? Nach welchen Modellen bzw. Schulen und Methoden geben Coaches und SupervisorInnen an zu arbeiten und setzen sie diese in der Praxis tatsächlich ein (Allegianz, Adhärenz)? Wie reagieren die KlientInnen auf unterschiedliche Interventionen (Responsiveness)? Methodisch wären hier neben Prozessskalen (z. B. zum Arbeitsbündnis in Anlehnung an Grawe, zum Selbstwirksamkeitserleben der KlientInnen oder zu Fantasien und Gegenübertragungsgefühlen der SupervisorInnen/Coaches in Anlehnung an analytische Prozessskalen) oder auch Intersessionskalen, die sich auf die Zeit zwischen den Sitzungen beziehen und damit den Arbeitsalltag miteinbeziehen, zielführend.

Nicht ohne Diagnostik

Für die skizzierten Forschungsfragen müssen die PraktikerInnen ihre Scheu, Vorbehalte oder gar Ablehnung der Diagnostik gegenüber überwinden, denn ohne vergleichbare Ausgangsdaten ist keine Wirksamkeitsforschung möglich! Coach- und KlientInnenvariablen und damit die Untersuchung ih-

requirements regarding the systematic evaluation and quality assurance of counselling services, in favour of clients and employers.

A lot of work needs to be done so let's get started! This requires the establishment of collaborative ventures, combining the interests and expert capabilities of the various stakeholders (coaches, supervisors, clients, client organisations, employer organisations, universities) and making them usable.

Bibliography

Arthur, W. Jr., Bennett, W. Jr., Edens, P.S., Bell, S.T. (2003). Effectiveness of Training in Organizations: A Meta-Analysis of Design and Evaluation Features. Journal of Applied Psychology, 88 (2), 234–245.

Benecke, C., & Krause, R. (2005). Initiales mimisch-affektives Verhalten und Behandlungszufriedenheit in der Psychotherapie von Patientinnen mit Panikstörungen. Zeitschrift für Psychosomatische Medizin und Psychotherapie, 51(4), 346–359.

Böning, U., & Fritschle, B. (2005). Coaching fürs Business. Bonn: ManagerSeminare.

Bozer, G., Sarros, J.C. (2012). Examining the Effectiveness of Executive Coaching on Coachees' Performance in the Israeli Context. International Journal of Evidence Based Coaching and Mentoring, 10(1), 14–32.

Brown, K. W. & Ryan, R. M. (2003). The benefits of being present: Mindfulness and its role in psychological well-being. Journal of Personality and Social Psychology, 84, 822–848.

Carey, W., Philippon, D., & Cummings, C. (2011). Coaching models for leadership development: An integrative review. Journal of Leadership Studies, 5(1), 51–69.

Cerni, T., Curtis, G., & Colmer, S. (2010). Executive coaching can enhance transformational leadership. International Coaching Psychology Review, 5(1), 81–85.

Cox, E., & Patrick, C. (2012). Managing Emotions at Work: How Coaching Affects Retail Support Workers' Performance and Motivation. International Journal of Evidence Based Coaching and Mentoring, 10(2), 34–51.

Curtis, D.F., Kelly, L.L. (2013). Effect of a quality of life coaching intervention on psychological courage and self-determination. International Journal of Evidence Based Coaching and Mentoring, 11(1), 20–38.

De Haan, E., Duckworth, A., Birch, D. & Jones, C. (2013). Executive coaching outcome research: The contribution of common factors such as relationship, personality match, and self-efficacy. Consulting Psychology Journal: Practice and Research, 65(1), 40–57.

De Meuse, K.P., Dai, G., Lee, R.J. (2009). Evaluating the effectiveness of executive coaching: beyond ROI? Coaching: An International Journal of Theory, Research and Practice, 2(2), 117–134.

res Einflusses auf Supervisions- oder Coachingprozess und -ergebnis müssen systematisch erhoben werden. Bislang sind sowohl die Merkmale der KlientInnen (Einstellungen, Persönlichkeit, Geschlecht, Grad an Freiwilligkeit des Coachings oder der Supervision, usw.) als auch die der Coaches und SupervisorInnen (Berufserfahrung, theoretisch-konzeptionelle Orientierung, etc.) noch kaum untersucht.

Eine sinnvolle Wirksamkeitsforschung kann ohne eine differenzierte Erfassung der KlientInnen-Charakteristika, der sie umgebenden Teamdynamik und der organisationalen Rahmenbedingungen des Coachings nicht erfolgen. Diagnostik geht auf das griechische Verb „diagignóskein" zurück, das verschiedene Facetten eines Wahrnehmungs- und Informationsverarbeitungsprozesses vom Erkennen bis zum Beschließen umfasst. Das Verb bedeutet „genau kennenlernen", „(sich) entscheiden", „beschließen" (vgl. Möller & Kotte, 2014). Versucht man sich einer „Diagnostik", also einem genauen Hinschauen, differenziert zu nähern, muss einerseits der möglicherweise eingeengte Blickwinkel reflektiert werden, den einzelne diagnostische „Brillen" nach sich ziehen können. Gleichzeitig ist ein systematisches diagnostisches Vorgehen die Grundlage für ein professionelles beraterisches Handeln im Gegensatz zu einem nur auf persönlichen Vorlieben und Vorannahmen begründeten Arbeiten. Das systematische Sammeln und Aufbereiten von Informationen mit dem Ziel, Entscheidungen für Interventionen zu begründen, zu kontrollieren und zu optimieren, ist als alltägliche „gute" beraterische Praxis zu verstehen. Es geht also darum, das Erkunden und Explorieren, das im Coaching und der Supervision ohnehin stattfindet, wissenschaftlich zu systematisieren und zu strukturieren, um das beraterische Handeln in möglichst optimaler Weise daraus abzuleiten.

Appell an die SupervisorInnen und Coaches

Sie als PraktikerInnen sind eingeladen, ihre Komfortzone und mögliche Abwehrmanöver zu verlassen und ihre Supervisionsprozesse für ForscherInnen zugänglich machen. Dies impliziert auch, sich die kritische Frage gefallen zu lassen, inwiefern das Argument, den Beratungsraum für KlientInnen zu schützen, wirklich im Vordergrund steht. Oder ist es nicht vielmehr ein willkommener Vorwand, sich einer Beobachtung und möglichen Bewertung durch externe Dritte (ForscherInnen) und den damit verbundenen eigenen Ängsten als SupervisorIn und Coach nicht stellen zu müssen? Es ist die Aufgabe der Wissenschaft, eine gleichberechtigte, symmetrische Kooperationsbeziehung zu gestalten, um mit den PraktikerInnen konstruktiv in einen

Drexler, A. & Möller, H. (2007). Berufliche Kompetenzentwicklung von Supervisorinnen in Ausbildung. Supervision, 3, 51–57.

Drexler, A., Uffelmann, P., Stippler, M. & Möller, H. (2009). Schulleitercoaching – Konzeption und Ausbildungsevaluation. Organisationsberatung, Supervision, Coaching, 1, 35–53.

Drexler, A. & Möller, H. (2009). Erfolgsmessungen von Weiterbildung – Das Innsbrucker Modell. In. H. Pühl (Hrsg.): Handbuch der Supervision 3, S. 381–398. Berlin: Leutner.

Drexler, A. & Möller, H. (2010).Coachinglehrgänge auf dem Prüfstand: Ein Evaluationsmodell, Wirtschaftspsychologie aktuell, 3, 9–13.

Ellam-Dyson, V. & Palmer, S. (2011). Leadership Coaching? No thanks, I'm not worthy. The Coaching Psychologist, 7(2), 108–117.

Ely, K, Boyce, L.A., Nelson, J.K., Zaccaro, S.J., Hernez-Broome, G., Whyman, W. (2010). Evaluating leadership coaching: a review and integrated framework. The Leadership Quarterly, 21, 585–599.

Ely, K. & Zaccaro, S.J. (2011) Evaluating the effectiveness of coaching – a focus on stakeholders, criteria, and data collection methods. In: G. Hernez-Broome & L.A. Boyce (Hrsg.) Advancing Executive Coaching – Setting the course for Successful Leadership Coaching. San Francisco: Jossey-Bass.

Grant, A.M., Green, L.S., & Rynsaardt, J. (2010). Developmental coaching for high school teachers: Executive coaching goes to school. Consulting Psychology Journal: Practice & Research September, 62(3), 151–168.

Greif, S. (2008). Coaching und ergebnisorientierte Selbstreflexion. Göttingen: Hogrefe.

Hayes, S. C., Follette, V. M. & Linehan, M. (Eds.) (2004). Mindfulness and acceptance: Expanding the cognitive behavioural tradition. New York: Guilford Press.

Haubl, R. (2009). Unter welchen Bedingungen nützt die Supervisionsforschung der Professionalisierung supervisorischen Handelns? In: Haubl, R. & Hausinger, B. (Hrsg.). Supervisionsforschung. Einblicke und Ausblicke (S. 179–207). Göttingen: Vandenhoeck & Ruprecht.

Hossiep, R. & Paschen, M. (2003). Bochumer Inventar zur berufsbezogenen Persönlichkeitsbeschreibung – BIP. 2., vollständig überarbeitete Auflage. Göttingen: Hogrefe.

Ianiro, P ., & Kauffeld, S. (2011). Black-Box Coaching-Prozess: Beziehungsaufbau und -gestaltung auf Grundlage interpersonaler Basisdimensionen. Vortrag beim 2. LOCCS-Symposium, 27.–29. Mai, München.

Kaufel, S., Scherer, S., Scherm, M. & Sauer, M. (2006). Führungsbegleitung in der Bundeswehr – Coaching für militärische Führungskräfte. In: W. Backhausen & J.-P. Thommsen (Hrsg.), Coaching, durch systemisches Denken zur innovativen Personalentwicklung (S. 419–438). Wiesbaden: Gabler.

Kauffeld, S. (2010). Nachhaltige Weiterbildung. Betriebliche Seminare und Trainings entwickeln, Erfolge messen, Transfer sichern. Berlin: Springer.

Dialog zu treten. Diese, so wünschen wir es uns, stellen der Forschung ihre eigenen Perspektiven, Ideen und Erwartungen zur Verfügung. Vielleicht hilft dabei der zunehmende Druck von außen, dass auf absehbare Zeit die Anforderungen an die systematische Evaluation und Qualitätssicherung von Beratungsleistungen auf Seiten der KundInnen und AuftraggeberInnen ohnehin steigen werden.

Es gibt viel zu tun, packen wir es an! Dazu braucht es die Schaffung von Kooperationsformen, die Interessen und Expertisen der verschiedenen Stakeholder (Coaches, SupervisorInnen, KlientInnen, KlientInnenorganisationen, auftraggebende Organisationen, Universitäten) bündeln und nutzbar machen.

Literatur

Arthur, W. Jr., Bennett, W. Jr., Edens, P.S., Bell, S.T. (2003). Effectiveness of Training in Organizations: A Meta-Analysis of Design and Evaluation Features. Journal of Applied Psychology, 88 (2), 234–245.

Benecke, C., & Krause, R. (2005). Initiales mimisch-affektives Verhalten und Behandlungszufriedenheit in der Psychotherapie von Patientinnen mit Panikstörungen. Zeitschrift für Psychosomatische Medizin und Psychotherapie, 51(4), 346–359.

Böning, U., & Fritschle, B. (2005). Coaching furs Business. Bonn: ManagerSeminare.

Bozer, G., Sarros, J.C. (2012). Examining the Effectiveness of Executive Coaching on Coachees' Performance in the Israeli Context. International Journal of Evidence Based Coaching and Mentoring, 10(1), 14–32.

Brown, K. W. & Ryan, R. M. (2003). The benefits of being present: Mindfulness and its role in psychological well-being. Journal of Personality and Social Psychology, 84, 822–848.

Carey, W., Philippon, D., & Cummings, C. (2011). Coaching models for leadership development: An integrative review. Journal of Leadership Studie, 5(1), 51–69.

Cerni, T., Curtis, G., & Colmer, S. (2010). Executive coaching can enhance transformational leadership. International Coaching Psychology Review, 5(1), 81–85.

Cox, E., & Patrick, C. (2012). Managing Emotions at Work: How Coaching Affects Retail Support Workers' Performance and Motivation. International Journal of Evidence Based Coaching and Mentoring, 10(2), 34–51.

Curtis, D.F., Kelly, L.L. (2013). Effect of a quality of life coaching intervention on psychological courage and self-determination. International Journal of Evidence Based Coaching and Mentoring, 11(1), 20–38.

Kessler, H., Bayerl, P., Deighton, R. M. & Traue, H. C. (2002). Facially Expressed Emotion Labeling (FEEL). Verhaltenstherapie und Verhaltensmedizin, 23(3), 297–306.

Kieser, A. (2005). Wissenschaft und Beratung. Heidelberg: Universitätsverlag Winter.

Kines, P., Anderson, L.P., Spangenberg, S., Mikkelsen, K.L., Dyreborg, J. & Zohar, D. (2010). Improving construction site safety through leader-based verbal safety communication. Journal of Safety Research, 41(5), 399–406.

Kirkpatrick, D. L. (1994). Evaluating training programs: The four levels. San Francisco: Berrett-Koehler.

Kochanowski, S., Seifert, C.F. & Yukl, G. (2010). Using coaching to enhance the effects of behavioral feedback to managers. Journal of Leadership and Organizational Studies, 17(4), 363–369.

Kotte, S., Schubert, D. & Möller, H. (in Vorber.). Why do coaches (not) participate in coaching research?

Kotte, S. & Möller, H. (2013). Coaching im Kontext von Führungsentwicklungsprogrammen. In: Wegener, R., Fritze, A., & Loebbert, M. (Hrsg.). Coaching-Praxisfelder. Forschung und Praxis im Dialog (Online-Teil, S. 31–49). Wiesbaden: Springer.

Kotte, S., Oellerich, K., Schubert, D. & Möller, H. (im Druck). Die Akademisierung von Coaching. Das ambivalente Verhältnis von Coachingforschung und -praxis: Dezentes Ignorieren, kritisches Beäugen oder kooperatives Miteinander? In: A. Schreyögg & Ch. Schmidt-Lellek: Die Professionalisierung von Coaching. Ein Lesebuch für den professionellen Coach. Wiesbaden: VS-Verlag.

Kühl, W. (2014). Wirkungen von Führungskräfte-Coaching in der Sozialen Arbeit. Organisationsberatung Supervision Coaching. Springer Fachmedien Wiesbaden 2.

Ladyshewsky, R. K. (2007). A strategic approach for integrating theory to practice in leadership development. Leadership & Organization Development Journal, 28(5), 426–443.

Leonard-Cross, E. (2010). Developmental Coaching: Business benefit – fact or fad? An evaluative study to explore the impact of coaching in the workplace. International Coaching Psychology Review, 5(1), 36–47.

Linley, P., Nielsen, K.M., Gillett, R., & Biswas-Diener, R. (2010). Using signature strengths in pursuit of goals: Effects on goal progress, need satisfaction, and well-being, and implications for coaching psychologists. International Coaching Psychology Review, 5(1), 6–15.

Looss, W. (2006). Unter vier Augen: Coaching für Manager. Bergisch Gladbach: EHP.

Mitmansgruber, H. (2005). Meta-Emotion-Scale. Unveröffentlichtes Manuskript.

Möller, H. & Kotte, S. (2011). Die Zukunft der Coachingforschung. Organisationsberatung Supervision Coaching, 18(4), 445–456.

Möller, H., Kotte, S. & Oellerich, K. (2013). Coaching-Praxis und Wissenschaft – ein unüberwindlicher Gap? CoachingMagazin, 2013, 1, 35–39.

Möller, H. (2012). Was ist gute Supervision? Kassel: kassel university press.

De Haan, E., Duckworth, A., Birch, D. & Jones, C. (2013). Executive coaching outcome research: The contribution of common factors such as relationship, personality match, and self-efficacy. Consulting Psychology Journal: Practice and Research, 65(1), 40–57.

De Meuse, K.P., Dai, G., Lee, R.J. (2009). Evaluating the effectiveness of executive coaching: beyond ROI? Coaching: An International Journal of Theory, Research and Practice, 2(2), 117–134.

Drexler, A. & Möller, H. (2007). Berufliche Kompetenzentwicklung von Supervisorinnen in Ausbildung. Supervision, 3, 51–57.

Drexler, A., Uffelmann, P., Stippler, M. & Möller, H. (2009). Schulleitercoaching – Konzeption und Ausbildungsevaluation. Organisationsberatung, Supervision, Coaching, 1, 35–53.

Drexler, A. & Möller, H. (2009). Erfolgsmessungen von Weiterbildung – Das Innsbrucker Modell. In. H. Pühl (Hrsg.):Handbuch der Supervision 3, S. 381–398. Berlin: Leutner.

Drexler, A. & Möller, H. (2010).Coachinglehrgänge auf dem Prüfstand: Ein Evaluationsmodell, Wirtschaftspsychologie aktuell, 3, 9–13

Ellam-Dyson, V. & Palmer, S. (2011). Leadership Coaching? No thanks, I'm not worthy. The Coaching Psychologist, 7(2), 108–117.

Ely, K, Boyce, L.A., Nelson, J.K., Zaccaro, S.J., Hernez-Broome, G., Whyman, W. (2010). Evaluating leadership coaching: a review and integrated framework. The Leadership Quarterly, 21, 585–599.

Ely, K. & Zaccaro, S.J. (2011). Evaluating the effectiveness of coaching – a focus on stakeholders, criteria, and data collection methods. In: G. Hernez-Broome & L.A. Boyce (Hrsg.) Advancing Executive Coaching–Setting the course for Successful Leadership Coaching. S.Francisco: Jossey-Bass.

Grant, A.M., Green, L.S., & Rynsaardt, J. (2010). Developmental coaching for high school teachers: Executive coaching goes to school. Consulting Psychology Journal: Practice & Research. Sept., 62(3), 151–168.

Greif, S. (2008). Coaching und ergebnisorientierte Selbstreflexion. Göttingen: Hogrefe.

Hayes, S. C., Follette, V. M. & Linehan, M. (Eds.) (2004). Mindfulness and acceptance: Expanding the cognitive behavioural tradition. New York: Guilford Press.

Haubl, R. (2009). Unter welchen Bedingungen nützt die Supervisionsforschung der Professionalisierung supervisorischen Handelns? In: Haubl, R. & Hausinger, B. (Hrsg.). Supervisionsforschung. Einblicke und Ausblicke (S. 179–207). Göttingen: Vandenhoeck & Ruprecht.

Hossiep, R. & Paschen, M. (2003). Bochumer Inventar zur berufsbezogenen Persönlichkeitsbeschreibung – BIP. 2., vollständig überarbeitete Auflage. Göttingen: Hogrefe.

Ianiro, P ., & Kauffeld, S. (2011). Black-Box Coaching-Prozess: Beziehungsaufbau und –gestaltung auf Grundlage interpersonaler Basisdimensionen. Vortrag beim 2. LOCCS-Symposium, 27.–29. Mai, München.

Möller, H. & Drexler, A. (2012). Bildungscontrolling: das Innsbrucker Modell zur Evaluation von Coachingausbildungen. In: G. Niedermair (Hrsg.): Kompetenzen entwickeln, messen und bewerten. Linz: Trauner, S. 555–562.

Möller, H. & Drexler, A. (2011). Bildungscontrolling in der Coachingausbildung. In: M. Stephan & P. Gross (Hrsg.): Organisation und Marketing von Coaching, S. 115–136. Wiesbaden: Verlag für Sozialwissenschaft.

Möller, H. & Kotte, S. (2014). Diagnostik im Coaching. Heidelberg: Springer.

Möller, H., Oellerich, K., Schubert, D. & Kotte, S. (2014). Beratungsforschung mit, für oder ohne die Praxis? Organisationsberatung, Supervision, Coaching, Jubiläumsband, 2, 313–327.

Scherf, M. (2010). Strukturen der Organisationsberatungsinteraktion. Interdisziplinäre Beratungsforschung. Göttingen: Vandenhoeck & Ruprecht.

Scherm, M. & Scherer, S. (2011). Feedbacksysteme im Coachingprozess: Forschungsergebnisse und Praxis. In: R. Wegener, A. Fritze, M. Loebbert (Hrsg.), Coaching entwickeln. Forschung und Praxis im Dialog (S. 135–147). Wiesbaden: VS Verlag für Sozialwissenschaften.

Schermuly, C. C., Schermuly-Haupt, M.-L., Schölmerich, F. & Rauterberg, H. (2014). Zu Risiken und Nebenwirkungen lesen Sie … Negative Effekte von Coaching. Zeitschrift für Arbeits- und Organisationspsychologie, 58(1), 17–33.

Schmidt, S., Strauß, B., Höger, D. & Brähler, E. (2004). Die Adult Attachment Scale (AAS). Psychotherapie, Psychosomatik, Medizinische Psychologie, 9/10, 375–382.

Schumacher, J., Eisemann, M. & Brähler, E. (2000). FEE Fragebogen zum erinnerten elterlichen Erziehungsverhalten. Bern: Verlag Hans Huber.

Seiger, C. & Künzli, H. (2011). Der Schweizerische Coachingmarkt 2010 aus der Sicht von Coachs. Züricher Hochschule für angewandte Wissenschaften [Online]. Available: http://pd.zhaw.ch/hop/544183222.pdf (21.02.2014)

Sherlock-Storey, M., Moss, M. & Timson, S. (2013). Brief coaching for resilience during organisational change – an exploratory study. The Coaching Psychologist, 9(1), 19–26.

Spencer, L. (2011). Coaching and training transfer: A phenomenological inquiry into combined training-coaching programmes. International Journal of Evidence Based Coaching and Mentoring, Special Issue 5, 1–18.

Theeboom, T., Beersma, B., van Vianen, A.E.M. (2014). Does coaching work? A meta-analysis on the effects of coaching on individual level outcomes in an organizational context. The Journal of Positive Psychology, 9(1), 1–18.

Wallis, G. (2010). Does a »blended« programme of development and coaching produce sustainable change? International Journal of Evidence Based Coaching and Mentoring, Special Issue 4, 105–113.

Kaufel, S., Scherer, S., Scherm, M. & Sauer, M. (2006). Führungsbegleitung in der Bundeswehr – Coaching für militärische Führungskräfte. In: W. Backhausen & J.-P. Thommsen (Hrsg.), Coaching, durch systemisches Denken zur innovativen Personalentwicklung (S. 419–438). Wiesbaden: Gabler.

Kauffeld, S. (2010). Nachhaltige Weiterbildung. Betriebliche Seminare und Trainings entwickeln, Erfolge messen, Transfer sichern. Berlin: Springer.

Kessler, H., Bayerl, P., Deighton, R. M. & Traue, H. C. (2002). Facially Expressed Emotion Labeling (FEEL). Verhaltenstherapie und Verhaltensmedizin, 23(3), 297–306.

Kieser, A. (2005). Wissenschaft und Beratung. Heidelberg: Universitätsverlag Winter.

Kines, P., Anderson, L.P., Spangenberg, S., Mikkelsen, K.L., Dyreborg, J. & Zohar, D. (2010). Improving construction site safety through leader-based verbal safety communication. Journal of Safety Research, 41(5), 399–406.

Kirkpatrick, D. L. (1994). Evaluating training programs: The four levels. San Francisco: Berrett-Koehler.

Kochanowski, S., Seifert, C.F. & Yukl, G. (2010). Using coaching to enhance the effects of behavioral feedback to managers. Journal of Leadership and Organizational Studies, 17(4), 363–9.

Kotte, S., Schubert, D. & Möller, H. (in Vorber.). Why do coaches (not) participate in coaching research?

Kotte, S. & Möller, H. (2013). Coaching im Kontext von Führungsentwicklungsprogrammen. In: Wegener, R., Fritze, A., & Loebbert, M. (Hrsg.). Coaching-Praxisfelder. Forschung und Praxis im Dialog (Online-Teil, S. 31–49). Wiesbaden: Springer.

Kotte, S., Oellerich, K., Schubert, D. & Möller, H. (im Druck). Die Akademisierung von Coaching. Das ambivalente Verhältnis von Coachingforschung und -praxis: Dezentes Ignorieren, kritisches Beäugen oder kooperatives Miteinander? In: A. Schreyögg & Ch. Schmidt-Lellek: Die Professionalisierung von Coaching. Ein Lesebuch für den professionellen Coach. Wiesbaden: VS-Verlag.

Kühl, W. (2014). Wirkungen von Führungskräfte-Coaching in der Sozialen Arbeit. Organisationsberatung Supervision Coaching. Springer Fachmedien Wiesbaden 2.

Ladyshewsky, R. K. (2007). A strategic approach for integrating theory to practice in leadership development. Leadership & Organization Development Journal, 28(5),426–443.

Leonard-Cross, E. (2010). Developmental Coaching: Business benefit – fact or fad? An evaluative study to explore the impact of coaching in the workplace. International Coaching Psychology Review, 5(1), 36–47.

Linley, P, Nielsen,K.M., Gillett,R., & Biswas-Diener, R. (2010). Using signature strengths in pursuit of goals: Effects on goal progress, need satisfaction, and well-being, and implications for coaching psychologists. International Coaching Psychology Review, 5(1), 6–15.

Looss, W. (2006). Unter vier Augen: Coaching für Manager. Bergisch Gladbach: EHP.

Mitmansgruber, H. (2005). Meta-Emotion-Scale. Unveröffentlichtes Manuskript.

Möller, H. & Kotte, S. (2011). Die Zukunft der Coachingforschung. Organisationsberatung Supervision Coaching, 18(4), 445–456.

Möller, H., Kotte, S. & Oellerich, K. (2013). Coaching-Praxis und Wissenschaft – ein unüberwindlicher Gap? CoachingMagazin, 2013, 1, 35–39.

Möller, H. (2012). Was ist gute Supervision? Kassel: kassel university press.

Möller, H. & Drexler, A. (2012). Bildungscontrolling: das Innsbrucker Modell zur Evaluation von Coachingausbildungen. In: G. Niedermair (Hrsg.): Kompetenzen entwickeln, messen und bewerten. Linz: Trauner, 555–562.

Möller, H. & Drexler, A. (2011). Bildungscontrolling in der Coachingausbildung. In: M. Stephan & P. Gross (Hrsg.): Organisation und Marketing von Coaching, 115–136. Wiesbaden: Verlag für Sozialwissenschaft.

Möller, H. & Kotte, S. (2014). Diagnostik im Coaching. Heidelberg: Springer.

Möller, H., Oellerich, K., Schubert, D. & Kotte, S. (2014). Beratungsforschung mit, für oder ohne die Praxis? Organisationsberatung, Supervision, Coaching, Jubiläumsband, 2, 313–327.

Scherf, M. (2010). Strukturen der Organisationsberatungsinteraktion. Interdisziplinäre Beratungsforschung. Göttingen: Vandenhoeck & Ruprecht.

Scherm, M. & Scherer, S. (2011). Feedbacksysteme im Coachingprozess: Forschungsergebnisse und Praxis. In: R. Wegener, A. Fritze, M. Loebbert (Hrsg.), Coaching entwickeln. Forschung und Praxis im Dialog (S. 135–147). Wiesbaden: VS Verlag für Sozialwissenschaften.

Schermuly, C. C., Schermuly-Haupt, M.-L., Schölmerich, F. & Rauterberg, H. (2014). Zu Risiken und Nebenwirkungen lesen Sie … Negative Effekte von Coaching. Zeitschrift für Arbeits- und Organisationspsychologie, 58(1), 17–33.

Schmidt, S., Strauß, B., Höger, D. & Brähler, E. (2004). Die Adult Attachment Scale (AAS). Psychotherapie, Psychosomatik, Medizinische Psychologie, 9/10, 375–382.

Schumacher, J., Eisemann, M. & Brähler, E. (2000). FEE Fragebogen zum erinnerten elterlichen Erziehungsverhalten. Bern: Verlag Hans Huber.

Seiger, C. & Künzli, H. (2011). Der Schweizerische Coachingmarkt 2010 aus der Sicht von Coachs. Züricher Hochschule für angewandte Wissenschaften [Online]. http://pd.zhaw.ch/hop/544183222.pdf (21.02.2014)

Sherlock-Storey, M., Moss, M. & Timson, S. (2013). Brief coaching for resilience during organisational change – an exploratory study. The Coaching Psychologist, 9(1), 19–26.

Spencer, L. (2011). Coaching and training transfer: A phenomenological inquiry into combined training-coaching programmes. International Journal of Evidence Based Coaching and Mentoring, Special Issue 5, 1–18.

Theeboom, T., Beersma, B., van Vianen, A.E.M. (2014). Does coaching work? A meta-analysis on the effects of coaching on individual level outcomes in an organizational context. The Journal of Positive Psychology, 9(1), 1–18.

Wallis, G. (2010). Does a »blended« programme of development and coaching produce sustainable change? International Journal of Evidence Based Coaching and Mentoring, Special Issue 4, 105–113.

Keeping fit, maintaining balance, gaining insight. How coaching and supervision provide quality assurance for organisations

Erik de Haan

Abstract

This article looks at how three professions (leadership, coaching & supervision) can work together to mitigate and balance the risks of the strong leadership that we have in our ever growing corporate and (non-)governmental organisations. Firstly, I explore how a leader who is brave and challenges herself to consider the converse of her leadership and to integrate her own vulnerable 'shadow side' is maintaining and enhancing her quality as a leader. Secondly, I consider how such leader in working with a challenging professional (executive coach or organisation-development consultant), who is brave enough to doubt the leader's narrative and to raise areas of need, vulnerability, doubt and self-deception, can take action to assure the quality of their leadership. Thirdly, I describe how those brave executive coaches can ensure their own quality of service by taking up supervision from a challenging outsider who 'holds their toes' and also holds them to the task of speaking their highly personal truth to leaders. It emerges that supervision often provides a final, timely opportunity to catch and consider hidden dynamics of leadership practice.

Keywords: Leadership, Executive Coaching, Supervision, Quality Assurance (QA).

Arbeitsfähig bleiben – Balance halten – Einsichten gewinnen. Wie Coaching und Supervision Qualität für Organisationen sichern

Erik de Haan

Abstract

Dieser Artikel befasst sich damit, wie drei Berufe (Management, Coaching & Supervision) zusammenarbeiten können, um die Risiken einer starken Führungsorientierung zu mildern und auszugleichen, die wir in unseren ständig wachsenden Profit- und Non-Profit-Organisationen beobachten können.

Zunächst untersuche ich, wie eine Führungskraft, die sich mutig den Herausforderungen stellt, ihr eigenes Leitungsverhalten zu ändern und ihre verletzliche „Schattenseite" zu integrieren, ihre Qualität als Führungskraft nicht nur aufrecht erhält, sondern verbessert.

Zweitens betrachte ich, wie solche Führungskräfte – sofern sie mit einem fordernden Coach oder Organisationsberater arbeiten, der das „Narrativ" mutig in Frage stellt und auch Themen wie Bedürftigkeit, Verletzlichkeit, Zweifel und Selbsttäuschung zur Sprache bringt, ein Führungshandeln entwickeln können, das die Qualität ihrer Führung gewährleistet.

Drittens beschreibe ich, wie Coaches ihre eigene Servicequalität durch Supervision mit einem Außenstehenden gewährleisten können, der sie immer wieder fordert, aus ihrer sehr persönlichen Wahrhaftigkeit heraus zu Führungskräften zu sprechen. Es zeigt sich, dass Supervision oftmals einmalige Gelegenheiten bietet, verborgene Dynamiken der Führungspraxis zu erfassen und zu bedenken.

Schlüsselwörter: Führung, Leitungscoaching, Supervision, Qualitätssicherung (QS).

1. The leadership shadow: the vulnerability of being a leader

In today's fast paced, interconnected, and mercilessly competitive business world, senior executives have to push themselves and others hard. In order to succeed, leaders have to live the paradox of closely attending to others and following as deeply as they lead. They have to listen well to others, understand their concerns, give them personal support, and at the same time motivate them for results or take decisions on their behalf.

Precisely those leaders who can adapt to these conditions and who can develop a tough and relentless focus on competitive advantage are most at risk of adopting unhelpful and ultimately unproductive patterns of demand, stubbornness, or frenetic activity. Instead of being open to possibility and ambiguity, and willing to engage in creative conversations with themselves and others, these executives instead become obstinate, resentful, inarticulate, or intense. They become a caricature of themselves and go into 'overdrive'.

Most often they are qualities executives have relied on to get them to the top and to achieve outstanding results, qualities that overshoot under stress and challenge, into unhelpful drives that lead to business and personal catastrophes (Claxton, Owen & Sadler-Smith, 2015). Hitherto high-performing executives suddenly find themselves facing the prospect of relationship breakdowns, strategic failures or the risks of derailment.

Stepping forward to make a leadership gesture always creates a rift within oneself: a rift between one's sunny, active, constructive, or aggressive side that has the ambition to contribute, create and prove something; and one's doubting, pessimistic, needy, vulnerable, careful and concerned side, which craves for connection with oneself and others. This shadow side is therefore part and parcel of leadership.

The rift and the play of light and dark accompanying this process may be very subtle; e.g., one may bring a very caring side of oneself to one's leadership role, bringing out one's particular warmth, care, and also concern and attentiveness. Even in such cases there is bound to be a whole 'other' side of our personalities which we push down in order to make such a bid for leadership, or for following the leadership role through. In the case of a very caring, concerned, warm leader there may be a whole side of oneself to do with conflict, resentment, self-importance, that one is keeping down. The 'leadership shadow' phenomenon is consistently present in all leadership roles. In order to make the 'bid' or put forward the 'drive' other aspects have to be left behind, pushed back and discarded, somewhere in the dark of our experiencing, including self-experiencing.

1. Die Schattenseite von Führung: die Verletzlichkeit in der Führungsfunktion

In der heutigen schnelllebigen, vernetzten und gnadenlos wettbewerbs-orientierten Geschäftswelt müssen Führungskräfte sich selbst und andere hart antreiben. Um erfolgreich zu sein, müssen Führungskräfte das Paradox handhaben, die Anderen sowohl engmaschig zu begleiten als auch sie zu führen. Sie müssen gut zuhören, die Anliegen Anderer verstehen, ihnen persönliche Unterstützung geben, sie aber gleichzeitig motivieren, Ergebnisse zu erzielen, und überdies Entscheidungen in ihrem Namen treffen.

Gerade diejenigen Führungskräfte, die sich gut an diese Bedingungen anpassen und einen harten und unnachgiebigen Fokus auf Wettbewerbsvorteile entwickeln können, sind am meisten gefährdet, wenig hilfreiche und letztlich unproduktive Muster des Forderns, der Sturheit oder der frenetischen Aktivität zu entwickeln. Statt offen für Möglichkeiten und Mehrdeutigkeit zu sein und in kreative Auseinandersetzungen mit sich selbst und anderen einzutreten, werden diese Führungskräfte hartnäckig, gereizt, artikulieren sich nicht oder überintensiv. Sie werden zu einer Karikatur ihrer selbst und „übersteuern".

Meistens sind dies Qualitäten, auf die Führungskräfte besonders vertraut haben, um an die Spitze zu kommen und hervorragende Ergebnisse zu erzielen. Qualitäten, die unter Stress und Druck zu überschießenden, wenig hilfreichen „Hamsterrädern" werden und zu geschäftlichen wie persönlichen Katastrophen (Claxton, Owen & Sadler-Smith, 2015) führen. Bisher hoch leistungsfähige Führungskräfte sehen sich plötzlich mit Beziehungsabbrüchen, strategischen Fehlern oder den Risiken einer Entgleisung konfrontiert.

Sich mit einem Leitungsanspruch zu zeigen, erzeugt immer einen Riss in sich selbst: eine Kluft zwischen einer sonnigen, aktiven, konstruktiven, bzw. aggressiven Seite in sich selbst, voll des Ehrgeizes, etwas zu schaffen und zu beweisen; und einer zweifelnden, pessimistischen, bedürftigen, verletzlichen, vorsichtigen und besorgten Seite, die sich nach Verbindung mit sich selbst und anderen sehnt. Diese Schattenseite ist daher stets ein wesentlicher Bestandteil von Führung.

Dieser Riss und das Spiel von Licht und Dunkel, die diesen Prozess begleiten, können sehr subtil sein; zum Beispiel kann man eine sehr fürsorgliche Seite von sich selbst in die Führungsrolle einbringen, eine besondere Wärme, Fürsorge, Achtsamkeit und Aufmerksamkeit. Auch in solchen Fällen existiert unweigerlich eine ganze „andere" Seite unserer Persönlichkeit, die wir zurückdrängen, um eine solche Führungsrolle durchzutragen.

Case Example

We are getting used to our daily dosage of corporate scandal at the very top of the organisations which deliver the products and services that we love to buy. As an example, today (21 July 2015) the CEO of Toshiba has resigned together with his predecessor and a swathe of senior executives.

The Financial Times writes "A panel of external lawyers and accountants said on Monday there was a 'systematic' and 'deliberate' attempt to inflate profit figures amid a corporate culture in which employees were afraid to speak out against bosses' pushes for unrealistic earnings targets. The CEO Mr Tanaka said in a news conference following a 15-second bow of contrition, that he 'felt the need to carry out a major overhaul in our management team to build anew our company'." Apparently Tanaka himself had been aware of the overstatement of profits and had not taken action to end the improper accounting. Top management would assign 'challenges', or earnings-improvement targets, at monthly meetings with the heads of in-house companies and subsidiaries, and this drive for improvement ultimately brought out the very opposite of what it was designed to achieve. Tanaka resigned together with his predecessor and five other Toshiba board members. Those that had pressured others with demands for blind loyalty and the achievement of impossible targets are now leaving the firm with more than a billion dollars unexplained and still greater damage to the brand.

The great challenge of leaders can be summed up by the same paradox of leaders this article began with. It is the art of maintaining a focused 'leadership agenda' or drive forward, together with the 'debris' of that same agenda: all the contradictions, doubts and vulnerabilities that leadership has relayed to the dark shadows of the leader's or the organisation's personality.

2. QA for leaders – how coaches and organisation-development consultants may help

The shadow side plays a role in every form of leadership and as long as the job is part-time and leaders have a strong-willed, confrontational spouse as well as assertive colleagues who remind them of their human fragility and fallibility, the leadership shadow can be processed so that it does not cause too many problems. Unfortunately many of our captains of industry and political leaders are not in such a fortunate position. They are dedicated and even devoted to the job, they put in an exorbitant amount of time and effort, and

Im Falle einer sehr fürsorglichen, besorgten, warmen Führungskraft kann es also eine Seite von sich selbst geben, die mit Konflikten, Ärger und Selbstwert zu tun hat und die es gilt, unten zu halten.

Das „Führungsschatten-Phänomen" ist in allen Führungspositionen ständig präsent. Um offensiv anzubieten oder auf „Vollgas" zu schalten, müssen andere Aspekte zurück gelassen werden, zurückgedrängt und verworfen, irgendwo in der Dunkelheit unseres Erlebens, einschließlich des Selbsterlebens.

Fallbeispiel

Wir haben uns an unsere tägliche Dosis von Unternehmensskandalen an der Spitze jener Organisationen gewöhnt, deren Produkte und Dienstleistungen wir nur allzu gerne kaufen. Ein Beispiel vom 21. Juli 2015: Der CEO von Toshiba ist zusammen mit seinem Vorgänger und einem Großteil der Führungskräfte zurückgetreten.

Die Financial Times schreibt: „Ein Gremium externer Anwälte und Wirtschaftsprüfer sagte am Montag, es habe ein „systematischer" und „gezielter" Versuch stattgefunden, Gewinnzahlen aufzublasen, und dies in einer Unternehmenskultur in der Mitarbeitende Angst hatten, Vorgesetzten zu widersprechen, die unrealistische Ergebnisziele einforderten."

Der Geschäftsführer Herr Tanaka sagte in einer Pressekonferenz nach einer zerknirschten 15-Sekunden-Verbeugung, dass er „eine Generalüberholung unseres Managementteams für notwendig halte, um unser Unternehmen neu aufzubauen." Tanaka waren die bewusst übertrieben ausgewiesenen Gewinne ganz offensichtlich bekannt, und er hatte keine Maßnahmen ergriffen, um die falsche Buchhaltung zu beenden. Das Top-Management sollte „Herausforderungen", oder Ertrags-Verbesserungs-Ziele in monatlichen Treffen mit den Leitern der In-House-Firmen sowie der Tochtergesellschaften festsetzen, und dieses Streben nach Verbesserung hatte letztlich das Gegenteil dessen hervorgebracht, was erreicht werden sollte. Tanaka trat mit seinem Vorgänger und fünf weiteren Toshiba Vorstandsmitgliedern zusammen zurück.

Diejenigen, die Andere mit Forderungen nach blinder Loyalität und nach Erreichung unmöglicher Ziele unter Druck gesetzt hatten, verlassen jetzt die Firma mit mehr als einer Milliarde Dollar ungeklärter Kosten und noch größeren Schäden an der Marke.

they are rarely criticised or challenged by those near to them. Under such conditions, how will leaders remain fresh, balanced, and inspired to keep reflecting openly and self-critically alongside their own firmly held convictions?

I believe that this kind of challenging, outspoken and fresh consultancy to (top) leaders exists and can help to remind them of their highly personal leadership shadows and of the fact that they do have (hidden) doubts, needs and vulnerabilities around their leadership targets and strategies. They may not say so in public but at some level they themselves know how intrinsically weak their leadership is and will always be, when considered in a larger context (De Haan & Kasozi, 2014). This fresh and challenging scrutiny of managers and leaders is provided by organisation-development consultants and executive coaches, if they are worth the considerable fees they are paid (Nelson & Hogan, 2009).

Some of the work that these coaches and consultants do is just spotting or guessing the shadow sides that leaders have forgotten about or for many reasons prefer not to consider. It is the coach's task to bring back awareness of vulnerability or neediness, corruptibility or hubris, depending on the highly personal contents of the leader's shadow. Coaching restores balance and looks after a leader's 'fitness to practise' precisely by generating insight and inspiration around the leader's most sensitive and vulnerable areas.

A form of leadership is now required in turn from the coach or consultant: namely the drive to speak their honest, fearless truth to power (De Haan, 2006) and to reflect freely and independently, alongside the leader and leadership questions of the day. The question presents itself: how do coaches remain fit for practice and make sure that they approach their clients with the requisite level of freshness and robustness? The answer to that question is: supervision.

3. QA for coaches – how supervisors look after those that are looking after leaders

Access to executive coaching is no longer viewed as a privilege restricted to an organisation's elite: over the last decade or so it has become widely used as a 'just in time' development intervention in a wide range or managerial and technical settings. For the in-house learning and development specialist, this widened access brings with it the challenge of ensuring that the coaching is 'fit for purpose'; not an easy task given the confidential nature of the vast majority of coaching relationships. Only a few years ago, it was easy to set yourself up as an executive coach, with credentials based on recommen-

Die große Herausforderung für Führungskräfte kann durch das gleiche Paradox von Führung zusammengefasst werden, mit dem dieser Artikel begann. Es ist die Kunst, proaktiv auf eine „Führungsagenda" zu fokussieren, und diese in Balance zu bringen mit dem „Schutt", den eben diese Agenda mit sich bringt: den Widersprüchen, Zweifeln und Schwachstellen – mit dem dunklen Schatten von Führung sowohl in der Persönlichkeit der Führungskraft, aber auch des Unternehmens.

2. Qualitätssicherung für Führungskräfte – wie Coaches und Organisationsentwickler helfen können

Die Schattenseite spielt eine Rolle in jeder Form der Führung, doch solange der Job nur einen Teil der Zeit in Anspruch nimmt, und Führungskräfte eine/n willensstarke/n, konfrontative/n EhepartnerIn sowie durchsetzungsfähige KollegInnen haben, die sie an ihre menschliche Zerbrechlichkeit und Fehlbarkeit erinnern, kann der Führungsschatten so verarbeitet werden, dass er nicht allzu viele Probleme verursacht. Leider sind viele unserer Industriekapitäne und politischen FührerInnen nicht in einer solch glücklichen Lage. Sie sind engagiert, ja hingebungsvoll in ihren Job, widmen ihm exorbitant viel Zeit und Mühe und werden selten von den Menschen in ihrer unmittelbaren Umgebung kritisiert oder in Frage gestellt. Wie sollen Führungskräfte unter solchen Bedingungen unverbraucht und ausgeglichen bleiben, bzw. offen und selbstkritisch ihre eigenen fest verwurzelten Überzeugungen reflektieren?

Ich glaube, dass anspruchsvolle, freimütige und offene Beratung von (Top-)Führungskräften ihnen helfen kann, sie an ihren sehr persönlichen Führungsschatten zu erinnern, und an die Tatsache, dass auch für sie (verdeckte) Zweifel, Bedürfnisse und Schwachstellen zu ihren Führungszielen und Strategien dazugehören. Sie mögen dies nicht so in der Öffentlichkeit sagen, aber auf einer bestimmten Ebene wissen sie selbst, wie in sich schwach ihre Führung in einem größeren Kontext betrachtet ist und immer sein wird (De Haan & Kasozi, 2014). Dieses offene und anspruchsvolle Infragestellen von Managern und Führungskräften wird durch OrganisationsentwicklerInnen und Leitungscoaches zur Verfügung gestellt, wenn sie die beträchtlichen Honorare, die ihnen bezahlt werden, wert sind (Nelson & Hogan, 2009).

Ein Teil der Arbeit, die Coaches und BeraterInnen tun, besteht darin, die Schattenseiten zu erkennen oder zu erraten, welche die Führungskräfte vergessen haben, oder aus vielen Gründen lieber nicht berücksichtigen. Es ist die Aufgabe des Coaches, Verletzlichkeit oder Bedürftigkeit, Bestechlichkeit

dations and past experience. Qualifications were unheard of and very few organisations thought to ask about prior training or ongoing arrangements for professional development.

All that is changing: most large corporations now make use of internal and external coaches, who are expected to have been trained and accredited by a recognised institution. In many ways this increased demand for professionally qualified coaches parallels the expectation that business leaders have themselves been professionally developed. This growing professionalisation of coaching and business leadership has contributed to the growth of qualification programmes at business schools, with MSc's in Organisational Consulting or Executive Coaching alongside the more traditional MBA's and other Master and Doctoral level programmes.

However, the achievement of a coaching qualification cannot be taken as evidence of professionalism and competence by itself. Coaching is an extremely demanding and isolated activity, full of struggles with finding one's voice to speak truth sensitively to power, doubts (De Haan, 2008), ethical dilemmas or invitations to collude with dysfunctional leadership behaviour (De Haan & Carroll, 2014). For this reason we expect executive coaches and organisational consultants to be in regular supervision and e.g. after qualifying we require our own Ashridge coaches to provide evidence of ongoing supervision if they wish to maintain their professional accreditation. Supervision is no longer a 'nice to have'; it is an essential prerequisite to maintaining quality, competence and professionalism of an executive coach (De Haan & Birch, 2010) and organisational consultant (De Haan & Birch, 2011).

Coaching supervision takes place either in groups or on a 1:1 basis. The purpose of supervision is to help the coach bring the best of themselves to their work with clients; in practical terms this means ensuring that the coach is sufficiently well-resourced to help their clients recognise their own leadership shadow and take responsibility for their leadership choices. Although supervision is a developmental process, its fundamental purpose is to monitor and improve the quality of the coach's work with their clients. By attending to their own emotional and intellectual resourcefulness, coaches will be in a stronger position to help their clients.

So what does this mean in practice? The essential feature of supervision is the regular provision of a confidential space where the coach is helped to reflect on their professional practice. Coaches are often very busy, combining their coaching with other professional roles which in turn have to be balanced with demands and responsibilities outside of work. Even though taking time out from a hectic schedule is always challenging, the benefits for the coach and their clients are potentially huge.

oder Hybris, entsprechend der sehr persönlichen Inhalte des Führungsschattens wieder ins Bewusstsein zu bringen. Coaching wirkt ausgleichend und Coaches kümmern sich um die „Fitness des Machens" genau dadurch, dass sie Einsicht in die empfindlichsten und gefährdeten Anteile der Führungskraft erzeugen.

In einer anderen Form der Selbstführung wird wiederum vom Coach oder vom/von der BeraterIn gefordert: ehrlich und furchtlos ihre persönliche Wahrheit Mächtigen gegenüber (De Haan, 2006) auszusprechen und frei und unabhängig mit den Führungskräften deren aktuelle Führungsfragen zu reflektieren. Die Frage stellt sich: Wie bleiben Coaches für die Praxis fit und stellen sicher, dass sie ihren KundInnen mit dem erforderlichen Maß an Klarheit und Stabilität gegenübertreten?

Die Antwort auf diese Frage lautet: Supervision.

3. Qualitätssicherung für Coaches – wie SupervisorInnen jene unterstützen, die Führungskräfte unterstützen

Zugang zu Leitungscoaching gilt längst nicht mehr als Privileg, beschränkt auf die Elite einer Organisation: in den letzten zehn Jahren ist es zu einer Entwicklungsmaßnahme bei akuten Anforderungen geworden, eingesetzt in einem breiten Spektrum betrieblicher und technischer Settings. Die Personalentwicklung stellt dieser erweiterte Zugang vor die Herausforderung sicherzustellen, dass das Coaching für den jeweiligen Zweck geeignet ist; keine einfache Aufgabe, ist doch die überwiegende Mehrheit der Coaching-Beziehungen durch strikte Vertraulichkeit gekennzeichnet. Noch vor wenigen Jahren war es leicht, mit Empfehlungen und Erfahrungen als Coach einzusteigen. Qualifikationen waren kein Thema, und nur sehr wenige Organisationen fragten nach Ausbildung oder gar kontinuierlicher beruflicher Weiterbildung.

All das ändert sich: Die meisten Großunternehmen setzen mittlerweile interne wie externe Coaches ein, von denen erwartet wird, dass sie von einer anerkannten Institution ausgebildet und akkreditiert sind. In vielerlei Hinsicht spiegelt diese zunehmende Anforderung an Professionalisierung von Coaches die Erwartung wider, dass auch Führungskräfte in der Wirtschaft sich professionell (weiter) zu entwickeln haben.

Diese wachsende Professionalisierung von Coaching und Unternehmensführung hat zum Wachstum von Business Schools beigetragen, mit MSc-Ausbildungen in Organisationsberatung oder Coaching, neben den traditionellen Master- und Doktorats-Programmen.

Case Example

An experienced executive coach was working with a client who was about to become a father and was under intense pressure both at home and in his leadership role. The coach had been working with the client for some time and they had built up a strong trust. During the early sessions the client hardly expressed any emotion but was now sharing immense anxiety, profound anger and a sense of helplessness. The coach felt overwhelmed by his client's strong feelings and was concerned that working with this level of emotion was beyond his level of competence. At the same time, he realised that the client was relying on their trusted relationship as one of very few places to bring his despair. During supervision the coach started processing his own emotional response to his client and discovered to his surprise that he was feeling very protective towards him. With this insight and the encouragement of his supervisor he felt strong enough to offer his client a clear boundary that would enable him to explore his emotions in a more detached way. The supervisor and coach agreed that if he felt he or his client was not coping, he would contact the supervisor again even if in between sessions.

Interestingly, the type of quality assurance that supervisors provide for coaches is comparable with the QA that coaches provide for leaders. Just like coaches with their clients, supervisors are helping coaches to reflect more honestly and deeply, and to recognise, accept and get a handle on 'shadowy' aspects of their services, such as not speaking up to certain leaders, accepting soothingly big presents from clients, or responding viscerally and unhelpfully to leadership shadows (only to name a few). Supervision is often a last opportunity to become aware of deeply hidden unhelpful dynamics in organisations. I have noticed on many occasions that a slightly stilted, awkward, or telling moment in supervision helped indicate a pattern which was ultimately at the core of a leader's problematic behaviour. And even though first noticed only in supervision, it helped the coach go back, respond and make a positive difference for many concerned.

4. Some ethical considerations behind QA for leaders and coaches

Similar to leadership focus going into damaging overdrive and derailment, there are substantial risks in coaching and supervision too, aside from the risk of simply not picking up one's client's practice going into overdrive.

Allerdings kann eine formale Coaching-Qualifikation nicht per se als Beweis für Professionalität und Kompetenz genommen werden. Coaching ist eine höchst anspruchsvolle und einsame Tätigkeit, voller Kämpfe darum, eine Sprache zu finden, die zugleich wahrhaftig und sensibel Macht, Zweifel, ethische Dilemmata oder die Verführung, dysfunktionales Führungsverhalten zu stützen, anspricht (De Haan, 2008; De Haan & Carroll, 2014). Aus diesem Grund erwarten wir von Coaches und OrganisationsberaterInnen, regelmäßig Supervision in Anspruch zu nehmen. Z. B. verlangen wir von unseren eigenen Ashridge Coaches nach Abschluss der Ausbildung Nachweise kontinuierlicher Supervision, wenn sie ihre berufliche Akkreditierung erhalten wollen. Supervision ist nicht länger ein „nützlicher Zusatz"; es ist eine wesentliche Voraussetzung für die Aufrechterhaltung der Qualität, Kompetenz und Professionalität eines Coaches (De Haan & Birch, 2010) und Organisationsberaters (De Haan & Birch, 2011).

Supervision von Coaching findet entweder in Gruppen oder auf einer 1:1 Basis statt. Die Supervision dient dem Zweck, den Coach bestmöglich in der Arbeit mit dessen KlientInnen zu unterstützen; in der Praxis bedeutet dies zu gewährleisten, dass der Coach über ausreichend Ressourcen verfügt, um seinen/ihren KundInnen dabei zu helfen, ihre Führungsschatten zu erkennen sowie die Verantwortung für ihre Entscheidungen zu übernehmen. Obwohl Supervision ein Entwicklungsprozess ist: sein grundlegendes Ziel besteht darin, die Qualität der Coaches in der Arbeit mit ihren KundInnen zu begleiten und zu verbessern. Je besser der Kontakt zu den eigenen emotionalen und intellektuellen Ressourcen gehalten werden kann, desto besser werden Coaches auch ihren KundInnen helfen.

Was bedeutet das in der Praxis? Das wesentliche Merkmal von Supervision ist die regelmäßige Zurverfügungstellung eines vertraulichen Raumes, in dem Coaches ihre berufliche Praxis reflektieren können. Coaches sind oft sehr damit beschäftigt, ihr Coaching mit anderen Berufsrollen zu kombinieren, die wiederum mit Anforderungen und Aufgaben außerhalb der Arbeit balanciert werden müssen. Auch wenn es immer eine Herausforderung darstellt, sich eine Auszeit von einem hektischen Zeitplan zu nehmen: die Vorteile für den Coach und seine KundInnen sind potenziell enorm.

Fallbeispiel

Ein erfahrener Coach arbeitete mit einem Kunden, der gerade Vater wurde und unter starkem Druck stand, sowohl zu Hause als auch in seiner Führungsrolle. Der Coach arbeitete schon seit längerem mit dem Kunden und

Berglas (2004) summarised the 'very real dangers of executive coaching' which in his view are often aggravated by a coach's lack of psychological understanding. He gives case examples of coaches

- misjudging the situation;
- aggravating the status quo; and
- abusing their own (the coach's) power.

Other ethical challenges in the coaching and consulting professions come from

1. The many new coaches, often (internal) consultants, HR Directors and CEOs, who still enter the profession with only minimal training.
2. Very low bargaining power of customers who negotiate a multitude of very small contracts.
3. A lack of regulation in the consulting and coaching professions.
4. Feelings of shame, anxiety and resulting client protection when there are difficulties or concerns.
5. A certain 'numbness' or resistance to external quality assurance, particularly with more experienced coaches and supervisors.

Compounding these risks are practices of what I would call 'toothless' quality assurance:

- Administrative systems that only tick boxes or look into the 'facts' of practice not the lived experience of it.
- Mindlessly applying codes of conduct through 'quandary' ethics and ethical vignettes which does little to prepare for real life ethics.
- 'Moral reasoning' which has demonstrably little impact on 'moral action'. It is long known that there are essentially two ethical people in all of us: (1) the future ethical me who will one day do those things I recommend for others and (2) the present-day ethical me who reacts from a different set of standards (Carroll & Shaw, 2012).
- 'Self-less' or 'un-relational' ethics where we forget the basic premise underlying all ethics and moral codes, the so-called golden rule "Don't do to others what you wouldn't want them to do to you" or put more positively, "treat others as you would like them to treat you".

Finally here are some aspects of quality assurance through coaching and supervision that I believe do make a positive impact in practice:

1. External quality assurance seems more reliable than peer quality assurance; so external coaching and supervision are better placed for quality assurance than internal coaching and supervision.

sie hatten eine stabile Vertrauensbasis aufgebaut. In den ersten Sitzungen hatte der Kunde kaum Emotionen geäußert, aber jetzt zeigte er immense Angst, tiefe Wut und ein Gefühl der Hilflosigkeit. Der Coach fühlte sich von den starken Gefühlen seines Kunden überwältigt und traute seiner eigenen Kompetenz nicht zu, mit diesem Ausmaß an Emotionen zu arbeiten. Zugleich erkannte er, dass für den Kunden ihre vertraute Beziehung einen der wenigen Orte bedeutete, wo er seiner Verzweiflung Ausdruck verleihen konnte. Während der Supervision untersuchte der Coach seine eigene emotionale Reaktion auf seinen Klienten und entdeckte zu seiner Überraschung einen stark beschützenden Impuls ihm gegenüber. Mit dieser Erkenntnis und der Ermutigung seines Supervisors fühlte er sich stark genug, um seinem Klienten eine klare Grenze zu setzen, die es diesem ermöglichte, seine Gefühle in einer distanzierteren Weise zu erkunden. Supervisor und Coach einigten sich, dass Letzterer, wenn er sich oder seinen Kunden als überwältigt erlebte, den Supervisor wieder kontaktieren würde, notfalls zwischen den Sitzungen.

Interessanterweise ist die Art der Qualitätssicherung, die Supervision für Coaches bietet, vergleichbar mit der Qualitätssicherungsfunktion der Coaches für Führungskräfte. Genau wie Coaches ihren KundInnen, helfen SupervisorInnen Coaches, ehrlicher und tiefgehender zu reflektieren, sowie die „Schattenaspekte" ihrer Dienstleistung zu erkennen, zu akzeptieren und handhabbar zu machen – wie etwa bestimmte Führungskräfte nicht zu konfrontieren, große Geschenke von KundInnen zu akzeptieren oder intuitiv und wenig hilfreich auf den Führungsschatten zu reagieren (um nur einige zu nennen).

Supervision ist oft eine letzte Gelegenheit, sich tief versteckter, nicht hilfreicher Dynamiken in Organisationen gewahr zu werden. Ich habe oft bemerkt, dass ein etwas gestelzter, ungeschickter, oder aufschlussreicher Moment in der Supervision auf ein Muster verwies, das letztlich den Kern des problematischen Verhaltens einer Führungskraft berührte. Und auch wenn zunächst nur in der Supervision bemerkt, half es dem Coach zurückzugehen, zu reagieren und einen positiven Unterschied für viele Beteiligten zu machen.

4. Ethische Überlegungen zur Qualitätssicherung für Führungskräfte und Coaches

Ähnlich wie ein Führungsfokus in schädliche Übersteuerung und Entgleisung gehen kann, gibt es auch erhebliche Risiken in Coaching und Super-

2. Market forces, the triangular relationship and the general custom of contracts of only limited duration: these play a containing role and guard against excesses.
3. Supervision is now most prevalent at the stage of education, whilst it can play a more important role for beginning (qualified) coaches and also for very experienced coaches, which are the two groups most at risk.

Case Example

A team of coaches working with 'High Potential' leaders at a government department had been meeting virtually for group supervision. Over time it became apparent that the content of many of the coaching sessions was about the coachees' poor relationships with the executive team, with many of the coachees blaming senior management for being remote and uninterested. Some of the coaches themselves felt similarly about senior management and wanted the supervisor to feed the concerns back to the executive via the Learning and Development manager. The supervisor helped the coaches recognise that they were colluding with their clients and may be part of a 'parallel process' (De Haan, 2012). He then helped the coaches reappraise their role and the coachees' personal responsibility for their interaction with senior management.

It is encouraging to see that increasingly leaders speak out about their reliance on executive coaches and similarly coaches communicate their supervisory support as well as development consultants being upfront about charging for group supervision on larger projects. Most of Ashridge's clients are agreeable with this approach and share our view that (group) supervision is an integral part of the Quality Assurance process – similar to other elements such as contractual meetings and evaluation processes.

To sum up and paraphrase Gary Embleton (2002): Ethics are not problems to be solved. They are relational issues to be lived. Get in touch with your own pain and -whatever happens- do not inflict that pain onto others. This is the real task of supervision: to penetrate the celluloid respectability of coaching and explore the often brutal, destructive and mad forces operating within and among the leader, coach and supervisor.

vision – ganz abgesehen von der Gefahr der einfach nicht richtig erfassten Praxis der eigenen KlientInnen – in Übersteuerung zu gehen.

Berglas (2004) fasst die „sehr realen Gefahren des Leitungscoaching" zusammen, die seiner Ansicht nach oft durch einen persönlichen Mangel an psychologischem Verständnis des Coaches verschärft werden. Er gibt Fallbeispiele von Coaches, die

- die Situation falsch einschätzen;
- den Status quo verschlimmern; und
- ihre eigene Macht missbrauchen.

Andere ethische Herausforderungen in Coaching und Beratungsberufen erwachsen aus:

1. den vielen neuen Coaches, oft (internen) Beratern, HR-Direktoren und CEOs, die immer noch diesen Beruf mit nur minimaler Ausbildung beginnen.
2. sehr geringer Verhandlungsmacht der KundInnen, die eine Vielzahl von sehr kleinen Kontrakten verhandeln.
3. einem Mangel an Regulierung in Beratungsberufen und Coaching.
4. Gefühlen der Scham, Angst und dem daraus resultierenden Kundenschutz, wenn es Schwierigkeiten oder Bedenken gibt.
5. einer gewissen „Taubheit" oder einem Widerstand gegen die externe Qualitätssicherung, insbesondere mit erfahrenen Coaches und SupervisorInnen.

Meiner Meinung nach sind die folgenden Praktiken relativ „zahnlose" Qualitätssicherung:

- Verwaltungssysteme, die nur Kästchen ankreuzen oder in die „Fakten" der Praxis schauen, nicht in deren gelebte Erfahrung.
- Gedankenlose Anwendung von Verhaltenskodizes als „Dilemma-Ethik" und über bloße ethische Vignetten, die wenig zu angewandter Ethik im wirklichen Leben beitragen.
- „Moralische Argumentation", die auf „moralisches Handeln" nachweislich wenig Einfluss hat. Es ist lange bekannt, dass im Wesentlichen zwei ethische Menschen in allen von uns stecken: (1) das zukünftige ethische Ich, das eines Tages diese Dinge tun wird, die ich für andere empfehle, und (2) das heutige ethische Ich, das aus einem anderen Set von Standards heraus reagiert (Carroll & Shaw, 2012).
- „Selbstlose" oder „beziehungslose" Ethik machen die Prämisse vergessen, die aller Ethik und moralischen Codes zugrunde liegt, die sogenannte gol-

References

Berglas, S. (2002). The very real dangers of executive coaching. Harvard Business Review, 80, 86–92.

Carroll & Shaw (2012). Ethical Maturity in the Helping Professions. Victoria (Australia), Psychoz.

Claxton, G., Owen, D. & Sadler-Smith, E. (2015). Hubris in leadership: a peril of unbridled intuition? Leadership, 11.1, 57–78.

De Haan, E. (2006). Fearless Consulting. Chichester: Wiley.

De Haan, E. (2008). I doubt therefore I coach – critical moments in coaching practice. Consulting Psychology Journal: Practice and Research, 60.1, 91–105.

De Haan, E. (2012). Supervision in action: a relational approach to coaching and organisation supervision. Columbus: McGraw-Hill/Open University Press, 2012.

De Haan, E., & Birch, D. (2010). Quality control for coaching. The Training Journal, August, 71–74.

De Haan, E., & Birch, D. (2011). Supervision for consultants. The Training Journal, January, 63–67.

De Haan, E. & Carroll, M. (2014). Moral Lessons – Part 1: what would you do? Coaching @ Work 9.1, January/February, 37–39. Part 2: further guidance. Coaching @ Work 9.2, March/April, 46–50.

De Haan, E. & Kasozi, A. (2014). The leadership shadow: how to recognise and avoid derailment, hubris and overdrive. London: Kogan Page.

Embelton, G. (2002). Dangerous liaisons and shifting boundaries in psychoanalytic perspectives on supervision, in McMahon, Mary & Patton, Wendy (Eds.), Supervision in the Helping Professions: A Practical Approach (119–130). French's Forest: Pearson. [Author's Note: I have changed 'analysis' into 'coaching' in this quote]

Nelson, E. and R. Hogan (2009). Coaching on the Dark Side. International Coaching Psychology Review, 4, 7–19.

dene Regel, zuerst formuliert von Konfuzius: „Behandle andere so, wie du von ihnen behandelt werden willst."

Schließlich noch einige Aspekte der Qualitätssicherung durch Coaching und Supervision, die, so glaube ich, positive Auswirkungen in der Praxis haben:
1. Externe Qualitätssicherung scheint zuverlässiger als Peer-Qualitätssicherung; externes Coaching und externe Supervision sind für die Qualitätssicherung internem Coaching und interner Supervision vorzuziehen.
2. Die Marktkräfte, die Dreiecksbeziehung und die allgemein üblichen befristeten Kontrakte spielen eine stabilisierende Rolle und bieten Schutz vor Überschreitungen.
3. Supervision wird zurzeit noch am häufigsten in der Ausbildung eingesetzt, könnte jedoch eine wichtigere Rolle für den Einstieg von (fertig ausgebildeten) Coaches und auch für sehr erfahrene Coaches spielen; sie sind die beiden am stärksten gefährdeten Gruppen.

Fallbeispiel

Ein Team von Coaches, die mit „High Potential"-Führungskräften einer Regierungsabteilung gearbeitet hatten, traf sich zur Gruppensupervision.

Im Laufe der Zeit wurde deutlich, dass es in vielen der Coaching-Sitzungen um die schlechten Beziehungen der Coachees zum Führungsteam ging, wofür viele der Coachees dem Senior Management die Schuld zuwiesen, das zurückhaltend und uninteressiert sei. Einige der Coaches sahen die Geschäftsleitung ähnlich und wollten, dass der Supervisor die Bedenken über die Personalentwicklung an das Management zurückmelden möge. Der Supervisor half den Coaches zu erkennen, dass sie die Sicht ihrer KlientInnen übernommen hatten und Teil eines „Parallelprozesses" (De Haan, 2012) waren. Er half dann den Coaches, sowohl ihre eigene Rolle zu überdenken als auch die persönliche Verantwortung der Coachees für ihre Interaktion mit dem Senior Management.

Es ist ermutigend, dass immer mehr Führungskräfte über ihr Vertrauen zu ihren Coaches sprechen, und in ähnlicher Weise Coaches die Unterstützung durch Supervision kommunizieren; PersonalentwicklerInnen finden sich an vorderster Front, wenn es darum geht, Gruppensupervision für größere Projekte vorzusehen. Die meisten Ashridge-KundInnen stimmen mit diesem Ansatz und unserer Ansicht überein, dass (Gruppen-)Supervision integraler Bestandteil des Qualitätssicherungsprozesses ist – ähnlich wie andere Elemente, etwa vereinbarte Sitzungen und Evaluation.

Um zusammenzufassend Gary Embleton (2002) zu paraphrasieren: Ethik bedeutet nicht, Probleme zu lösen. Es geht um Fragen gelebter Beziehungen. Halten Sie Kontakt zu Ihrem eigenen Schmerz und – was auch immer geschieht – stülpen Sie diesen Schmerz nicht anderen über. Dies ist die eigentliche Aufgabe der Supervision: die dünnwandige Respektabilität des Coachings zu durchbrechen und die oft brutalen, destruktiven und verrückten Kräfte zwischen Führungskraft, Coach und SupervisorIn zu erkunden.

Literatur

Berglas, S. (2002). The very real dangers of executive coaching. Harvard Business Review, 80, 86–92.

Carroll, M. & Shaw, E. (2012). Ethical Maturity in the Helping Professions. Victoria (Australia), PsychOz.

Claxton, G., Owen, D. & Sadler-Smith, E. (2015). Hubris in leadership: a peril of unbridled intuition? Leadership, 11.1, 57–78.

De Haan, E. (2006). Fearless Consulting. Chichester: Wiley.

De Haan, E. (2008). I doubt therefore I coach – critical moments in coaching practice. Consulting Psychology Journal: Practice and Research, 60.1, 91–105.

De Haan, E. (2012). Supervision in action: a relational approach to coaching and organization supervision. Columbus: McGraw-Hill/Open University Press, 2012.

De Haan, E., & Birch, D. (2010). Quality control for coaching. The Training Journal, August, 71–74.

De Haan, E., & Birch, D. (2011). Supervision for consultants. The Training Journal, January, 63–67.

De Haan, E. & Carroll, M. (2014). Moral Lessons – Part 1: what would you do? Coaching @ Work 9.1, January/February, 37–39. Part 2: further guidance. Coaching @ Work 9.2, March/April, 46–50.

De Haan, E. & Kasozi, A. (2014). The leadership shadow: how to recognize and avoid derailment, hubris and overdrive. London: Kogan Page.

Embelton, G. (2002). Dangerous liaisons and shifting boundaries in psychoanalytic perspectives on supervision, in McMahon, Mary & Patton, Wendy (Eds.), Supervision in the Helping Professions: A Practical Approach (119–130). French's Forest: Pearson.

Nelson, E. and R. Hogan (2009). Coaching on the Dark Side. International Coaching Psychology Review, 4, 7–19.

ECVision

Results

A European Glossary of Supervision and Coaching

Marina Ajdukovic
Lilja Cajvert
Michaela Judy
Wolfgang Knopf
Hubert Kuhn
Krisztina Madai
Mieke Voogd

ECVision

Ergebnisse

Ein europäisches Glossar für Supervision und Coaching

Marina Ajdukovic
Lilja Cajvert
Michaela Judy
Wolfgang Knopf
Hubert Kuhn
Krisztina Madai
Mieke Voogd

Supervision – Scope of Concept

These descriptions aim at giving an overview of the mainstream concepts of supervision in Europe today. This glossary covers the definitions given under 1 (1.1.–1.4.).

1. Supervision as a counselling profession focuses on the interaction of persons, professional tasks and organisations

Supervision provides ample space and time to reflect professional functioning in complex situations.

Supervision primarily serves the development of individuals, teams and organisations. It improves the professional lives of individuals and teams with regard to their roles in an institutional context. It also focuses on ensuring and developing the quality of communication among staff members and methods of cooperation in various working contexts.

Additionally, supervision offers support in different reflection and decision-making processes and in challenging and demanding professional situations and conflicts. It supports clarification and processing of tasks, functions and roles. It assists in the handling of processes of change, in finding innovative solutions for new challenges and measures to combat mobbing and burnout.

The following differentiations refer to different foci of supervision.

1.1   Supervision for work with clients

Supervision provides a reflective space to professionals (who work with clients, e.g. social workers, therapists in psychosocial work fields) to serve the assurance and development of the quality of their professional attitude and performance. The focus is on the supervisees' clients and on how the supervisees work with their clients.

Supervision – Schwerpunktkonzepte

Diese Beschreibungen geben einen Überblick über die gängigen Konzepte von Supervision in Europa. Das Glossar deckt die unter Punkt 1 gegebenen Definitionen (1.1.–1.4.) ab.

1. Supervision berät die Interaktion von Personen, beruflichen Anforderungen und Organisationen

Supervision bietet einen strukturierten und geschützten Rahmen, um professionelles Handeln in komplexen Situationen zu reflektieren.

Supervision dient in erster Linie der Entwicklung von Personen, Teams und Organisationen. Sie erweitert die berufliche Handlungsfähigkeit von Personen und Teams in ihrem Eingebunden-Sein in einen institutionellen Kontext. Sie leistet Qualitätsentwicklung, indem sie die Kommunikation und Kooperation der Mitarbeitenden in verschiedenen Arbeitswelten verbessert. Außerdem bietet Supervision Unterstützung bei Reflexions- und Entscheidungsprozessen sowie in fordernden beruflichen Situationen und Konflikten. Sie unterstützt die Klärungen von Aufgaben, Funktionen und Rollen, hilft bei der Bewältigung von Veränderungsprozessen, beim Finden innovativer Lösungen für neue Herausforderungen und bietet Maßnahmen gegen Mobbing und Burnout.

Die folgenden Differenzierungen beziehen sich auf unterschiedliche Schwerpunktsetzungen von Supervision.

1.1 Supervision der Arbeit mit KlientInnen

Supervision bietet einen Reflexionsraum für Menschen, die mit KlientInnen arbeiten, also z. B. SozialarbeiterInnen, TherapeutInnen oder in psychosozialen Arbeitsfeldern Tätige. Ziel ist, dass die SupervisandInnen ihre Einstellungen und ihr professionelles Handeln überprüfen und weiterentwickeln,

This approach often – but not necessarily – means that the supervisor is an experienced practitioner in the work field s/he supervises.

1.2 Educational Supervision for trainees in professional training courses

The key component of this kind of supervision is part of the development of professional competences in training programmes. It serves the integration of knowledge, skills and values/attitudes the trainees have acquired during their professional training. It is necessarily related to a specific curriculum of a training provider. It **focuses on learning** to master specific methods, skills or approaches to the expected outcome of developing competences of professionals in a particular method or approach. Therefore, the supervisor should be an experienced practitioner of that same method or approach.

1.3 Supervision as improvement of professional functioning

Supervision focuses on the improvement of individuals, teams and organisations in all work fields. The main aims include higher quality, more effectiveness and work efficiency in professional contexts. All professions or work fields can profit from supervision in that understanding.

According to this approach, the supervisor is an expert for counselling the interaction of persons, professional tasks and organisations, but he is not a practitioner of a specific work field.

1.4 Organisation supervision

This approach contributes to the effective functioning of an organisation. It is carried out during regular meetings of superiors and their subordinates and members of professional teams while being supervised. In this case, the emphasis is on reflecting the relationship between the team and the wider organisational environment. It enlightens power positions and institutional and subjective understanding of roles and tasks. Thus, organisational supervision contributes to the improvement of organisational culture.

und so dessen Qualität sichern. Der Fokus liegt auf der Beziehung zwischen den SupervisandInnen und deren KlientInnen, und darauf, wie die SupervisandInnen mit ihren KlientInnen arbeiten.Dieser Ansatz bedeutet oft – aber nicht notwendigerweise – dass die/der SupervisorIn ein/e erfahrene/r PraktikerIn im Arbeitsfeld ist, das sie/er supervidiert.

1.2 Lehrsupervision für AusbildungskandidatInnen

Kernelement dieser Form von Supervision ist, dass sie zur Entwicklung professioneller Kompetenzen in Ausbildungen beiträgt. Sie dient der Integration von Wissen, Fertigkeiten, Werten und Einstellungen, die AusbildungskandidatInnen während ihrer Ausbildung erworben haben. Sie bezieht sich verpflichtend auf einen bestimmten Lehrplan eines Ausbildungsanbieters. Sie fokussiert auf Lernen und soll den Lernenden die Aneignung und Entwicklung spezifischer Methoden, Fähigkeiten und Fertigkeiten ermöglichen. Ein/e SupervisorIn sollte deshalb ein/e erfahrene/r PraktikerIn der gleichen Methode sein.

1.3 Supervision als Beratung beruflichen Handelns

Supervision berät die Interaktion von Personen, Teams und Organisationen in allen Arbeitsfeldern. Sie fokussiert auf die Verbesserung des professionellen Handelns, höhere Qualität, sowie mehr Wirksamkeit und Effizienz in beruflichen Zusammenhängen. Alle Berufe oder Arbeitsfelder können von Supervision in diesem Verständnis profitieren.

In diesem Ansatz ist der/die SupervisorIn ExpertIn für das Beraten der Interaktion von Personen, professionellen Aufgaben und Organisationen, nicht aber PraktikerIn im Arbeitsfeld, das sie/er supervidiert.

1.4 Organisationssupervision

Dieser Ansatz trägt zum wirksamen Funktionieren einer Organisation bei. Organisationssupervision findet in regelmäßigen Treffen von Vorgesetzten und ihren Untergebenen bzw. von Mitgliedern unterschiedlicher Teams statt, wobei diese Treffen supervidiert werden. In diesem Verständnis von Supervision liegt der Schwerpunkt auf dem Reflektieren der Beziehung zwischen Teams und dem organisatorischen Umfeld. Sie macht Machtkonstel-

2. Supervision as a managerial function

It takes place in an organisation at an operative level. It includes the managing and controlling of defined and communicated tasks. The supervisor is therefore part of the organisational hierarchy.

This understanding of supervision has its origins in Anglo-Saxon countries and is mainly used by globally working enterprises.

lationen ebenso transparent wie institutionelles und subjektives Verständnis von Rollen und Aufgaben. Damit trägt sie v. a. zur Verbesserung der Organisationskultur bei.

2. Supervision als Funktion des Management-Handelns

Supervision findet in einer Organisation auf einer operativen Ebene statt. Als Unternehmensfunktion bedeutet sie das Management und Controlling definierter und kommunizierter Aufgaben. Supervision ist daher Teil der Organisationshierarchie. Dieses Supervisionsverständnis hat sine Ursprünge in angelsächsischen Ländern und wird v. a. von globalen Unternehmen verwendet.

Coaching – Scope of Concept

Many definitions of coaching used in Europe can be reduced to some of the five different concepts mentioned below.

Concepts 4 and 5 are beyond the present work that focuses on dealing with counselling the interaction between persons, work, and organisation.

1. Coaching is a form of professional counselling that inspires the coachees to maximise their personal and professional potential. It aims at initiating a transformational process. Goals and solutions are discovered along the way. Coach and coachees work together in a partnering relationship. The coachees are experts on the content level; the coach is an expert in professional counselling.

2. Coaching primarily aims at managers working with specific objectives, methodology and approach. Typical features are topic-specific support provided by a limited number of consultations, as well as teaching of skills at short training intervals. This approach prevails in German-speaking countries.

3. Coaching is a form of professional guidance focusing on the professional and personal growth of the coachees. It is a structured and purposeful process whereby the coach encourages the effective behaviour of the coachees. The coach is likely to use directive approaches to support the coachees to accomplish their goals.

These three definitions of coaching concern individuals, groups, teams and organisations.

4. Coaching is one of many competences that professionals such as managers, teachers or social workers have acquired.

5. Coaching is a synonym for training or mentoring in very different fields (e.g. health, job etc.).

Coaching – Schwerpunktkonzepte

Die meisten der in Europa verwendeten Definitionen von Coaching können auf eines der fünf unten dargelegten Konzepte reduziert werden.

Das Glossar deckt die Coaching-Verständnisse der Punkte 1–3 ab. Die Konzepte 4 und 5 stehen jenseits des Ansatzes dieses Glossars, der auf die Beratung der Interaktion von Personen, Arbeit und Organisation abstellt.

1. Coaching ist eine Beratungsform, die Coachees dabei unterstützt, ihr persönliches und professionelles Potenzial zu maximieren. Es zielt auf einen Transformationsprozess ab. Ziele und Lösungen werden in diesem Prozess entdeckt. Coach und Coachee arbeiten zusammen in einer partnerschaftlichen Beziehung. Der Coachee ist ExpertIn für seine/ihre eigene Arbeit; der Coach ist Experte für professionelle Beratung.

2. Coaching zielt vorrangig auf Manager ab und arbeitet mit definierten Zielen sowie einer spezifischen Methodik. Typische Merkmale sind die Orientierung auf themenspezifische Unterstützung in einer beschränkten Anzahl von Beratungen, sowie das Einüben von Fertigkeiten in Trainingssequenzen mit kurzen Intervallen. Dieser Ansatz herrscht in deutschsprachigen Ländern vor.

3. Coaching ist eine Form professioneller Begleitung, die sich auf professionelles und persönliches Wachstum der Coachees konzentriert. Es ist ein strukturierter und zielgerichteter Prozess, in dem der Coach effektive Verhaltensweisen der Coachees ermutigt. Der Coach verwendet auch direktive Ansätze, um Coachees bei der Erreichung ihrer Ziele zu unterstützen.

Diese drei Definitionen von Coaching betreffen Personen, Gruppen, Teams und Organisationen.

4. Coaching ist eine von vielen Kompetenzen, die Professionalisten wie Manager, LehrerInnen oder SozialarbeiterInnen erwerben.

5. Coaching ist ein Synonym für Training oder Mentoring in sehr verschiedenen Arbeitsfeldern (z. B. Gesundheit, Job, etc.)

Stakeholders

Stakeholders are the persons and bodies involved in and responsible for the process of supervision or coaching.

1. Training Provider

Supervision   *Coaching*
Organisation that offers and runs training programmes for supervision and coaching.

2. Clients

Supervision
Clients of the supervisees are party in the supervision process though not physically present.
Related concept: client system.

Coaching
Coaching literature uses client as a synonym for coachee.

3. National Organisations

Supervision
Consortium of professional supervisors and coaches (and in some countries also training providers) under national law, accepting ANSE standards and ANSE ethics.

Coaching
Consortium of professional coaches and training providers under national law accepting professional standards and ethics either set by international associations (e.g., EMCC or ICF) or set by the consortium itself.

Akteure

Akteure sind Personen oder Institutionen, die in den Prozess von Supervision oder Coaching einbezogen, bzw. dafür verantwortlich sind.

1. Ausbildungsträger

Supervision   *Coaching*
Organisation, die Ausbildungslehrgänge für Supervision und Coaching anbietet und durchführt.

2. KlientInnen

Supervision
Die KlientInnen der SupervisandInnen sind ebenfalls Akteure im Supervisionsprozess, wenn auch nicht physisch anwesend.
Verwandtes Konzept: Klientensystem.

Coaching
Die Coaching-Literatur verwendet KlientIn synonym mit Coachee.

3. Nationale Verbände

Supervision
Konsortium professioneller SupervisorInnen und Coaches (und in einigen Ländern auch Ausbildungsanbieter), die unter nationalem Recht sowie der Selbstverpflichtung auf ANSE Standards und der ANSE Ethik agieren.

Coaching
Konsortium professioneller Coaches, die unter nationalem Recht agieren und die professionellen Standards und eine Ethik akzeptieren, die entweder von internationalen Verbänden (z. B. EMCC oder ICF), oder durch das Konsortium selbst festgelegt sind.

4. Supervisees/Coachees

Supervision

The users of supervision.
The supervisees assume responsibility for:
- their part of the conditions and cooperation;
- their process of development and learning;
- the transformation of new insights gained into their professional situation.

Coaching

The users of coaching. The coachees are responsible for their process of development. They are supposed to be open, bring in their experiences, thoughts and feelings, be on time, and keep appointments. The coachees are responsible for defining the goals they want to work on as well as progressing according to steps set by themselves.

5. Supervisor/Coach

Supervision

A supervisor is:
- a trained professional according to an approved curriculum – following ANSE standards and national regulations,
- a graduate/postgraduate trained professional with more than three years of work experience,
- responsible for creating a viable space which supports the supervisees in pursuing their goals.

Coaching

A coach is a trained professional who guides a coachee, group or a team in pursuit of a contracted goal.
In principle, everybody can call himself/herself a coach. International professional associations, such as ICF and EMCC, develop professional standards that are based on education, experience, performance evaluation and the level of service, or on continuous professional development. The emphasis is more on performance and output criteria than on training hours.

4. SupervisandIn/Coachee

Supervision

NutzerIn von Supervision.
SupervisandInnen übernehmen die
Verantwortung für die eigene Mitarbeit, für ihren Entwicklungs- und
Lernprozess, sowie für den Transfer
neuer Erkenntnisse in ihren beruflichen Alltag.

Coaching

NutzerIn von Coaching.
Coachees sind für ihren Entwicklungsprozess verantwortlich. Sie sollen eigene Erfahrungen, Gedanken
und Gefühle einbringen, pünktlich
sein und Termine einhalten.
Coachees sind für die Festlegung der
Ziele, an denen sie arbeiten wollen
sowie für Fortschritte bezüglich der
selbstgesetzten Ziele verantwortlich.

5. SupervisorIn/Coach

Supervision

Ein/e SupervisorIn ist:

• Eine ausgebildete Fachkraft ge-
  mäß eines nach ANSE-Standards
  und nationalen Regelungen
  anerkannten Ausbildungscurri-
  culums.
• Ein/e BeraterIn mit (post)-gra-
  dualer professioneller Ausbildung
  und mit mehr als drei Jahren
  Berufserfahrung.
• Für die Schaffung eines adäqua-
  ten Reflexionsraumes verantwortlich, der SupervisandInnen
  beim Entwickeln und Verfolgen
  ihrer Ziele unterstützt.

Coaching

Ein Coach ist eine ausgebildete Fachkraft, die einen Coachee, eine Gruppe oder ein Team beim Verfolgen
eines vertraglich vereinbarten Zieles
anleitet.
Im Prinzip kann sich jede/r Coach
nennen.
Internationale Berufsverbände,
wie ICF & EMCC, haben Standards
entwickelt, die auf Ausbildung, Erfahrung, Leistungsbewertung, dem
Niveau der Leistungserbringung
oder auf kontinuierlicher beruflicher
Weiterentwicklung basieren. Der
Schwerpunkt liegt mehr auf Leistung
und Output-Kriterien als auf Trai-
ningsstunden.

6. Contractual partner

| *Supervision* | *Coaching* |

Is the responsible manager in an organisation who orders, finances and evaluates supervision/coaching. S/he is involved in the selection of the supervisor/coach and in the contracting process. This involvement may cover a power of veto up to even a direct personal selection. Most often public bodies or organisations have internal regulations for supervision/coaching and lists of recommended/authorised supervisors/coaches.

6. Vertragspartner

Supervision   *Coaching*

Ist der zuständige Manager in einer Organisation, die Supervision/Coaching anordnet, zahlt und evaluiert. Er/Sie ist an der Auswahl der/des SupervisorIn/Coaches sowie der vertraglichen Vereinbarung beteiligt. Die Involviertheit kann von einem Vetorecht bis zu einer direkten, persönlichen Auswahl reichen. Oft haben öffentliche Einrichtungen oder Organisationen interne Regelungen für die Supervision/Coaching sowie Empfehlungslisten bzw. zugelassene SupervisorInnen/Coaches.

Core qualities

Core qualities are necessary basic characteristics of professional work in supervision and coaching. A supervisor/coach needs a clear and reflected understanding of the following core qualities.

1. Ambiguity Tolerance

Supervision   *Coaching*
Discussing and reflecting conflicts, allowing contradictory approaches to show up. This may change perspectives and goals. This includes tolerating tension and exploring the various feelings, which arise during a counselling process. Ambiguity (also: complexity, ambivalence) is an integral part of the human condition and encompassing feelings, notions, and attitudes about something or somebody. Ambiguity often creates worry, anxiety or confusion within a person or a group.

2. Diversity Awareness

Supervision   *Coaching*
Knowing and factoring in how values, communication styles and assumptions guide human action generally. Having come to terms with one's own biases as a supervisor/coach enables to support supervisees/coachees in exploring their own stereotyping.
This includes recognising, reflecting and managing processes of power and the distribution of resources in a way that enhances the supervisees'/coachees' abilities of dealing with them.

Kernqualitäten

Kernqualitäten sind unverzichtbare fundamentale Charakteristika professioneller Beratung in Supervision und Coaching. Ein/e SupervisorIn/Coach braucht ein klares und reflektiertes Verständnis aller Kernqualitäten.

1. Ambiguitätstoleranz

Supervision   *Coaching*
Das Auftauchen widersprüchlicher Gefühle und Sichtweisen in Konflikten wahrnehmen, erörtern und reflektieren. Dies zu erfahren kann Perspektiven und Ziele verändern. Es beinhaltet, Spannung auszuhalten und die verschiedenen Gefühle, die während des Beratungsprozesses auftauchen, zu erkunden. Mehrdeutigkeit (auch: Komplexität, Ambivalenz) ist integraler Bestandteil des Menschseins und umfasst Gefühle, Annahmen und Einstellungen zu etwas oder jemandem. Mehrdeutigkeit schafft oft Unruhe, Angst oder Verwirrung, sowohl in einer Person als auch in einer Gruppe.

2. Diversity

Supervision   *Coaching*
Wissen um und Einbeziehen dessen, wie Werte, Kommunikationsstile und handlungsleitende Annahmen menschliches Verhalten steuern. Vertrautsein mit den eigenen handlungsleitenden Annahmen und Vorurteilen als SupervisorIn/Coach; dies ermöglicht es, SupervisandInnen/Coachees in der Erforschung ihrer eigenen Stereotypisierungen zu unterstützen.
Dazu gehört es, Prozesse der Macht- und der Ressourcenverteilung so zu thematisieren, dass die SupervisandInnen/Coachees neue Handlungsspielräume im Umgang mit ihnen entwickeln können.

3. Empathy

Supervision   *Coaching*

Empathy is a way of recognising the emotional state of the supervisees and separating it from the supervisor's own emotional response on 'what comes from the supervisees'.

It includes being aware of transference/countertransference and one's own preoccupations.

4. Experience Orientation

Supervision   *Coaching*

Expressing an event in a way that supports supervisees/coachees to link their experience here and now to their work, to how they deal with the views of others, the way they express their opinions or make decisions.

5. Ethics/Values

Supervision   *Coaching*

In dealing with power, trust and responsibility, supervisors and coaches maintain their personal and professional integrity by positioning themselves autonomously in relation to constituents, clients and colleagues. Supervisors and coaches are bound to keep confidentiality, handle the process of contracting carefully and avoid becoming a party in conflicting interests.

Acting responsibly is part of professionalism for supervisors and coaches. They care for maintaining their skills, for the reliability of the profession they exercise and for supporting the learning process of supervisees and coachees. Most professional organisations for supervision and coaching have established a 'Code of Ethics' which reflects the state of professionalism.

3. Empathie

Supervision   *Coaching*

Empathie ist die Fähigkeit, die emotionale Befindlichkeit der SupervisandInnen zu erkennen und sie von den eigenen emotionalen Reaktionen auf diese trennen zu können. Das erfordert Kenntnis und Bewusstheit von Übertragung/Gegenübertragung und eigenen Voreingenommenheiten.

4. Erfahrungsorientierung

Supervision   *Coaching*

Ein Ereignis oder Verhalten in einer Weise zur Sprache bringen, die SupervisandInnen/Coachees unterstützt, ihre Erfahrungen hier und jetzt mit jenen in ihrer Arbeit in Verbindung zu bringen: wie sie mit den Sichtweisen anderer umgehen, wie sie ihre Meinungen formulieren, oder wie sie Entscheidungen treffen.

5. Ethik & Werte

Supervision   *Coaching*

Im Umgang mit Macht, Vertrauen und Verantwortung halten SupervisorInnen und Coaches ihre persönliche und berufliche Integrität durch selbstverantwortliche Positionierung gegenüber ihren KundInnensystemen und KollegInnen aufrecht.

SupervisorInnen und Coaches sind zu Vertraulichkeit verpflichtet, handhaben Vereinbarungsprozesse sorgfältig und vermeiden Parteinahme bei widerstreitenden Interessen.

Verantwortungsvolles Handeln ist integraler Bestandteil der Professionalität von SupervisorInnen und Coaches. Sie sorgen für die Weiterentwicklung ihrer Fähigkeiten, für die Vertrauenswürdigkeit ihres Berufsstandes und unterstützen die Lernprozesse der SupervisandInnen/Coachees.

Die meisten professionellen Verbände für Supervision und Coaching haben einen „Code of Ethics" etabliert, der den aktuellen Stand der Professionalitätsentwicklung widerspiegelt.

6. Leadership and Management

Supervision   *Coaching*

Integration of organisational components into the process, especially those issues that most frequently arise such as authority, subservience and competition.

7. Function and Role

Supervision   *Coaching*

In a group-dynamic approach, function means the formal activities negotiated by the members in a social system. The members are bound to activities in a special frame and contract of working together. Role in this case means behaviour and expectations of behaviour in social systems between two or more persons.

Other approaches use function and role more or less as synonyms. Nevertheless, supervision and coaching take into account both formal and informal activities and attitudes of the supervisees/coachees.

6. Führung und Management

Supervision   *Coaching*

Integration organisationaler Anforderungen in den Prozess, insbesondere die sich häufig ergebenden Thematiken Autorität, Unterordnung und Konkurrenz.

7. Funktion und Rolle

Supervision   *Coaching*

In einem gruppendynamischen Ansatz bezeichnet Funktion die formellen Tätigkeiten und Zuständigkeiten, die Mitglieder in sozialen Systemen aushandeln. Die Mitglieder sind an vertraglich und organisational vereinbarte Tätigkeiten und Zuständigkeiten in der Zusammenarbeit gebunden. Rolle bedeutet in diesem Fall Verhalten und Verhaltenserwartungen in sozialen Systemen zwischen zwei oder mehreren Personen.

Andere Ansätze verwenden die Begriffe Funktion und Rolle mehr oder weniger synonym.

Doch ziehen Supervision und Coaching stets sowohl formelle als auch informelle Tätigkeiten und Einstellungen der SupervisandInnen/Coachees in Betracht.

8. Integration of Theory and Practice

Supervision

Exploring the supervisees' implicit and explicit theories. Their content-related, emotional and body language-related messages are reflected and clarified referring to the supervisors' concepts and theories. This approach adds a new perspective to the supervisees' situation and assumptions and supports the application of a theory for deeper understanding.

Coaching

Integrating a new feature into an existing bigger picture. It can take place within an individual, a group, an organisation or on community level. During the coaching process, the coachees grow towards a level of conscious competence. The coachees apply lessons learned in various contexts and circumstances. The new behaviour becomes part of the person's identity.

9. Interactive Process

Supervision   *Coaching*

An interactive process ‚happens' in supervision/coaching between the supervisees/coachees and the supervisor/coach. It concerns how they jointly shape their working relationship and deal with the verbalised and non-verbalised content of the conversation between the supervisor/coach and supervisees/coachees.

10. Communication

Supervision   *Coaching*

Communication comprises any act of exchanging verbal and/or nonverbal signs. Communication as a core quality means a conscious and reflected approach to that ongoing exchange.

8. Integration von Theorie und Praxis

Supervision

Erkunden der impliziten und expliziten Theorien der SupervisandInnen. Ihre inhaltlichen, emotionalen und körpersprachlichen Botschaften werden reflektiert und mit den Konzepten und Theorien der/des SupervisorIn in Beziehung gesetzt.

Dieser Zugang eröffnet eine neue Perspektive auf die Situation der SupervisandInnen und deren Annahmen. Er unterstützt ein tieferes Verständnis einer Theorie und deren Anwendbarkeit. Dies integriert ein neues Element in ein vorhandenes größeres Bild. Diese Integration kann in einer Person, einer Gruppe, einer Organisation stattfinden.

Coaching

Entwickeln zunehmend bewusster Kompetenz von Coachees während eines Coaching-Prozesses.
Die Coachees wenden Gelerntes in verschiedenen Kontexten und Situationen an. Das neue Verhalten wird Teil der Identität der Person.

9. Interaktiver Prozess

Supervision   *Coaching*

„Geschehen" in Supervision/Coaching zwischen SupervisandInnen/Coachees und SupervisorIn/Coach. In diesem Prozess gestalten sie gemeinsam ihre Arbeitsbeziehung und ihren Umgang mit den verbalisierten und nichtverbalisierten Inhalten des Gesprächs zwischen SupervisandInnen/Coachees und SupervisorIn/Coach.

10. Kommunikation

Supervision   *Coaching*

Kommunikation umfasst jede Handlung, den Austausch von verbalen und/oder nonverbalen Zeichen. Kommunikation als Kernqualität bedeutet einen bewussten und reflektierten Umgang mit diesem ständigen Austausch.

11. Contracting

Supervision

Identifying the participants' expectations and relating them to a contracted and thereby testable way of working in supervision. Basic methodic framework of the supervision process.

The contracting may be dyadic – if an individual personally requests supervision – or triangular – between the supervisees' organisation, the supervisees and the supervisor in case the supervision takes place in context and on request of the organisation.

Coaching

Identifying the participants' expectations and relating them to a contracted and thereby testable way of working in coaching.

The contracting may be dyadic – if the individual personally asks for coaching – or triangular – between the coachees' organisation, the coachees and the coach in case the coaching takes place in context and on request of the organisation.

Coaching always has a determined duration, a defined goal and measurable results.

12. Context awareness

Supervision   *Coaching*

Reflecting the influence and the effects of the supervisees'/coachees' wider social interactions.

13. Learning Process

Supervision   *Coaching*

The process whereby knowledge, skills and competences are acquired through reflecting experience.

Characteristics and goals are related to the following forms of learning:

• Experiential learning. Learning from personal experience. Initiating from the practical experience of the individual and connecting it with the effects of a certain attitude or approach.

• Reflective learning. Plays an important role in the cycle of experiential learning. The concept of reflection in learning as an active persistence and careful consideration of any belief or form of knowledge in light of the data that support them and lead to new conclusions.

11. Kontrakt

Supervision

Herausarbeiten der Erwartungen aller Beteiligten, die danach in eine vereinbarte und daher überprüfbare Form gebracht werden. Methodisches Grundelement jedes Supervisionsprozesses.

Der Kontrakt kann dyadisch vereinbart werden – wenn eine Person selbst Supervision anfragt – oder als Dreieckskontrakt zwischen der Organisation, den SupervisandInnen, und der/dem SupervisorIn, sofern die Supervision im Kontext und im Auftrag der Organisation stattfindet.

Coaching

Herausarbeiten der Erwartungen aller Beteiligten, die danach in eine vereinbarte und daher überprüfbare Form gebracht werden. Coaching hat immer eine definierte Dauer, definierte Ziele und messbare Ergebnisse.

12. Kontext

Supervision   *Coaching*

Reflektieren des Einflusses und der Wirkungen der sozialen Interaktionen der SupervisandInnen/Coachees in einem weiteren Kontext.

13. Lernprozess

Supervision   *Coaching*

Prozess, in dem Wissen, Fertigkeiten und Kompetenzen durch reflektierte Erfahrung erworben werden.

Charakteristika und Ziele beziehen sich auf unterschiedliche Lernformen:

• Erfahrungslernen: Lernen aus persönlicher Erfahrung. Ausgehend von den praktischen Erfahrungen der Person werden diese mit den Wirkungen eines bestimmten Verhaltens in Verbindung gebracht.

• Reflexives Lernen: Spielt eine wichtige Rolle im Zyklus des Erfahrungslernens. Reflexion beim Lernen bedeutet kontinuierliche, nachhaltige und sorgfältige Befragung jeder Annahme und jedes Wissens im Licht von Fakten, die sie stützen und/oder zu neuen Schlüssen führen können.

- Integrated learning. The learning process by which the integration of professional, personal and methodological knowledge and skills is enabled.
- Individualised learning. Process in which the supervisees are unique in their knowledge, beliefs, abilities and learning styles.
- Dialogic learning. The central didactic device of learning in supervision is the dialogue: The supervisor/coach and supervisees/coachees affirm and improve their relationship and conversational exchanges by which the supervisor/coach joins the supervisees/coachees by listening, checking what was heard and giving very specific feedback.
- Double loop learning: By reflecting an experience, supervisees/coachees are able to modify a goal in the light of that experience. This approach shifts the effort from how to solve a problem to questioning the goal.
- Model learning: When the supervisees/coachees experience an attitude of the supervisor/coach and integrate parts of that attitude into their own behaviour.

14. Organisation

Supervision   *Coaching*

Taking into account not only the dyadic relationship between supervisor/coach and supervisees/coachees, but also the organisation as a set of meanings and adjustments comprising a set of processes and activities. End users/clients who are the final recipients of the supervisees'/coachees' professional actions also have to be taken into account.

It is important to be clear on which understanding, on which theory of organisation the supervisor/coach and the supervisees/coachees base their thinking and reflecting.

15. Parallel Process

Supervision   *Coaching*

Parallel processes are described as problems, impasses, feelings, and difficulties occurring simultaneously in two separated relationships: between supervisee – client and supervisor/coach – supervisee/coachee. Parallel processes

- Integratives Lernen: Prozess, der die Integration von professionellem, personalem sowie methodischem Wissen und den entsprechenden Fertigkeiten ermöglicht.
- Individualisiertes Lernen: Prozess auf Basis des einzigartigen Wissens, der Annahmen, Fähigkeiten und des Lernstils einer/eines SupervisandIn/Coachee.
- Dialogisches Lernen: Die zentrale Methode des Lernens in der Supervision ist der Dialog. SupervisorIn und SupervisandInnen/Coachees bestätigen und entwickeln ihre Beziehung und ihren Austausch im Gespräch. Der/Die SupervisorIn begleitet die SupervisandInnen/Coachees durch Zuhören, Überprüfen des Gehörten sowie durch gezieltes Feedback.
- Lernen in einer „doppelten Reflexionsschleife": das Reflektieren einer Erfahrung befähigt SupervisandInnen/Coachees, ein Ziel im Lichte dieser Erfahrung zu modifizieren. Das verschiebt das Anliegen von der Lösung eines Problems zu einem Infragestellen des Ziels.
- Modelllernen: Wenn SupervisandInnen/Coachees eine Haltung oder Verhaltensweise der/des SupervisorIn erleben und Teile davon in eigenes Verhalten integrieren.

14. Organisation

Supervision   *Coaching*

Miteinbeziehen nicht nur der dyadischen Beziehung zwischen SupervisorIn/Coach und SupervisandIn/Coachee, sondern auch der Organisation als Struktur von Bedeutungen und Anpassungsanforderungen, die in Zielformulierungen, Prozessen und Handlungen zusammenwirken. KlientInnen/KundInnen als „EndnutzerInnen" der SupervisandInnen/Coachees sind dabei ebenfalls in den Blick zu nehmen.

Zu klären ist auch, auf welchem – auch theoretischen – Verständnis von Organisation SupervisorIn/Coach und SupervisandIn/Coachee ihr Denken und Reflektieren aufbauen.

15. Parallelprozess/Spiegelphänomen

Supervision   *Coaching*

Parallelprozesse (auch: Spiegelphänomene) werden als Verhaltensweisen, Probleme, Gefühle, Schwierigkeiten beschrieben, die zeitgleich in zwei Beziehungen auftreten: zwischen SupervisandIn und KlientIn sowie Super-

are unconscious and cannot be recognised or understood in advance. What has occurred between a client and a supervisee or within a team may then be transferred to the actual supervision session between supervisee/coachee and supervisor/coach.

16. Performance

Supervision

Developing a new, creative element that will enrich and direct the work of the supervisees.

Coaching

Making the coachees' actions more effective both on a personal and professional level.

17. Professional Exploration

Supervision   *Coaching*

Increasing the professionalism of the supervisees/coachees by discussing certain experiences and issues such as beliefs, attitudes, ways of behaviour, aims and visions.

This requires a safe space for the very personal exploration of one's work with regard to obstacles, hindrances, successes, and dilemmas.

18. Quality Development

Supervision   *Coaching*

Continuous purposeful process of keeping up one's own professional skills and abilities. This includes taking care of one's own personal and professional development, and contributing to a professional community.

visorIn und SupervisandIn. Es können sich auch Verhaltensweisen oder Schwierigkeiten innerhalb eines Teams in der Beziehung zur/zum SupervisorIn/Coach spiegeln.

Parallelprozesse sind unbewusst und können im Voraus weder erkannt noch verstanden und daher auch nicht vorhergesagt werden.

Was zwischen KlientIn und SupervisandIn oder in einem Team aufgetreten ist, kann in der Supervisons-/Coachingsitzung auf ähnliche Art zwischen Super-visandInnen/Coachees und Supervisor/Coach auftreten.

16. Performance

Supervision
Entwickeln eines neuen, kreativen Elements, das die Arbeit der SupervisandInnen bereichert und leitet.

Coaching
Die Handlungen der Coachees sowohl auf persönlicher wie auch auf professioneller Ebene effektiver machen.

17. Professionelle Exploration

Supervision   *Coaching*

Steigern der Professionalität von SupervisandInnen/Coachees, indem Erfahrungen, Überzeugungen, Einstellungen, Verhaltensweisen, sowie Ziele und Visionen erörtert werden.

Dies erfordert einen geschützten Raum für sehr persönliche Erkundungen der Arbeitssituation einer Person mit Blick auf Hindernisse, Behinderungen, Erfolge und Dilemmata.

18. Qualitätsentwicklung

Supervision   *Coaching*

Zielgerichteter kontinuierlicher Prozess der Weiterentwicklung der eigenen beruflichen Fähigkeiten und Fertigkeiten.

Dies schließt Achtsamkeit gegenüber der eigenen persönlichen und beruflichen Entwicklung ein, ebenso wie Beiträge zur Professionsentwicklung in einer Berufsvereinigung zu leisten.

19. Reflection

Supervision   *Coaching*

Observing and articulating own experiences, feelings, thoughts and beliefs. By doing so, the present attitudes are connected, both with their origins in the past, and with the future attitudes the supervisees/coachees want to adopt. Reflection needs a stance taken towards the social patterns human beings are co-creating when communicating.

Certain techniques support the supervisees/coachees to become aware of their own influence in different situations. One may reflect on the contents, on the process and on the way of reflecting (meta-reflection).

Besides the metacognitive component (thinking about one's own thought processes), reflection includes an emotional component: consideration of personal emotional states and behavioural components, analysing behaviour, decisions and the consequences of one's own actions in a certain context. This allows drawing one's own conclusions about necessary changes to achieve wished-for outcomes in the future.

Therefore, reflection may not lead to quick solutions. It requires the ability to withstand tension without trying to eliminate it by immediate action.

20. Resource Orientation

Supervision	*Coaching*
Focusing on the supervisees' resources, knowledge, skills, and competences and supporting the supervisees by bringing them in as effectively as possible.	Assumption that individuals or teams are capable of generating their own solutions, with the coach supplying supportive, discovery-based approaches and frameworks. The process builds on the personal strengths and competences; it focuses on the solution the client finds and on his/her hidden strengths.

19. Reflexion

Supervision   *Coaching*

Wahrnehmen, Beobachten und Beschreiben von eigenen Erfahrungen, Gedanken, Gefühlen und Überzeugungen.

Dadurch werden gegenwärtige Einstellungen sowohl mit ihren Ursprüngen in der Vergangenheit als auch mit den zukünftigen Haltungen, die die SupervisandInnen/Coachees einnehmen wollen, in Zusammenhang gebracht.

Reflexion bedarf einer grundsätzlichen Haltung, welche die sozialen Muster, die Menschen ständig in ihrer Kommunikation schaffen, in den Blick nimmt und kontinuierlich befragt.

Bestimmte Techniken unterstützen die/den SupervisandIn/Coachee, ihren eigenen Einfluss auf verschiedene Situationen zu erkunden. Man kann den Inhalt, den Prozess sowie die Art zu reflektieren (Metareflexion) reflektieren.

Neben der metakognitiven Komponente (nachdenken über das eigene Nachdenken) beinhaltet Reflexion eine emotionale Komponente: das Erkunden eigener emotionaler Befindlichkeiten und Verhaltensweisen. Es bedeutet das Analysieren eigenen Verhaltens, eigener Entscheidungen und der Wirkungen des eigenen Tuns. Erst dann können eigene Schlüsse über Veränderungen, die gewünschte Ergebnisse erst möglich machen, gezogen Deshalb darf Reflexion nicht zu schnellen Lösungen führen. Sie erfordert die Fähigkeit, Spannung auszuhalten, statt sich ihrer durch schnelles Handeln zu entziehen.

20. Ressourcenorientierung

Supervision

Das Fokussieren auf Ressourcen, Wissen, Fertigkeiten und Kompetenzen von SupervisandInnen. Diese werden dadurch unterstützt, sie so wirksam wie möglich einzusetzen.

Coaching

Annahme, dass Personen oder Teams in der Lage sind, eigene Lösungen zu kreieren, während der Coach unterstützende, Entdeckungen fördernde Ansätze und den entsprechenden Rahmen beiträgt. Das Verfahren basiert auf persönlichen Kompetenzen; es fokussiert auf die Lösungen der Coachees und auf deren verborgene Stärken.

21. Responsibility and Accountability

Supervision
The motivation and ability of a person, group or team to follow their goals and use the supervisor's support to reach them.
Furthermore, the supervisees are responsible for transferring the outcomes of the supervision to their daily practices.

Coaching
The motivation of the coachees to reach their goals is crucial in coaching.
During the whole process, the coach focuses on keeping the coachees connected with their goals and on taking action towards attaining them.

22. Change

Supervision
Focusing on possible changes concerning a supervisee/a team/an organisation within the process of supervision. This can be a change of perspective as well as a change of attitude or behaviour.

Coaching
Focusing on one or all of a three-level change. Level 1: a more complex understanding of the problem situation. Level 2: a better understanding of personal responsibilities and action areas in solving the problem. Level 3: finding a solution on the personal or system level. It aims at developing the personality (based on self-awareness and self-esteem) and the system the individual is part of. The goal of coaching is to achieve change.

21. Selbstverantwortung und Verbindlichkeit

Supervision
Die Motivation und Fähigkeit einer Person, Gruppe oder eines Teams, ihre Ziele zu verfolgen und die Unterstützung der/des SupervisorIn zu nützen, um diese zu erreichen. Überdies sind SupervisandInnen für die Übertragung der Ergebnisse der Supervision in ihre tägliche Praxis verantwortlich.

Coaching
Die Motivation der Coachees, ihre Ziele zu erreichen, ist von entscheidender Bedeutung im Coaching. Während des gesamten Prozesses fokussiert der Coach auf die Ziele der Coachees, und was diese zu deren Erreichung tun.

22. Veränderung

Supervision
Fokussieren auf mögliche, bzw. sinnvolle Veränderungen für SupervisandInnen/Teams/Organisationen im Prozess der Supervision.
Dies können Veränderungen der Perspektive, der Einstellung oder des Verhaltens sein.

Coaching
Fokussieren auf eine oder alle der folgenden 3-Ebenen-Veränderung:
Stufe 1: komplexeres Verständnis der Problemsituation.
Stufe 2: besseres Verständnis persönlicher Verantwortung und der Handlungsspielräume beim Problemlösen.
Stufe 3: Finden einer Lösung auf der Ebene der Person oder des Systems.
Zielt auf Persönlichkeitsentwicklung (basierend auf Selbsterfahrung und Selbstwert), wie auch auf das System, dem die Person angehört.
Das Ziel von Coaching ist Veränderung.

23. Reciprocity

Supervision   *Coaching*

Factoring in and reflecting the supervisees'/coachees' context dealing with the question which roles the supervisor/coach may play through their do-ings or non-doings in the course of acting professionally, be it with clients or in any other course of action.

In addition, the effect of the observer, describer, reflector or analyser of a reciprocal action on the examined action needs to be taken into account: everyone and everything involved influences any situation.

24. Goal and Need Orientation

Supervision

Double function of supervision, being both bound to contracted goals as well as to the supervisees' needs.

Requires a space of freedom and creativity of supervisor and super-visees for individually agreeing upon how the supervisees will pursue their goals and how they will meet their own developmental needs.

The goals and needs of the super-visees/teams/contracting organisa-tions are transparent and in focus of the supervisor (related to contract).

Coaching

Primary focus on creating actionable strategies for achieving specific goals in one's work or personal life.

The emphasis in a coaching relation-ship is on action, accountability and follow-through.

Feelings and needs play an important role in any learning and decision making process.

23. Wechselwirkung

Supervision   *Coaching*

Miteinbeziehen und Reflektieren des Kontexts der SupervisandInnen/Coachees, wobei gleichzeitig die Wirkungen zu berücksichtigen sind, die SupervisorIn/Coach durch ihr Handeln oder Unterlassen im Beratungsprozess haben, auf die SupervisandInnen/Coachees, KlientInnen oder auf ein anderes Geschehen.

Es muss also die Wirkung des Beobachtenden, Beschreibenden, Reflektierenden oder Analysierenden auf die Themen der SupervisandInnen/Coachees in Betracht gezogen werden: Alle Geschehen hängen miteinander zusammen.

24. Ziel- und Bedürfnisorientierung

Supervision

Doppelte Funktion von Supervision, die sowohl vereinbarte Ziele als auch Bedürfnisse der SupervisandInnen miteinbezieht. Erfordert einen kreativen Freiraum, innerhalb dessen SupervisorIn und SupervisandInnen sich individuell darauf einigen, wie die SupervisandInnen ihre Ziele verfolgen, und wie sie ihre eigenen Entwicklungsbedürfnisse erfüllen.

Die Ziele und Bedürfnisse der SupervisandInnen/Teams/auftraggebenden Organisationen sind transparent und – bezogen auf den Kontrakt – im Fokus der/des SupervisorIn.

Coaching

Primärer Fokus beim Entwickeln erfolgversprechender Strategien, damit Coachees bestimmte Ziele in ihrer Arbeit oder ihrem persönlichen Leben erreichen können.

Der Schwerpunkt in einer Coachingbeziehung liegt auf Handlungs- und Umsetzungsorientierung sowie auf Verantwortlichkeit.

Gefühle und Bedürfnisse spielen eine wichtige Rolle in jedem Lern- und Entscheidungsprozess.

Types

The different types of supervision and coaching indicate the various reasons for undergoing a supervision and/or coaching process within an organisational frame. These types refer – in contrast to settings – to certain aims of supervision and coaching.

1. Educational Supervision/Educational Coaching

Supervision
Learning to perform professional work within the framework of a professional education programme (curricula) including monitoring the fulfilment of specific professional standards.
Related terms:
Learning supervision: The aim is to master specific methods, skills or approaches to accomplish the anticipated outcome of being a competent professional.
It guides supervision trainees through their learning supervision.
Synonym: supervision in education.
Learner supervision:
supervision performed by a trainee acting as a supervisor during his/her education. Mandatorily accompanied by learning supervision.

Coaching
Coaching within the framework of a training programme on coaching or leadership and management at university or postgraduate level. There are explicit coaching formats for students apart from mentoring or tutoring to help them integrate theory and practice on a professional level.

Arten

Die verschiedenen Arten von Supervision und Coaching verweisen auf die verschiedenen Gründe für einen Supervisions- und/oder Coaching-Prozess innerhalb einer Organisation. Arten beziehen sich – im Gegensatz zu Settings – auf vordefinierte Ziele von Supervision und Coaching.

1. Ausbildungssupervision/Ausbildungscoaching

Supervision

Dient dazu, im Rahmen einer Ausbildung professionelles Handeln zu erlernen, einschließlich der Überprüfung, wie professionelle Standards erfüllt werden.
Verwandte Begriffe:
Lehr-Supervision: diese Art von Supervision zielt darauf ab, dass AusbildungskandidatInnen spezifische Methoden und Fähigkeiten meistern und sich zu kompetenten Profis entwickeln. AusbildungskandidatInnen werden durch ihre Lern-Supervision geleitet und begleitet.
Synonym: Ausbildungssupervision.
Lern-Supervision: Supervision, die Auszubildende im Rahmen ihrer Ausbildung durchführen. Wird verpflichtend durch Lehr-Supervision begleitet.

Coaching

Coaching im Rahmen einer Ausbildung für Coaching, Führung oder Management auf universitärer oder postgradualer Ebene.
Es gibt explizite Coaching-Formate für StudentInnen – abgesehen von Mentoring oder Tutoring – die ihnen helfen, Theorie und Praxis auf einer professionellen Ebene zu integrieren.

2. Business Coaching

Supervision

Coaching
Coaching within an organisational context. The coach does not have to be a member of the organisation. The questions tackled in coaching arise from the work context.

3. Coaching Supervision/Coach the Coach

Supervision

Coaching
Used by experienced coaches after their training programme as a form of quality assurance and for their professional development.
Quality assurance for coaches, assessing competence and supporting professional development.
It has a normative, formative and supportive function.

4. Internal/External Supervision/Coaching

Supervision
Internal supervision:
Supervision within an organisation/by a member of the organisation.
External supervision:
Supervision by an independent supervisor not responsible for the work of the supervisees and not taking a monitoring function on the work of the supervisees.

Coaching
Internal coaching:
Coaching within an organisation/by a member of the organisation.
External coaching:
Coaching by an independent coach neither responsible for the work of the coachees nor taking a monitoring function on the work of the coachees.

2. Business Coaching

Supervision

Coaching
Coaching im Unternehmenskontext.
Der Coach muss nicht Mitglied der
Organisation sein. Fragen, die im
Coaching behandelt werden, ergeben
sich aus dem Arbeitskontext.

3. Coaching Supervision/Coach the Coach

Supervision

Coaching
Qualitätssicherung für Coaches, dient
der Kompetenzbeurteilung sowie der
Unterstützung der professionellen
Entwicklung. Es hat eine normative,
formative und unterstützende Funk-
tion. Wird von Coaches nach ihrer
Ausbildung als Form der Qualitäts-
sicherung und für ihre berufliche
Entwicklung eingesetzt.

4. Externe/Interne Supervision/Coaching

Supervision
Interne Supervision:
Innerhalb einer Organisation/durch
ein Mitglied der Organisation.
Externe Supervision:
Durch eine/n unabhängige/n SupervisorIn, die/der nicht für die Arbeit
der SupervisandInnen verantwortlich ist und keine Kontrollfunktion
für die Arbeit der SupervisandInnen
wahrnimmt.

Coaching
Internes Coaching:
Coaching innerhalb einer Organi-
sation/durch ein Mitglied der
Organisation.
Externes Coaching:
Coaching durch einen unabhängigen
Coach, die/der nicht für die Arbeit
der Coachees verantwortlich ist und
keine Kontrollfunktion bezüglich der
Arbeit der Coachees wahrnimmt.

5. Case Supervision

Supervision

The supervisees bring their professional interactions with their clients forward as reference material for the supervision process.
There are two different perspectives on case supervision:
1. The supervisor is an expert in the work field of the supervisees, because the supervision focuses on how to apply professional competences, sometimes also referred to as consultation.
2. The supervisor is an expert on leading the process and thereby opens to the supervisees new perspectives on the cases.

Coaching

6. Group Supervision/Group Coaching

Supervision

Supervision with participants who are not in any formal professional or organisational contact. The participants may come from similar or different professions or professional fields.
There are two main approaches to group supervision: In the first approach, the groups are small (a supervision group may not exceed four, sometimes six participants) in order to give each participant the opportunity to present their own topics and allow for discussion. The second approach aims at working with the group process and the group resources, which allows work with bigger groups.

Coaching

Coaching with participants who are not in any formal professional or organisational contact.
The participants may come from similar or different professions and professional fields.

5. Fallsupervision

Supervision

Die SupervisandInnen bringen ihre professionellen Interaktionen mit ihren KlientInnen als Referenzmaterial in den Supervisionsprozess ein.

Es gibt zwei verschiedene Perspektiven auf die Fallsupervision:

1. Der/Die SupervisorIn ist ExpertIn im Arbeitsfeld der SupervisandInnen, die Supervision fokussiert auf die Anwendung spezifischer beruflicher Kompetenzen. Manchmal auch als Konsultation bezeichnet.

2. Der/Die SupervisorIn ist ExpertIn dafür, den Prozess zu gestalten und eröffnet dadurch den SupervisandInnen neue Perspektiven auf ihre Praxis.

Coaching

6. Gruppensupervision/Gruppencoaching

Supervision

Supervision mit Teilnehmenden, die in keinem formellen beruflichen oder organisationalen Kontakt stehen. Die SupervisandInnen können aus ähnlichen oder verschiedenen Berufsfeldern kommen.

Es gibt zwei Hauptkonzepte der Gruppensupervision:

1. Im ersten Konzept sind die Gruppen klein (vier bis maximal sechs Teilnehmende), um allen Teilnehmenden Gelegenheit zu geben, ihre eigenen Themen zu bearbeiten.

2. Der zweite Ansatz arbeitet mit dem Gruppenprozess und den Gruppenressourcen, was die Arbeit mit größeren Gruppen ermöglicht.

Coaching

Coaching mit Teilnehmenden, die in keinem formellen beruflichen oder organisationalen Kontakt stehen. Die Teilnehmenden können aus ähnlichen oder verschiedenen Berufen oder professionellen Feldern kommen.

7. Intervision/Peer Coaching

Supervision   *Coaching*

Refers to a specific form of supervision/coaching carried out among colleagues.

It has no permanent supervisor/coach because the members of the group take turns in adopting the role of the supervisor/coach and thus provide supervision/coaching to each other. All members are responsible for the supervision/coaching process.

Synonyms: "Peer Supervision", "Collegial Coaching".

8. Career Coaching

Supervision

Coaching

This type of coaching supports clients to achieve and fulfill their career and employment goals. It focuses on career change, employment, job search and other career related topics, often based in the field of existential questions. Coachees expect to gain career confidence, insight, encouragement, and inspiration.

9. Clinical Supervision

Supervision

The term clinical supervision is used in Anglo-Saxon literature, referring to supervision connected to any treatment/therapeutic/client work, in both, medical and social field.

Coaching

7. Intervision/Peer Coaching

Supervision   *Coaching*

Form der kollegialen Supervision/Coaching.
Es gibt keine/n permanente/n SupervisorIn/Coach, die Mitglieder der Gruppe übernehmen abwechselnd die Funktion der/des SupervisorIn/Coaches und supervidieren/coachen/intervidieren einander auf diese Art gegenseitig. Alle Mitglieder sind für den Prozess gleichermaßen verantwortlich.
Synonyme: Peer Supervision, Kollegiales Coaching.

8. Karrierecoaching

Supervision   *Coaching*

Diese Art des Coaching unterstützt Coachees beim Erreichen ihrer Karriere- und Berufsziele. Es konzentriert sich auf berufliche Veränderung, Beschäftigung, Jobsuche, Karriere und verwandte Themen, die oft in existentiellen Fragen gründen. Coachees erwarten sich, Vertrauen in die eigene Karriere, Einsicht, Ermutigung und Inspiration zu gewinnen.

9. Klinische Supervision

Supervision   *Coaching*

Der Begriff klinische Supervision wird in der angelsächsischen Literatur verwendet und bezieht sich auf Supervision in Verbindung mit Behandlung/Therapie/KlientInnenarbeit, sowohl im medizinischen wie im sozialen Bereich.

10. Meta-Supervision

Supervision   *Coaching*

Supervison the supervisor uses for
developing his/her skills and for
having his/her own space for reflection on his/her own work as a
supervisor.
Synonym: supervison of supervision.

11. Leadership Supervision/Leadership Coaching

Supervision

Supervising the special tasks a leading function/role requires in the
public and the non-profit sector. It
focuses on leadership performance
and attitudes. It is recommended
that the supervisors have some
personal experience and knowledge in organisation and management.
Another approach applied in the
public, the non-profit and the
profit sector uses the term coaching
which is more common. Other
approaches have leaders as a special
target group; the format is concep-
tualised as individual or group
supervision.
The various approaches overlap
according to supervisees' needs as
well as to national or methodological concepts of supervision. In any
case, leaders require a well-reflected
relationship to and a way of dealing
with power and authority.

Coaching

Leadership coaching can be understood in three different ways:
Coaching on the subject of leadership.
Coaching of professionals with managerial tasks in the hierarchy of organisations.
Coaching of higher management or
board members. Also called (Top)
"Executive Coaching".

10. Meta-Supervision

Supervision   *Coaching*
Supervision, die SupervisorInnen
als Reflexionsraum für ihre supervisorische Arbeit nützen, um ihre
Fertigkeiten weiterzuentwickeln.
Synonym: Supervision von Supervision.

11. Leitungssupervision/Leitungscoaching

Supervision

Das Supervidieren der speziellen
Aufgaben, die eine Führungs-
funktion erfordert. Fokussiert auf
Führungsleistung und Haltungen.
Es wird empfohlen, dass die/der
SupervisorIn über Erfahrung und
Wissen zu Organisation und
Management verfügt.
Supervision für Führungspersonen
im Non-Profit- und Profit-Bereich.
Hohe Überschneidung mit Coa-
ching, das als Begriff in Wirtschafts-
unternehmen üblicher ist.
Supervision für die Zielgruppe Füh-
rungspersonen, das Format ist als
Einzel- oder Gruppensupervision
konzeptualisiert.
Die verschiedenen Ansätze über-
lappen sich sowohl hinsichtlich der
Bedürfnisse der SupervisandInnen
als auch national oder methodolo-
gisch unterschiedlicher Konzepte. In
jedem Fall benötigt die/der SupervisorIn eine reflektierte Beziehung
zu und eine elaborierte Form des
Umgangs mit Macht und Autorität.

Coaching

Leitungscoaching kann auf drei un-
terschiedliche Weisen verstanden
werden:
Coaching zum Thema Führung.
Coaching von Berufstätigen mit
leitenden Aufgaben innerhalb der
Hierarchie von Organisationen.
Coaching von höheren Leitungsper-
sonen oder Aufsichtsratsmitgliedern.
Dies wird üblicherweise „Top-" oder
„Executive Coaching" genannt.

12. Organisational Supervision/Organisational Coaching

Supervision

Contributes to the effective functioning of the organisation. It takes place through regular and supervised contacts of superiors and subordinates, and members of professional teams. The emphasis is on reflecting the relationship between the team and the wider organisational environment, on illuminating power positions, and on institutional and subjective understanding of roles and tasks. This organisational supervision approach contributes to organisational culture.

Related types:

Organisational consulting is the generic term for all professional guidance interventions aimed at organisations, or parts of them, in order to sustainably change, develop and stabilise them. Its focus is – in contrast to supervision and coaching – on the organisations with their structures and communication, less on persons. Organisational development is a specific form of organisation consulting which involves the stakeholders and employees in the process of development.

Coaching

Means an integral coaching approach. It aims at a change related to organisations as complex systems. This approach was recently developed.

The characteristics are:

demand-driven and an on-the-job method of organisational development;

the coach has a facilitating role and begins with the client (system);

it is an interactive and action oriented approach.

In individual- and team-coaching lies a strong focus on the organisation as the dominant system the coachees function in.

12. Organisationssupervision/Organisationscoaching

Supervision

Organisationssupervision trägt zum wirksamen Funktionieren der Organisation bei. Sie findet durch regelmäßige und supervidierte Kontakte von Vorgesetzten und Untergebenen sowie von Mitgliedern unterschiedlicher Teams statt.

Der Schwerpunkt liegt auf dem Reflektieren der Beziehung zwischen Team und organisationalem Umfeld, auf dem Klären von Machtpositionen sowie auf institutionellem und subjektivem Verständnis von Rollen und Aufgaben.

Dieser organisationale Supervisionsansatz trägt zur Entwicklung der Organisationskultur bei.

Verwandte Begriffe:

Organisatonsberatung: bezeichnet die Beratung von Leitungsinterventionen, die auf Organisationen oder Teile von ihnen ausgerichtet sind, mit dem Ziel, sie nachhaltig zu verändern, sie zu entwickeln und zu stabilisieren. Organisationsberatung fokussiert – im Gegensatz zu Supervision und Coaching – auf Strukturen und Kommunikation der Organisation und weniger auf Personen.

Organisationsentwicklung: ist eine Form der Organisationsberatung, die Interessengruppen und Mitarbeitende in den Entwicklungsprozess der Organisation miteinbezieht.

Coaching

Organisationscoaching bezeichnet einen integralen Coaching-Ansatz, der auf eine Veränderung des komplexen Systems „Organisation" abzielt. Dieser Ansatz wurde erst vor kurzem entwickelt.

Die Charakteristika sind:
- bedarfsgesteuerte „On-the-Job"-Methode organisationaler Entwicklung.
- Die/Der Coach hat eine begleitende Rolle, fokussiert auf das KundInnen-System;
- interaktiver und handlungsorientierter Ansatz.

Im Einzel- wie Teamcoaching liegt ein starker Fokus auf der Organisation als dominierendes System innerhalb dessen die Coachees agieren.

13. Team Supervision/Team Coaching

Supervision

Supervision with teams.

A team comprises a group of people linked by a common purpose. Teams are especially appropriate for conducting tasks that are highly complex and have many interdependent subtasks.

Supervision focuses on team relationships, communication boundaries, team roles, power relations and competition, the atmosphere in the team etc.

The Anglo-Saxon or Dutch approach mainly uses the term "Organisation Consulting".

Coaching

Coaching with teams.

A team comprises a group of people linked by a common purpose. Teams are especially appropriate to conduct tasks that are highly complex and have many interdependent subtasks. The overall goal is the improved functioning and performance of the team.

Triangle acquisition and triangle contracting are of special importance.

13. Teamsupervision/Teamcoaching

Supervision

Supervision mit Teams.

Ein Team umfasst eine Gruppe von Menschen, die gemeinsam ein Arbeitsziel verfolgen. Teams sind besonders geeignet, hoch komplexe Aufgaben auszuführen.

Viele Aufgaben sind nur in Abhängigkeit der Teammitglieder voneinander erfüllbar.

Teamsupervision fokussiert auf Teambeziehungen, Kommunikationsbarrieren, Teamrollen, Macht und Einfluss, Konkurrenz, die Atmosphäre im Team usw.

Im angelsächsischen oder niederländischen Ansatz ist für diese Form der Supervision der Ausdruck „Organisationsberatung" gebräuchlich.

Coaching

Coaching mit Teams.

Ein Team umfasst eine Gruppe von Menschen, die gemeinsam ein Arbeitsziel verfolgen. Teams sind besonders geeignet, hoch komplexe Aufgaben auszuführen.

Viele Aufgaben sind nur in Abhängigkeit der Teammitglieder voneinander erfüllbar.

Das übergeordnete Ziel ist es, das Funktionieren und die Leistung des Teams zu verbessern.

Dreiecksakquise und Dreieckskontrakte sind von besonderer Bedeutung.

Teamcoaching kann von einem Tag bis zu mehreren Sitzungen über längere Zeit variieren.

Settings

Settings describe the number of participants, the ways the participants are organised, the frequency and the media in use.

1. Single

Supervision
Dyadic form of supervision, one supervisor and one supervisee.
The approaches differ according to frequency, interval and number of sessions. Sometimes only one session may take place; other approaches strictly define a minimum of sessions and intervals.

Coaching
Dyadic form of coaching, one coach and one coachee.
The approaches differ according to frequency, interval and number of sessions. Sometimes, only one session may take place. The duration of the coaching process varies depending on needs and preferences.

2. Face to Face

Supervision   *Coaching*
Face to face presence of supervisor and supervisees, coach and coachees.

Settings

Settings beschreiben die Zahl der Teilnehmenden, die Organisationsformen der Teilnahme, die Frequenz sowie verwendete Medien.

1. Einzel

Supervision
Dyadische Form der Supervision, ein/e SupervisorIn und ein/e SupervisandIn.
Ansätze unterscheiden sich nach Häufigkeit, Intervall zwischen und Anzahl von Sitzungen. Manchmal findet nur eine Sitzung statt; andere Ansätze definieren ein striktes Minimum von Sitzungen und Intervallen.

Coaching
Dyadische Form von Coaching, ein Coach und ein Coachee.
Ansätze unterscheiden sich nach Häufigkeit, Intervall zwischen und Anzahl von Sitzungen. Manchmal findet nur eine Sitzung statt; Die Dauer des Coaching-Prozesses variiert je nach Bedarf und Vorlieben.

2. Face-to-face

Supervision   *Coaching*
Face-to-face-Präsenz von SupervisorIn/SupervisandInnen, bzw. Coach und Coachee.

3. Remote/Online/New Media/Telephone

Supervision   *Coaching*

Using new media to perform a (part of a) supervision/coaching process.

4. Group

Supervision   *Coaching*

Supervision/coaching with participants who are not in formal professional or organisational contact. The participants may come from similar or different professions and professional fields. There are various approaches to the number of supervisees/coachees, the frequency, and the interval and number of sessions.

5. Organisation

Supervision   *Coaching*

To supervise/coach the organisation as a system consisting of many parts such as individuals, teams, leaders, customers, suppliers, structures, culture(s), formal and informal relationships etc.

It is clearly process-oriented and strongly linked to the management. Which parts of the system should be involved has to be decided during the process with regard to the contracted goals.

6. Team

Supervision   *Coaching*

A team comprises a group of persons linked by a common purpose. Teams are especially suitable to conduct tasks that are highly complex and have many interdependent subtasks.

Options: Team supervision/coaching with or without a team leader. The duration can vary from one day to many sessions during a longer period.

3. Fernbeziehung/Online/Neue Medien/Telefon

Supervision

Das Verwenden neuer Medien um einen Prozess (oder einen Teil davon) durchzuführen.

Coaching

Das Verwenden neuer Medien um einen Prozess (oder einen Teil davon) durchzuführen, v. a. einen Coachingprozess.

4. Gruppe

Supervision   *Coaching*

Supervision/Coaching mit Teilnehmenden, die in keinem formellen beruflichen oder organisationalen Kontakt stehen. Die Teilnehmenden können aus ähnlichen oder verschiedenen Berufen oder professionellen Feldern kommen. Es gibt verschiedene Ansätze zur Anzahl der SupervisandInnen, sowie zur Häufigkeit, zu den Intervallen und der Anzahl der Sitzungen.

5. Organisation

Supervision   *Coaching*

Das Supervidieren/Coachen der Organisation als System, das aus vielen Teilen wie Personen, Teams, LeiterInnen, KundInnen, Lieferanten, Strukturen, Kultur(en), formellen und informellen Beziehungen usw. besteht.
Das Setting ist prozessorientiert und eng an die Leitung gekoppelt. Welche Teile des Systems miteinbezogen werden, muss während des Prozesses mit Blick auf die vereinbarten Ziele immer wieder entschieden werden.

6. Team

Supervision   *Coaching*

Supervision/Coaching mit Teams. Ein Team bezeichnet eine Gruppe von Menschen, die gemeinsam ein Arbeitsziel verfolgen. Teams sind besonders geeignet, hoch komplexe Aufgaben auszuführen, viele Aufgaben sind nur in Abhängigkeit der Teammitglieder voneinander erfüllbar.
Optionen: Team-Supervision/Coaching mit oder ohne Teamleitung.

Methods

Methods are specific techniques to facilitate the process for the supervisees or coachees in order to improve the interaction between persons, their work and the organisation.

1. The Use of Empathy

Supervision

The use of empathy is a way of recognising the supervisees' emotional state and of separating it from the supervisor's own emotional response on 'what comes from the supervisees'. Being aware of (counter)transference and one's own preoccupations, the next step is to give feedback to the supervisees using it as an input for their process of development.

Coaching

Empathy is a way of recognising the emotional state of the coachees from within. It aims at seeing the coachees' world from their point of view.

Methoden

Methoden sind spezifische Techniken, die den Supervisions- bzw. Coaching-prozess fördern und erleichtern; Fokus ist dabei stets die Verbesserung der Interaktion von Person, Berufsrolle und Organisation.

1. Arbeiten mit Empathie

Supervision

Arbeiten mit Empathie bedeutet, den emotionalen Zustand der SupervisandInnen ebenso wahrzu-nehmen wie eigene emotionale Reaktionen als SupervisorIn – und beides voneinander trennen zu können.
Sich der eigenen (Gegen-)Über-tragung und der eigenen Voran-nahmen bewusst zu sein, ist eine notwendige Voraussetzung, um den SupervisandInnen entwicklungs-fördernde Rückmeldungen geben zu können.

Coaching

Empathie ist eine Möglichkeit, den emotionalen Zustand des Coachees wahrzunehmen. Sie zielt darauf ab, die Welt des Coachees aus ihrer/ seiner Perspektive zu sehen.

2. The Use of Group Process

Supervision

The extent of using the group process in supervision depends on the theoretical approach of the supervisor.

Supervision groups are important for the learning processes and the self-awareness of supervisees through group feedback, both on the content and the relational level. A supervisor can use the group process to discover and highlight the "parallel process" when the supervisory relationship "here-and-now" is mirroring the relationship between the supervisees and their clients.

Coaching

The extent of using the group process in coaching depends on the theoretical approach of the coach.

Coaching groups are important for the learning processes and self-awareness of coaches by means of group feedback, both on the content and the relational level.

3. Contracting

Supervision   *Coaching*

Decision-making before starting a supervision/coaching process. A contract is agreed upon between the relevant participants (supervisor/coach, supervisees/coachees, and organisation). Decisions are made according to the different roles, responsibilities and expectations of the participants, and according to the financial conditions, rules of confidentiality, relevant organisational aspects, evaluation and outcomes. Contracting sets a clear working agreement as a frame for the supervisory/coaching relationship, and is a basis for quality assurance.

2. Arbeiten mit dem Gruppenprozess

Supervision

Wie Gruppenprozesse in der Supervision genützt werden, hängt vom theoretischen und methodischen Konzept der/des SupervisorIn ab. Supervisionsgruppen unterstützen die Lernprozesse und die Selbstwahrnehmung der SupervisandInnen durch Gruppen-Feedback, sowohl auf der Inhalts- wie auch der Beziehungsebene.

Der/Die SupervisorIn kann den Gruppenprozess nützen, um im „Hier und Jetzt" der Supervision den „Parallelprozess", die Spiegelung der Beziehung zwischen SupervisandInnen und ihren KlientInnen zu entdecken und darauf hinzuweisen.

Coaching

Das Ausmaß der Nutzung des Gruppenprozesses im Coaching hängt vom theoretischen Ansatz des Coaches ab. Coaching-Gruppen ermöglichen erweiterte Lernprozesse und Selbstwahrnehmung der Coachees durch Gruppenfeedback, sowohl auf der Inhalts- wie auch der Beziehungsebene.

3. Auftragsklärung

Supervision   *Coaching*

Auftragsklärung meint eine Entscheidungsfindung vor Beginn eines Supervisions-/Coaching-Prozesses.

Sie basiert auf einem Kontrakt zwischen den relevanten Akteuren (SupervisorIn/Coach, SupervisandIn/Coachee und Organisation). Festgelegt werden Funktionen/Rollen, Verantwortlichkeiten und Erwartungen der Teilnehmenden, sowie finanzielle Bedingungen, Regeln der Vertraulichkeit, relevante organisatorische Aspekte, Auswertungen und Ergebnisse. Vereinbarungen werden in einem klaren Arbeitsvertrag niedergelegt. Sie bilden den Rahmen für die Supervisions-/Coaching-Beziehung und sind eine Grundlage der Qualitätssicherung.

4. Dialogue

Supervision   *Coaching*

Narrative concept of reflection in which language plays a central role. It is the conversation of two equal participants: between the supervisor/coach and the supervisees/coachees, who mutually respect the way in which each of them experiences reality. A prerequisite to achieving authenticity of dialogue is a genuine curiosity and a desire for mutual understanding.

The supervisors'/coaches' questions support the supervisees/coachees to find their own answers. They challenge the supervisees/coachees to comprehend the situation in which s/he has found herself/himself. Questions support the taking on of responsibility and the start of problem solving. Different creative techniques can facilitate the dialogue.

5. Measurement of Effects

Supervision	*Coaching*
See evaluation.	External indicators of performance and internal indicators of success are both incorporated in the coaching process from the beginning in order to register changes and boost confidence.

6. Expanding Theoretical Knowledge

Supervision   *Coaching*

By sharing the theoretical concepts of both the supervisees/coachees and the supervisor/coach, their theoretical knowledge expands. They have to be related to and connected with the concrete situation of the supervisees/coachees. It supports them to act in a more purposeful way.

4. Dialog

Supervision   *Coaching*

Narratives Konzept der Reflexion, Sprache spielt eine zentrale Rolle. Es ist ein Austausch zweier gleichberechtigter Teilnehmender: SupervisorIn/Coach und SupervisandIn/Coachee. Dieser setzt beidseitigen Respekt vor der unterschiedlichen Art, Realität zu erleben, voraus. Authentizität des Dialogs entsteht aus genuiner Neugier und der Lust auf gegenseitiges Verständnis.

Die Fragen der/des SupervisorInnen/Coaches unterstützen die SupervisandInnen/Coachees, ihre eigenen Antworten zu finden. Sie fordern von den SupervisandInnen/Coachees, die Situation, in der sie sich befinden, zu begreifen. Fragen unterstützen die Übernahme von Verantwortung und initiieren so Problemlösung. Verschiedene kreative Techniken erleichtern den Dialog.

5. Ergebnismessung

Supervision   *Coaching*

Siehe Evaluation.   Externe Leistungsindikatoren und interne Erfolgsindikatoren werden in den Coaching-Prozess von Anfang an einbezogen, um Veränderungen zu registrieren und das Vertrauen zu stärken.

6. Erweiterung theoretischen Wissens

Supervision   *Coaching*

Durch den Austausch der theoretischen Konzepte sowohl der SupervisandInnen/Coachees wie auch der/des SupervisorInnen/Coaches, erweitert sich das gemeinsame theoretische Wissen. Die Theorie muss handlungsleitend und an die konkrete Situation der SupervisandInnen/Coachees gekoppelt werden. Dies unterstützt sie, zielgerichteter zu handeln.

7. Feedback

Supervision   *Coaching*

Feedback refers to information provided to the other person about one's impression of her/his behaviour. Answers are supposed to be given to the following questions: What can I see? What do I feel? How does it affect me? The most important value is the opportunity to bring intentions closer to each other and the effect of one's behaviour. Feedback both reinforces and challenges one's thinking and behaviour. In group settings, feedback facilitates individual and mutual learning, and it fosters the collaborative process.

8. The Use of Hypotheses

Supervision   *Coaching*

As one can only communicate by sharing assumptions, doing so is a core issue in reflecting. By sharing views/hypotheses on a certain relation or question, the persons may co-create patterns of understanding that usually include new perspectives.

Hypotheses may also be applied by the supervisor/coach as a certain idea about a group's or a supervisee's/coachee's needs which then shape the further interventions of the supervisor/coach. In this case, the supervisor/coach does not necessarily share the hypothesis with the group members.

9. Meta-Communication

Supervision   *Coaching*

Communication about the different aspects of communication such as content, relation, appeal and expressing self-disclosure, expressed both verbally and non-verbally.

Synonyms: second order communication, communication on communication.

7. Feedback

Supervision   *Coaching*

Feedback bedeutet, dass einer Person von Anderen Informationen über deren Eindruck von ihrem/seinem Verhalten zur Verfügung gestellt werden. Die Informationen sollen sich auf folgende Fragen beziehen: Was nehme ich wahr? – Was fühle ich? – Wie beeinflusst mich das?

Der wichtigste Wert ist die Möglichkeit, Absicht und Wirkung des eigenen Verhaltens in Beziehung zu bringen. Feedback verstärkt das Denken und Verhalten einer Person und stellt es gleichzeitig in Frage. In Gruppensettings unterstützt Feedback individuelles Lernen sowie voneinander Lernen und es fördert Kooperation.

8. Hypothesenbildung

Supervision   *Coaching*

Da Menschen nur über eigene Wahrnehmungen kommunizieren können, ist der Austausch von Wahrnehmungen das Kernthema von Reflexion. Durch die Untersuchung von Sichtweisen/Hypothesen zu einer Frage können Menschen gemeinsame Muster der Verständigung schaffen, die insbesondere neue Perspektiven fördern. Hypothesen können auch durch die/den SupervisorIn/Coach eingebracht werden, als eine Idee über die Bedürfnisse einer Gruppe oder SupervisandIn/Coachee, die dann die weiteren Interventionen des/der SupervisorIn/Coach mitbestimmen. In diesem Fall wird die Hypothese nicht unbedingt offen den Gruppenmitgliedern mitgeteilt.

9. Meta-Kommunikation

Supervision   *Coaching*

Kommunikation über die verschiedenen Aspekte der Kommunikation, wie Inhalt, Beziehung, Attraktivität und Selbstoffenbarung, die sowohl verbal als auch nonverbal ausgedrückt werden.

Synonyme: Kommunikation zweiter Ordnung, Kommunikation über Kommunikation.

10. Meta-Reflection

Supervision

Reflection about the outcome and the process of reflection (double-loop reflection) aiming at a deepened understanding of the client professional relationship, in the sense of professionally reflecting about herself/himself, the clients and their relationships.

Coaching

Reflection on the reflection process, the relationship and the outcome is an important competence for coaches.
Meta-reflection is not explicitly and regularly used as a methodological device in Coaching.

11. Focusing Problems

Supervision

Dividing the problem into sub-problems in order to make them more concrete and visible. Is indicated when a current problem proves to be chaotic and consequently produces anxiety. It serves to help the supervisees to take a step back from the problem and view it from a new perspective.

Coaching

When acute problems and anxiety arise the coach is aware that feelings of anxiety and insecurity may occur in the short term, caused by the insight that action or change is necessary. The crucial point is to proceed from words and insights to new and unfamiliar action.

12. Evaluation of Process

Supervision   *Coaching*

Evaluation as a systematic methodological means is an integral and integrated part of the supervision and coaching process that runs through all stages of the development of the relationship by using criteria agreed upon. It focuses on the process, on development and on expected and achieved outcomes.

10. Meta-Reflexion

Supervision
Reflexion über das Ergebnis und den Prozess der Reflexion (Doppelte Feedbackschleife). Ziel ist ein vertieftes Verständnis der KlientInnen (-systeme). Dies geschieht, indem die SupervisandInnen ihre professionelle Beziehung zu ihren KlientInnen sowie ihre Anteile an dieser Beziehung reflektieren.

Coaching
Reflexion über den Reflexionsprozess, die Beziehung und das Ergebnis. Meta-Reflexion ist eine wichtige Kompetenz für Coaches, wird jedoch nicht explizit und regelmäßig als Methode im Coaching verwendet.

11. Probleme fokussieren

Supervision
Reduktion eines aktuellen Problems in Teilprobleme, um sie konkreter, sichtbarer und handhabbarer zu machen.
Dies ist angezeigt, wenn sich ein Problem als chaotisch und angstbesetzt erweist.
Es hilft den SupervisandInnen, einen Schritt zurück zu treten und das Problem aus einer neuen Perspektive zu betrachten.

Coaching
Wenn akute Probleme oder auch Angst auftauchen, ist sich der Coach bewusst, dass Gefühle von Angst und Unsicherheit oft kurz vor der Einsicht entstehen, dass Maßnahmen oder Veränderungen nötig sind.
Die entscheidende Änderung ist, von Worten und Erkenntnissen in neues und ungewohntes Handeln zu kommen.

12. Prozessevaluation

Supervision   *Coaching*
Evaluation als systematisches methodisches Mittel ist ein wesentlicher und integraler Bestandteil von Supervisions- und Coaching-Prozessen, der durch alle Phasen der Entwicklung der Beziehung läuft. Dazu werden die gemeinsam vereinbarten Kriterien genützt. Die Evaluation fokussiert auf den Prozess, auf die Entwicklung sowie die erwarteten bzw. erzielten Ergebnisse.

13. Moderating the Process

Supervision   *Coaching*

Purposeful use of all methods with regard to structuring the process and achieving contracted goals.

14. Reflecting

Supervision

Reflection is the basic method of learning and developing in supervision. Reflecting on one's own thoughts, needs and feelings can contribute to the strengthening of the supervisory relationship.
See also core qualities under term reflection.

Coaching

Reflection is one among many methods of learning and development in coaching. Reflecting on one's own thoughts, needs and feelings can contribute to the strengthening of the coaching relationship. To stimulate reflection and self-analysis, certain tools are used.

15. Building a Stable Working Relationship

Supervision   *Coaching*

In order to strengthen the working relationship in the process, the supervisor/coach purposely uses contracting, empathy, reflecting, feedback etc. A strong working relationship is essential for a successful supervisory or coaching process.

13. Prozessmoderation

Supervision   *Coaching*

Gezielter Einsatz aller Methoden im Hinblick auf die Strukturierung des Prozesses und die Erreichung vertraglich vereinbarter Ziele.

14. Reflexion

Supervision	*Coaching*
Reflexion ist die grundlegende Methode des Lernens und der Entwicklung in der Supervision.	Reflexion ist eine von vielen Methoden des Lernens und der Entwicklung im Coaching.
Über eigene Gedanken, Bedürfnisse und Gefühle im Arbeitsprozess zu reflektieren trägt darüber hinaus zur Stärkung der supervisorischen Arbeitsbeziehung bei.	Reflexion der eigenen Gedanken, Bedürfnisse und Gefühle kann zur Stärkung der Arbeitsbeziehung beitragen.
Siehe auch unter „Reflexion" in Kernqualitäten.	Reflexion und Selbstanalyse werden durch Anwendung von Übungsmethoden angeregt.

15. Stabile Arbeitsbeziehung schaffen

Supervision   *Coaching*

Um die Arbeitsbeziehung im Prozess zu stärken, setzt der/die SupervisorIn/Coach zielgerichtet Empathie, Reflexion, Feedback etc. ein. Eine stabile Arbeitsbeziehung ist grundlegend für jeden erfolgreichen Supervisions- bzw. Coaching-Prozess.

Outcomes

Outcomes describe the effects of supervision/coaching on the supervisees/coachees.

1. Better Professional Performance

Supervision
Implies a change in thinking and practice of the supervisees, which has effects also on the supervisees' professional, sometimes even personal surroundings.
The result of supervision should be a new, creative element, which will enrich and direct the work of the supervisees. Awareness of new demands may appear.

Coaching
It implies that the coachees engage in new action or behaviour successfully. It has an effect on the coachees' professional, sometimes even personal, surroundings.
Awareness of new demands and suggestions for change may appear.

2. Effective Handling of Conflicts and Contradictions

Supervision
By reflecting and discussing conflicts and contradictions from different perspectives, supervisees develop more effective coping strategies.

Coaching
By reflecting and assessing conflicts and contradictions from different perspectives and experimenting with new behaviour, coachees develop more effective coping strategies.

Ergebnisse

Ergebnisse beschreiben die Effekte von Supervision/Coaching auf die Super-visandInnen/Coachees.

1. Bessere berufliche Leistung

Supervision
Impliziert eine Veränderung im Denken und Handeln von Super-visandInnen, die Auswirkungen auf deren professionelles, manchmal auch persönliches Umfeld hat.
Das Ergebnis der Supervision sollte in einem neuen, kreativen Element bestehen, das die Arbeit der Super-visandInnen bereichert und neu ausrichtet.
Bewusstsein für neue Anforderun-gen kann sich einstellen.

Coaching
Impliziert, dass Coachees erfolgreich neue Verhaltensweisen ausprobieren und nutzen, was auch Auswirkungen auf deren professionelles, manchmal auch persönliches Umfeld hat.
Bewusstsein für neue Anforderungen und Ideen für Veränderung können sich einstellen.

2. Effektive Handhabung von Konflikten und Widersprüchen

Supervision
Reflexion und Diskussion von Kon-flikten und Widersprüchen aus ver-schiedenen Perspektiven ermöglicht SupervisandInnen, effektivere Be-wältigungsstrategien zu entwickeln.

Coaching
Über Reflexion und Bewertung von Konflikten und Widersprüchen aus verschiedenen Perspektiven sowie durch Experimentieren mit neuem Verhalten entwickeln Coachees effek-tivere Bewältigungsstrategien.

3. Clarification of Roles and Functions in Organisations

Supervision
Clarification of the formal activities (functions) negotiated and communicated on an organisational level. Clarification of roles in the sense of behavioural patterns in social systems between persons.

Coaching
The coachees will become aware of their role and contribution and limits within the organisation and, if necessary, will try to change/develop behaviour and/or position.

4. Learning

Supervision
In supervision, learning is the result of a self-organised process during which supervisees create a reflective space for themselves, thereby: understanding more about the complexity of an actual situation; understanding organisational issues and including them into their personal goals; developing increasing competences in building decisions on self-reflection.

Coaching
Learning is understood as an ongoing dynamic process to face and handle different situations.

3. Klärung von Rollen und Funktionen in Organisationen

Supervision   *Coaching*

Klärung der formalen Tätigkeiten (Funktionen), die innerhalb der Organisation ausgehandelt und kommuniziert sind.

Klärung der Rollen im Sinne von Verhaltensmustern, die in sozialen Systemen zwischen Personen stattfinden. Die SupervisandInnen/Coachees werden sich ihrer Rollen bewusst sowie der Handlungsspielräume und Grenzen innerhalb der Organisation. Wenn nötig, versuchen sie, ihr Verhalten sowie die eigene Position zu ändern oder zu entwickeln.

4. Lernen

Supervision

In der Supervision ist Lernen das Ergebnis eines selbstorganisierten Prozesses, in dem SupervisandInnen einen Reflexionsraum für sich selbst schaffen.

Dadurch entwickelt sich ein vertieftes Verstehen der Komplexität einer Situation einschließlich jener der Organisation. Das ermöglicht, diese in persönliche Ziele einzubeziehen und zunehmende Kompetenz zu entwickeln, um Entscheidungsfindung auf (Selbst-)Reflexion aufzubauen.

Coaching

Lernen wird als ein fortlaufender dynamischer Prozess verstanden, um verschiedene Situationen besser akzeptieren und handhaben zu können.

5. New Insights

Supervision
Supervision leads supervisees to-wards new perspectives on thinking about work relevant situations, their capabilities, options and res-ponsibilities.
It encourages the supervisees to search for a changed understanding of professional relationships and processes and behaviour consistent with this understanding.

Coaching
The coach fosters shifts in thinking that reveal fresh perspectives.
The development of new insights is an important outcome of coaching.
A distinction is made between insight into external conditions and context, insight into others and into oneself.

6. Organisational Benefits

Supervision   *Coaching*
On an organisational level supervision/coaching leads to better professional performance within the organisation by
• clarification of functions and roles;
• effective handling of tensions and contradictions;
• prevention and reduction of stress and burnout;
• getting new insights;
• supporting professionalisation processes on all hierarchy levels and for all members.
Thereby, supervision/coaching supports a better professional performance of the organisation and serves as an integrated part of Quality Management as well as Change Management.

7. Professional Development

Supervision   *Coaching*
Supervision/Coaching is part of the supervisees' professionalisation proc-esses. The supervisees are supported in growing professionally.

5. Neue Erkenntnisse

Supervision

Supervision eröffnet SupervisandInnen neue Perspektiven der Wahrnehmung, sowohl in Bezug auf arbeitsrelevante Situationen, als auch hinsichtlich der eigenen Fähigkeiten, Handlungsspielräume und Verantwortlichkeiten.

Dies ermutigt SupervisandInnen zur Suche nach einem veränderten Verständnis professioneller Beziehungen und Abläufe und hilft, das Verhalten in Einklang mit diesem veränderten Verständnis zu bringen.

Coaching

Die/Der Coach fördert Verschiebungen im Denken, die neue Perspektiven eröffnen.

Die Entwicklung von neuen Erkenntnissen ist ein wichtiges Ergebnis des Coachings. Es wird unterschieden zwischen einerseits Einblick in äußere Bedingungen und den Kontext, andererseits Einfühlung in andere und in sich selbst.

6. Nutzen für die Organisation

Supervision *Coaching*

Auf der Ebene der Organisation führt Supervision/Coaching zu einer besseren beruflichen Leistung innerhalb der Organisation durch:

• Klärung von Funktionen und Rollen;
• effektiven Umgang mit Spannungen und Widersprüchen;
• Prävention und Reduzierung von Stress und Burnout;
• Gewinnen neuer Erkenntnisse;
• Unterstützung von Professionalisierungsprozessen auf allen Hierarchieebenen und für alle Mitarbeitenden.

Auf diese Weise unterstützt Supervision/Coaching eine bessere berufliche Leistungsfähigkeit der Organisation und dient als integrierter Bestandteil des Qualitätsmanagements sowie Change Management.

7. Professionalisierung

Supervision *Coaching*

Supervision/Coaching sind Teil der Professionalisierungsprozesse der SupervisandInnen. Diese werden in ihrem professionellen Wachstum unterstützt.

8. Quality Management

Supervision   *Coaching*

Supervision maintains or improves the professional competences of the person and clarifies working procedures and standards for the benefit of the clients.

9. Self Awareness

Supervision

It indicates the supervisees' developing an awareness of themselves, their attitudes and aspirations in order to work professionally. Self-awareness is achieved by continuous enhancement of self-reflective skills.

Coaching

Coaching is an exercise in self-understanding and self-change.

10. Prevention and Reduction of Stress

Supervision   *Coaching*

Supervision/coaching provides personal and professional help and support that enables empowerment. This prevents and reduces the risk of discomfort and stress. Thereby, resilience in the professional context might be enhanced.

11. Wellbeing/Health

Supervision

Supervision provides mental relief and renewed energy in a demanding job.
A significant aspect of supervision is to recognise and accept the feelings of the supervisees and to identify and reflect unhealthy patterns. Supervision is a way of taking care of one's own health.

Coaching

Coaching works on the assumption that all human actions are directed towards wellbeing.
Wellbeing is related to: wholeness, strength, skills and potential, inner wisdom, personal and professional development and responsibility.
Coaching can aim at maximising the coachees' personal and professional potential by achieving transformations on the level of beliefs, values, personality and identity.

8. Qualitätsmanagement

Supervision *Coaching*

Supervision/Coaching erhält oder verbessert die beruflichen Kompetenzen einer Person, und klärt Arbeitsabläufe und Standards in Bezug auf die KlientInnen.

9. Selbsterkenntnis

Supervision

Die SupervisandInnen entwickeln Bewusstsein ihrer selbst, ihrer Haltungen und Erwartungen, um zunehmend professionell zu arbeiten. Selbsterkenntnis wird durch kontinuierliche Verbesserung der Fähigkeit zur Selbstreflexion erreicht.

Coaching

Coaching ist eine Übung in Selbsterkenntnis und Selbstveränderung.

10. Stressprävention

Supervision *Coaching*

Supervision/Coaching bieten persönliche und professionelle Hilfestellung, und ermöglichen so Selbstermächtigung. Dies verhindert bzw. reduziert die Gefahr von Stress, schafft Handlungsspielräume und erhöht die Resilienz.

11. Wohlbefinden/Gesundheit

Supervision

Supervision bietet psychische Entlastung und fördert so die Gewinnung neuer Energie für anspruchsvolle Berufe. Ein wesentlicher Aspekt von Supervision ist es, die Gefühle der SupervisandInnen wahrzunehmen sowie zu akzeptieren, ungesunde Muster zu erkennen und darüber zu reflektieren. Supervision ist daher eine Möglichkeit, für die eigene Gesundheit zu sorgen.

Coaching

Coaching geht davon aus, dass alle menschlichen Handlungen auf Wohlbefinden ausgerichtet sind. Wohlbefinden steht in Beziehung mit: Ganzheit, Stärke, Fähigkeiten und Potenzialen, mit innerem Wissen um persönliche und berufliche Entwicklung und Verantwortung. Coaching strebt die Maximierung des persönlichen und beruflichen Potenzials der Coachees an.

ECVision
A European Competence Framework
of Supervision and Coaching

Marina Ajdukovic
Lilja Cajvert
Michaela Judy
Wolfgang Knopf
Hubert Kuhn
Krisztina Madai
Mieke Voogd

ECVision

Ein europäisches Kompetenzprofil
für Supervision und Coaching

Marina Ajdukovic
Lilja Cajvert
Michaela Judy
Wolfgang Knopf
Hubert Kuhn
Krisztina Madai
Mieke Voogd

Professional Identity

This present concept assumes that a supervisor/coach has a professional self-concept at hand and shows a professional attitude relating to it. A professional identity is a complex and dynamic equilibrium constantly undergoing the process of a two-dimensional integration, of the personal self and the professional demands.

Furthermore, one develops her/his professional identity by the interaction of the 'personal self' and the 'professional community'. This also is the broader context to monitor actions and activities according to existing professional cultures and standards.

The development of a professional identity is one of the core goals of vocational training of supervisors/coaches.

Professionelle Identität

Dieses Konzept impliziert, dass ein/e SupervisorIn/Coach über ein professionelles Selbstverständnis verfügt und ein entsprechendes Verhalten an den Tag legt. Eine berufliche Identität ist kein stabiles Konstrukt, sondern befindet sich in einem komplexen und dynamischen Fließgleichgewicht. Die Entwicklung einer beruflichen Identität ist ein kontinuierlicher Prozess, der zweidimensional sowohl die Integration des persönlichen Selbst wie auch jene der beruflichen Anforderungen einschließt.

Man entwickelt berufliche Identität durch die Wechselwirkung des „persönlichen Selbst" mit den Anforderungen der fachlichen Umwelt(en). In diesem Kontext findet ein ständiger Abgleich eigenen Tuns mit bestehenden Berufskulturen und Standards statt.

Die Entwicklung einer beruflichen Identität ist eines der Kernziele der Berufsausbildung von SupervisorInnen/Coaches.

1. Professional Attitude

Competence	Knowledge	Skills	Performance
Reflectivity	Knowledge about • Unconscious processes and related theories. • Theories of human perception, cognition and emotion. Knowledge about the importance of sharing ways of professional behaviour, professional experiences, facts, thoughts and feelings. Knowledge about how to reflect one's own personal style of reflection.	Having a clear and theory-based approach to unconscious processes and ways of dealing with them personally and professionally. Maintaining a self-reflecting approach towards one's own professional and personal attitudes. Performing self-reflective techniques. Expressing thoughts and feelings comprehensibly.	Observing and articulating own experiences, thoughts and beliefs. Recognising indications of unconscious processes and dealing with them. Challenging and questioning observations. Gaining insight from questioning. Observing the impact of own actions and deciding whether and how to change such actions. Deciding whether the expression of own insights is contextually appropriate. Using indicators to encourage a shift in perspective.

1. Professionelle Haltung

Kompetenz	Kenntnisse	Fähigkeiten	Performance
Reflexions-vermögen	Wissen über • unbewusste Prozesse und Theorien über sie. • Theorien der menschlichen Wahrnehmung, Kognition und Emotion. Wissen um die Bedeutung, eigenes professionelles Handeln, berufliche Erfahrung, Fakten, Gedanken und Gefühle mitzuteilen. Wissen über Formen der Reflexion und den eigenen, persönlichen Stil des Reflektierens.	Klarer und theorie-basierter Ansatz, um unbewusste Prozesse persönlich und professionell zu handhaben. Eine selbstreflexive Haltung gegenüber den eigenen beruflichen und persönlichen Verhaltensweisen pflegen. Selbstreflexive Techniken anwenden. Gedanken und Gefühle verständlich zum Ausdruck bringen zu können.	Beobachtet und artikuliert eigene Erfahrungen, Gedanken und Überzeugungen. Erkennt Hinweise auf unbewusste Prozesse und kann mit ihnen umgehen. Befragt diese Beobachtungen und stellt sie gegebenenfalls in Frage. Gewinnt Erkenntnisse aus dieser Befragung. Beobachtet die Wirkungen des eigenen Handelns und entscheidet, ob und wie dieses Handeln zu ändern wäre. Entscheidet, ob das Aussprechen eigener Einsichten situativ passend ist. Verwendet Formulierungen, die einen Perspektivenwechsel fördern.

Competence	Knowledge	Skills	Performance
Integrating Theory and Practice	Knowledge of one's own beliefs and implicit theories.	Recognising own implicit theories. Reflecting upon one's own experiences with the same or similar roles of the supervisee/coachee.	Articulating own beliefs and implicit theories. Reflecting upon their impacts on supervision/coaching processes in a given situation. Deciding if one's own experiences could be supportive for the supervisee/coachee.
	Good overall knowledge of the most important theoretical frameworks.	Referring to other theoretical frameworks.	Distinguishing common ground, similarities and differences among different theoretical approaches. Flexibility with the application of different approaches according to a specific task that arises within a supervision/coaching process.
	In-depth knowledge of at least one theoretical framework (depth psychology, integrative theory, systemic theory, etc.).	Adapting this theory to the various and contradictory situations that arise within a supervision/coaching process	Presenting this theory and its application in various contexts. Discussing options and limitations of this theory. Applying theoretical insights easily to different situations. Reducing the complexity of a given situation by referring to the theoretical framework. Choosing interventions that reduce the complexity for the supervisees/coachees.
		Questioning the relevance of specific theoretical insights.	Estimating theory as systematically applied descriptions of experience ("The map isn't the landscape.") Deciding on how to deal with the dynamics of one's own implicit theories (set of beliefs, values, action-prompting assumptions and behaviour, and how individuals choose to explain them rationally) and evidence-based scientific references.
		Understanding the difference between theory and methods/techniques.	Setting up interventions according to theoretical and methodological reflection. Using techniques from various theoretical approaches by clearly distinguishing the theoretical (epistemological) foundations.

Kompetenz	Kenntnisse	Fähigkeiten	Performance
Integration von Theorie und Praxis	Wissen um die eigenen Überzeugungen und impliziten Theorien.	Eigene implizite Theorien erkennen. Reflektieren eigener Erfahrungen mit gleichen oder ähnlichen Rollen von SupervisandInnen/Coachees.	Artikuliert eigene Überzeugungen und implizite Theorien. Reflektiert ihre Wirkungen auf Supervisions-/Coaching-Prozesse in einer bestimmten Situation. Entscheidet, ob eigene Erfahrungen für die SupervisandInnen/Coachees hilfreich sein könnten.
	Gute Kenntnisse der wichtigsten theoretischen Ansätze.	Bezugnahme auf andere theoretische Ansätze.	Unterscheidet Gemeinsamkeiten, Ähnlichkeiten und Unterschiede zwischen verschiedenen theoretischen Ansätzen. Setzt verschiedene Ansätze flexibel ein, je nach den spezifischen Anforderungen, die in einem Supervisions-/Coaching-Prozess auftauchen.
	Fundiertes Wissen über mindestens einen theoretischen Ansatz (Tiefenpsychologie, Integrative Theorie, systemische Theorie, etc.)	Adaptieren der Theorie an die verschiedenen und widersprüchlichen Situationen, die im Rahmen eines Supervisions-/Coaching-Prozesses entstehen.	Präsentiert die Theorie und ihre Anwendung in verschiedenen Kontexten. Erörtert Möglichkeiten und Grenzen der Theorie. Wendet theoretische Erkenntnisse gekonnt auf unterschiedliche Situationen an. Reduziert die Komplexität einer gegebenen Situation unter Bezugnahme auf einen theoretischen Rahmen. Wählt Interventionen, die Komplexität für die SupervisandInnen/Coachees reduzieren.
		Die Relevanz der spezifischen theoretischen Erkenntnisse untersuchen.	Vermittelt Theorie als systematisch angewendete Beschreibungen von Erfahrung („Die Landkarte ist nicht die Landschaft"). Entscheidet situationsspezifisch über den Umgang mit der Dynamik zwischen eigenen impliziten Theorien (dem Set aus Überzeugungen, Werten, handlungsleitenden Annahmen und Verhaltensweisen, und wie Menschen diese rational zu erklären suchen) und evidenzbasierten wissenschaftlichen Referenzsystemen.

Competence	Knowledge	Skills	Performance
Ambiguity Tolerance	Knowledge about • Ambiguity and am-bivalence as integral parts of the human condition. • Ambiguity and am-bivalence as part of professional work. • Social cognition.	Reflecting upon per-sonal reactions and perceptions even if they are associated with unpleasant insights. Reviewing results of reflection before taking appropriate action.	Staying connected both with herself/himself and others when conflicting feelings, messages and situations arise. Withstanding tension without seeking immediate relief or quick solutions. Coping with situations where worry, anxiety or confusion arise.

2. Ethics

Competence	Knowledge	Skills	Performance
Ethical Conduct	Knowledge about • The Codes of Ethics of the national and European profes-sional organisations. • The national and European legal framework.	Following the Codes of Ethics of the national and European profes-sional organisations. Considering ethical dilemmas related to supervisees/coachees, their organisations and their workplaces. Aligning with the national and European legal framework.	Dealing with power, trust and competition in such a way that it allows maintaining one's personal and professional integrity and responsibility. Keeping confidentiality within the legal and contractual framework. Adopting a neutral stance towards all parties. Assessing one's own conflict-ing interests and making an appropriate decision in accor-dance with ethical conduct. Identifying ethical dilemmas of supervisees/coachees and dealing with them pro-actively. Keeping within the boundaries of supervision/coaching. Differentiating between pro-fessional, ethical and political issues.

Kompetenz	Kenntnisse	Fähigkeiten	Performance
		Den Unterschied zwischen Theorie und Methoden verstehen.	Setzt Interventionen sowohl nach theoretischen wie auch methodologischen Überlegungen. Verwendet Techniken aus verschiedenen theoretischen Ansätzen ohne Vermischung der theoretischen (epistemologischen) Grundlagen.
Ambiguitäts-toleranz	Wissen um: • Mehrdeutigkeit und Ambivalenz als integrale Bestandteile des menschlichen Daseins. • Mehrdeutigkeit und Ambivalenz als integrale Bestandteile professioneller Arbeit. • Theorien der sozialen Kognition.	Reflexion eigener Reaktionen und Empfindungen, auch wenn dies mit unangenehmen Einsichten verbunden ist. Überprüfung der eigenen Einsichten ehe weiteres Handeln darauf aufgebaut wird.	Bleibt auch bei widersprüchlichen Gefühlen, Botschaften und Situationen sowohl mit sich selbst wie auch mit den Anderen in Kontakt. Hält Spannung (aus), ohne schnelle Abhilfe oder schnelle Lösungen zu suchen. Bleibt auch in Situationen, in denen Ärger, Angst oder Verwirrung entstehen, handlungsfähig.

2. Ethik

Kompetenz	Kenntnisse	Fähigkeiten	Performance
Ethisches Verhalten	Wissen um: • die ethischen Codes und Richtlinien der eigenen nationalen und europäischen Berufsverbände. • die nationalen und europäischen Rechtsrahmen für Supervision und Coaching.	Handeln nach den ethischen Richtlinien der eigenen nationalen und europäischen Berufsorganisationen. Bewusstes mit Bedenken ethischer Dilemmata von SupervisandInnen/Coachees mit und in ihren Organisationen. Orientierung an den nationalen und europäischen Rechtsrahmen.	Geht mit Macht, Vertrauen und Konkurrenz in einer Weise um, die sowohl die persönliche wie auch berufliche Integrität und Verantwortlichkeit wahrt. Wahrt die Vertraulichkeit im Rahmen der gesetzlichen Bedingungen sowie des vereinbarten Kontraktes. Nimmt eine allparteiliche Haltung ein. Schätzt eigene widersprüchliche Interessen bewusst ein, und entscheidet nach ethischen Gesichtspunkten. Erkennt ethische Dilemmata der SupervisandInnen/ Coachees und arbeitet proaktiv an ihnen. Bleibt innerhalb der Grenzen von Supervision/Coaching. Unterscheidet zwischen beruflichen, ethischen und politischen Fragen.

3. Quality Development

Competence	Knowledge	Skills	Performance
Ascertaining Continuous Professional Development	Knowledge about relevant professional bodies of knowledge.	Establishing communication with professional communities.	Staying connected with professional associations, standards and ethical codes. Committing to a professional procedure when dealing with complaints.
	Knowledge about evaluation methods and techniques.	Gathering information on the effectiveness of one's own practice. Applying personal, theoretical, practical and tacit knowledge to evaluate and improve one's practice.	Demonstrating planned evaluation and improvement of one's practice. Processing the results of differentiated evaluations with stakeholders. Demonstrating one's work to peers/the professional field.
	Familiarity with emerging theories, research areas and methods.	Reviewing ideas and perspectives.	Participating in regular peer-supervision, supervision on supervision, coaching or intervision. Studying professional journals and literature frequently.
Ascertaining Continuous Personal Development	Knowledge about stress, burnout and secondary trauma theory. Knowledge of personal strengths and limitations. Knowledge of one's own biographical patterns, vulnerabilities and biophysical reactions.	Recognising personal signs of stress at an early stage. Establishing measures for one's own stress management. Identifying personal needs by using a structured process to deal with them.	Dealing with stress in a way that does not harm others. Identifying one's own needs, personal resources and limitations. Realising and using methods of deliberate reflection and actions to deal with them. Realising personal biophysical reactions and hypothesising about them as a source of information about ongoing processes.
Contributing to Professional Standards and Development	Knowledge of general developments in • society, • organisational theory and practice, • professional discourses.	Assessing the impact level of one's work on • supervisees/coachees, organisations and the professional community. • Participating in research.	Connecting to developments in the professional field. Discussing professional standards, research and development pro-actively within professional communities. Acting as a teacher, trainer, consultant, coach or supervisor for peers. Contributing to research. Publishing articles or books.

3. Qualitätsentwicklung

Kompetenz	Kenntnisse	Fähigkeiten	Performance
Sicherstellen beruflicher Weiterentwicklung	Wissen um relevante Berufsverbände.	Etablieren und Halten der Kommunikation mit Berufsverbänden.	Pflegt die Verbindung zu Berufsorganisationen, und hält deren Standards und ethische Richtlinien ein. Verpflichtet sich zu einem professionellen Vorgehen im Umgang mit Beschwerden.
	Wissen um Selbst-Evaluation	Sammeln von Informationen über die Wirksamkeit der eigenen Praxis. Anwendung von persönlichem, theoretischem, praktischem und implizitem Wissen zur Evaluation und Verbesserung der eigenen Praxis.	Betreibt geplante und systematische Evaluation zur Verbesserung der eigenen Praxis. Bearbeitet die Ergebnisse differenzierter Evaluation mit allen Beteiligten weiter. Macht die eigene Arbeit für KollegInnen sowie im Berufsumfeld sichtbar.
	Vertraut sein mit neuen Theorien, Forschungsfeldern und Methoden.	Überprüfung eigener Ideen und Perspektiven.	Beteiligt sich regelmäßig an Peer-Supervision, Supervision von Supervision/Coaching oder Intervision. Studiert regelmäßig Fachzeitschriften und Fachliteratur.
Sicherstellen persönlicher Weiterentwicklung	Wissen um Stress-, Burnout- und Sekundäre Trauma-Theorie. Wissen um eigene persönliche Stärken und Grenzen. Wissen um eigene biographische Muster, deren Schwachstellen und eigene körperliche Reaktionen.	Erkennen persönlicher Anzeichen von Stress in einem frühen Stadium. Handhabung des eigenen Stress-Managements. Identifizieren eigener Bedürfnisse und ihnen in einem strukturierten Prozess begegnen.	Geht mit Stress in einer Weise um, die anderen nicht schadet. Identifiziert eigene Bedürfnisse, persönliche Ressourcen und Grenzen. Kennt und verwendet Methoden der Reflexion, um Ressourcen und Grenzen bewusst zu nutzen. Nimmt eigene körperliche Reaktionen wahr und nützt dies als Informationsquelle, um Hypothesen über den Prozessverlauf zu bilden.
Mitarbeiten an professionellen Standards und Entwicklungen	Wissen um allgemeine Entwicklungen in: • Gesellschaft, • Theorie und Praxis der Organisation, • professionellen Diskursen.	Beurteilung der Wirkung der eigenen Arbeit auf: • SupervisandInnen/Coachees, • Organisationen und im eigenen Berufsumfeld. Durchführung von bzw. Teilnahme an Forschung.	Nimmt an Entwicklungen im Berufsfeld aktiv teil. Diskutiert professionelle Standards und Entwicklungen sowie Forschung proaktiv innerhalb von Berufsorganisationen. Fungiert als UnterrichtendeR, TrainerIn und BeraterIn für Peers. Leistet einen Beitrag zur Forschung. Veröffentlicht Artikel bzw. Fachbücher.

4. Perspective on Person, Work and Organisation

Competence	Knowledge	Skills	Performance
Relating to Different Personal, Professional and Organisational Values and Cultures	Knowledge about • different types of organisations and their legal and environmental implications. • different concepts of organisational analysis. • various counselling formats within organisations and the function of supervision/coaching within them. • parallel processes in organisations.	Recognising types of organisations. Recognising conflicts between personal and organisational values. Dealing with conflicts of values. Applying concepts of organisational analysis. Recognising organisational/professional cultures. Recognising parallel processes in organisations.	Clarifying on which level and in which formats supervision/coaching is likely to be successful. Encouraging supervisees/coachees to explore conflicts between personal and organisational values. Designing supervision/coaching proposals according to the type of organisation, its environment and needs. Adapting concepts of organisational analysis to the existing situation and the needs of the supervisees/coachees, their organisations and workplaces. Supporting managerial staff to perform analysis of the organisational culture within which they are working. Communicating outcomes to supervisees/coachees in a clear and appropriate way. Supporting supervisees/coachees in transforming their acquired insight into action.
	Knowledge about sociological theories of labour including the history of the division of labour.	Being familiar with practice, theory and academic discourse of employment/work in society. Being familiar with relevant codes of employment/work in society. Keeping up with developments on the labour market.	Linking the actual work situation of supervisees/coachees to employment-related development. Fostering the supervisees'/coachees' understanding of how the personal work situation interweaves with the societal and political environment.

4. Perspektive auf Person, Arbeit und Organisation

Kompetenz	Kenntnisse	Fähigkeiten	Performance
Unterschiedliche persönliche, berufliche und organisatorische Werte und Kulturen einbeziehen	Wissen um: • verschiedene Typen von Organisationen und deren rechtliche und ökologische Implikationen. • verschiedene Konzepte der Organisationsanalyse. • verschiedene Beratungsformate innerhalb von Organisationen und die Funktion von Supervision/Coaching in ihnen. • Spiegelphänomene (Parallelprozesse) in Organisationen.	Erkennen von Organisationstypen Erkennen von Konflikten zwischen persönlichen und organisatorischen Werten. Handhaben dieser Wertekonflikte. Anwenden von Konzepten der Organisationsanalyse. Erkennen von Organisationskulturen bzw. professionellen Kulturen. Erkennen von Spiegelphänomenen in Organisationen.	Legt fest, auf welchem Level und innerhalb welcher Beratungsdesigns Supervision/Coaching erfolgversprechend sind. Ermutigt SupervisandInnen/ Coachees dazu, Konflikte zwischen persönlichen und organisatorischen Werten zu erkunden. Entwickelt Supervisions-/ Coaching-Angebote anhand der jeweiligen Art der Organisation, ihrem Umfeld und ihren Bedürfnissen. Passt Konzepte der Organisationsanalyse an die Gegebenheiten wie auch die Bedürfnisse der SupervisandInnen/ Coachees und ihrer Organisationen an. Unterstützt Führungskräfte bei der Analyse der Unternehmenskultur, in der sie arbeiten. Kommuniziert SupervisandInnen/Coachees Ergebnisse klar und angemessen. Unterstützt SupervisandInnen/ Coachees bei der Umsetzung von Erkenntnissen in konkretes Handeln.
	Wissen über soziologische Theorien der Arbeit, einschließlich der Entwicklung der arbeitsteiligen Gesellschaft.	Miteinbeziehen von Praxis, Theorie und akademischem Diskurs zur Arbeitswelt. Miteinbeziehen von relevanten Richtlinien der Arbeitswelt. Miteinbeziehen von Entwicklungen am Arbeitsmarkt.	Bringt die konkrete Arbeitssituation von SupervisandInnen/Coachees in Zusammenhang mit Entwicklungen am Arbeitsmarkt. Fördert das Verständnis von SupervisandInnen/Coachees für die Verwobenheit ihrer persönlichen Arbeitssituation mit gesellschaftlichen und politischen Rahmenbedingungen.

Competence	Knowledge	Skills	Performance
Dealing with Function, Role and Status within an Organisation	Knowledge about the formal activities that members of organisations negotiate. Knowledge about the various behavioural patterns and expectations of behaviour in social systems, i.e. about the interdependency impact of the formal position and the role. Knowledge about the dynamics of power and hierarchy.	Distinguishing between formal position and personal approaches. Making that distinction transparent for the supervisees/coachees. Linking roles with biographical, organisational and cultural background.	Exploring the requirements of any formal position in a way that makes it clear to the supervisees/coachees that there is a variety of individual ways of fulfilling them. Intervening in view of both the formal position and the role and supporting reflection on their interdependency. Setting interventions according to the formal position within the organisational hierarchy. Exploring the impact of the formal position and the role, supporting conscious decisions in this context.
Focussing on Leadership Issues	Knowledge about theories of leadership and management.	Assessing organisational aspects such as authority, subservience and competition. Recognising the supervisees'/coachees' personal behavioural patterns and style of leadership.	Recognising organisational aspects such as authority, subservience and competition. Co-creating with the supervisees/coachees feasible strategies for achieving specific goals for both themselves and the managerial task. Exploring ways of dealing with authority, subservience and competition. Integrating the supervisees'/coachees' personal patterns and styles into the process. Referring to the supervisees'/coachees' leadership resources.

Kompetenz	Kenntnisse	Fähigkeiten	Performance
Funktion, Rolle und Status innerhalb einer Organisation gestalten	Wissen um: • die formalen Aktivitäten, die Mitglieder der Organisationen verhandeln. • die verschiedenen Verhaltensmuster und Verhaltenserwartungen in sozialen Systemen, v. a. um Wechselwirkungen des Rollenhandelns. • die Dynamik von Macht und Hierarchie.	Unterscheiden zwischen formaler Funktion & persönlichen Zugängen. Transparentmachen dieser Unterscheidung für die SupervisandInnen/ Coachees. Verknüpfen von Rollen mit einem biographischen, organisatorischen und kulturellen Hintergrund.	Untersucht die Anforderungen jeder formalen Funktion in einer Weise, die SupervisandInnen/ Coachees deutlich macht, dass es verschiedene persönliche Möglichkeiten gibt, sie zu erfüllen. Interveniert mit Bezug auf beide und unterstützt die Reflexion über ihre gegenseitige Abhängigkeit. Setzt Interventionen entsprechend der formalen Position innerhalb der Organisationshierarchie. Untersucht die Wechselwirkungen des Rollenhandelns – wie Rollen gestaltet und übernommen werden – und unterstützt diesbezüglich bewusste Entscheidungen.
Auf Führung fokussieren	Wissen um Theorien von Führung und Management.	Einschätzen organisationaler Komponenten wie Autorität, Unterordnung und Konkurrenz. Erkennen der persönlichen Muster und des Führungsstils der SupervisandInnen/Coachees.	Erkennt organisationale Komponenten wie Autorität, Unterordnung und Konkurrenz. Entwickelt gemeinsam mit den SupervisandInnen/ Coachees umsetzbare Strategien zur Zielerreichung für sich selbst wie auch die Managementaufgabe. Erforscht Umgangsweisen mit Autorität, Unterordnung und Konkurrenz. Integriert die persönlichen Verhaltensweisen und Stile der SupervisandInnen/ Coachees in den Prozess. Fokussiert die SupervisandInnen/Coachees auf deren eigene Führungsressourcen.

Professional Conduct

Professional supervisors/coaches realise their professional behaviours according to the specific situations of the supervisees/coachees, the sponsors, the contracted goals and the varied relationships.

To be able to professionally handle these complex relationships and navigate social dynamics, supervisors/coaches need a rich repertoire of viable interventions and extensive knowledge about the dynamics of these situations and the persons acting in them. Therefore, the continuous evaluation of their own acting and processes they are part of is mandatory.

To sum up: Supervisors/coaches need – based on a (self-)reflective attitude – skills which enable them to perform reflection before, during and after their professional acting, and to intervene accordingly.

Professionelles Verhalten

Professionelle SupervisorInnen/Coaches passen ihr berufliches Verhalten flexibel der spezifischen Situation der SupervisandInnen/Coachees, den Auftraggebern, den vertraglich vereinbarten Zielen und der Beziehungsdynamik an.

Für den Umgang mit komplexen beruflichen Beziehungen und für die Steuerung sozialer Dynamiken müssen sie über ein reiches Repertoire viabler Interventionen verfügen sowie über theorie- und erfahrungsgeleitetes Wissen, um Interventionen zielgerichtet einsetzen zu können.

Kontinuierliche Reflexion des eigenen Handelns und der Prozesse, deren Bestandteil sie sind, ist obligatorisch. Daher brauchen SupervisorInnen/Coaches – basierend auf einer (selbst-)reflexiven Einstellung – Fähigkeiten, die es ihnen ermöglichen, Reflexion vor, während und nach dem Supervisionsprozess durchzuführen und entsprechend zu handeln.

1. Building a Professional Relationship

Competence	Knowledge	Skills	Performance
Contracting	Knowledge about • The function of contracting; • Issues to be contracted in supervision; • Dyadic, triangular and quadrangular contracting.	Establishing a working agreement as a framework for the supervision/coaching process. Reflecting on functions, roles, responsibilities, boundaries of the relationship in accordance with the contract.	Differentiating between dyadic, triangular and quadrangular contracting and contracts accordingly. Clarifying the different functions and roles within the supervision/coaching process. Clarifying the expectations of the parties involved, relating them to a contracted and thereby verifiable working method in supervision/coaching. Facilitating the unification process until common and viable goals for all parties, including legal implications and framework, have been established. Reviewing expectations and recommending formats suitable for the parties' goals and expectations. Clarifying financial conditions, rules of confidentiality, relevant organisational aspects, evaluation and outcomes. Providing a written contract if appropriate. Clarifying ways of reporting. Reviewing the contracted goals regularly during the process and re-contracting them if necessary.

1. Arbeitsbeziehung gestalten

Kompetenz	Kenntnisse	Fähigkeiten	Performance
Auftrags-klärung	Wissen um: • die Funktion des Kontrakts; • Bestandteile eines Supervisions-/Coaching-Kontrakts • jene supervisions-relevanten Fragen, die in einem Kontrakt zu vereinbaren sind; • dyadische, Drei-ecks- und Vierecks-Kontrakte.	Sicherstellen einer funktional passenden Vereinbarung als Rah-men für den Supervisi-ons-/Coaching-Prozess. Reflektieren über Funktionen, Rollen, Verantwortlichkeiten und Grenzen der pro-fessionellen Beziehung und deren Überein-stimmung mit dem Kontrakt.	Unterscheidet zwischen dyadi-schen, Dreiecks- und Vierecks-Kontrakten und gestaltet den Kontrakt entsprechend. Verdeutlicht unterschiedli-che Funktionen und Rollen innerhalb des Supervisions-/Coaching-Prozesses. Klärt Erwartungen der Be-teiligten und bezieht sie auf einen vertraglich vereinbarten und damit überprüfbaren Su-pervisions-/Coaching-Prozess. Ermöglicht den Einigungspro-zess, bis eine Vereinbarung mit gemeinsamen und tragfähigen Zielen für alle Beteiligten festgelegt ist, einschließlich der rechtlichen Auswirkungen und Rahmenbedingungen. Überprüft Erwartungen und empfiehlt Formate, die den Zielen und Erwartungen der Teilnehmenden am besten dienen. Klärt finanzielle Bedingungen, Regeln der Vertraulichkeit, organisatorische Aspekte, Aus-wertung und Ergebnisse. Bietet gegebenenfalls einen schriftlichen Vertrag an. Klärt Formen der Berichter-stattung. Gleicht die vertraglich verein-barten Ziele regelmäßig mit dem Prozessverlauf ab und verhandelt sie, wenn nötig, neu.

Competence	Knowledge	Skills	Performance
Structuring the Process	Mastering different theories of • Social psychology • Relational theories and models of inter-vention • Context and power dimensions Knowledge about • Components of supervision/coaching contract • Characteristics of the supervisory relation-ship • Concepts of phases of the supervisory relationship • How the subcon-scious and parallel processes may influ-ence relationships within the process of supervision • Specific difficul-ties and barriers in supervision/coaching relationships.	Establishing a profes-sional relationship by • Observing and reflecting the initial stage of the super-vision/coaching relationship. • Basing the rela-tionship on a clear contract. • Clarifying which elements within the professional relation-ship need negotia-tion. • Forming a working alliance and clarify-ing goals, limits and responsibilities of all parties.	Assessing how both super-visor/coach and supervisee/coachee present themselves at the initial stage. Building trust, encouraging openness and self-revelation by fostering accountability, recognising the supervisees'/coachees' needs and establish-ing an appropriate method of feedback. Applying appropriate methods according to the specific issues of the supervision/coaching relationship. In-group supervision establish-ing relationships with both individuals and the group as a whole.
		Maintaining and de-veloping the relation-ship by • Creating a dynamic learning process. • Supporting super-visees'/coachees' needs and encourag-ing development.	Continuously assessing the interpersonal connection with the supervisees/coachees. Creating a safe environment by accepting mistakes and vulnerabilities as learning opportunities.
		Giving and receiving feedback.	Offering opportunities to ex-press needs and feelings and to give and receive feedback.
		Containing of and ac-curately responding to emotions of the super-visees/coachees within subconscious and parallel processes.	Identifying attachment pat-terns, transference and coun-ter-transference dynamics and handling them as a relational mechanism. Recognising the feelings of others and responding in an empathic way.
		Managing relationship conflicts and alliance breaking.	Dealing with the importance of individual similarities and differences in a supervisory relationship. Providing an ap-propriate balance of challenge and support. Addressing processes of competition and rivalry and supporting the supervisees/coachees in dealing with them.

Kompetenz	Kenntnisse	Fähigkeiten	Performance
Prozesse strukturieren	Beherrscht Theorien der: • Sozialpsychologie, relationalen Theorien sowie Interventionsmodelle. • Kontext- und Machtdimensionen. Wissen um: • Merkmale einer Supervisions-/Coaching-Beziehung • Konzepte der Phasen dieser Beziehung • unbewusste Prozesse und Spiegelphänomene und deren Einfluss auf Beziehung und Prozess. • Spezifische Schwierigkeiten und Hindernisse in Supervisions-/Coaching-Beziehungen.	Aufbau einer professionellen Beziehung durch: • Beobachten und Reflektieren der Anfangsphase. • Aufbau der Beziehung auf einem klaren Vertrag. • Klären, welche Elemente innerhalb der Beziehung verhandelt werden müssen. • Aufbau einer funktionierenden Allianz durch Klärung der Ziele, Grenzen und Pflichten aller Beteiligten.	Untersucht, wie sich sowohl SupervisorIn/Coach als auch SupervisandInnen/Coachees in der Anfangsphase präsentieren. Entwickelt Vertrauen, Offenheit und Selbstoffenbarung durch Förderung von Verantwortlichkeit, Erkennen der Bedürfnisse der SupervisandInnen/Coachees und durch passende Formen des Feedbacks. Setzt Methoden gemäß der Besonderheiten jeder Supervisions-/Coaching-Beziehung ein. Baut Beziehungen sowohl mit den einzelnen Personen als auch mit der Gruppe als Ganzes auf.
		Aufrechterhalten und Entwickeln der professionellen Beziehung durch: • Gestalten eines dynamischen Lernprozesses. • Unterstützen der Bedürfnisse der SupervisandInnen/Coachees. • Ermutigen von Entwicklung.	Überprüft ständig die relationale Verbundenheit mit den SupervisandInnen/Coachees. Schafft einen sicheren Rahmen durch Akzeptieren von Fehlern und Verletzlichkeit als Lernmöglichkeiten.
		Feedback geben und nehmen.	Schafft Möglichkeiten, um Bedürfnisse und Gefühle zu äußern und um Feedback zu geben und zu erhalten.
		Halten von und adäquates Reagieren auf Emotionen bei unbewussten Prozessen und Spiegelphänomenen.	Identifiziert Beziehungsmuster sowie Übertragungs- und Gegenübertragungs-Dynamiken, und handhabt sie als relationale Mechanismen. Erfasst die Gefühle anderer und reagiert empathisch auf sie.
		Handhaben von Beziehungskonflikten und Vertragsbruch.	Handhabt die Bedeutung individueller Gemeinsamkeiten und Unterschiede in einer Arbeitsbeziehung. Bietet ein ausgewogenes Verhältnis von Forderung und Unterstützung. Spricht Konkurrenz und Rivalität an und unterstützt die SupervisandInnen/Coachees im Umgang mit ihnen.

Competence	Knowledge	Skills	Performance
		Handling reciprocity.	Taking into account the impact of the observer of an action on this action. Observing the impact of one's own action. Intervening according to this observation.
		Ending the professional relationship by: • Planning and preparing the termination of a supervision/coaching relationship. • Managing issues arising from the termination of the relationship.	Identifying expressions and patterns of separation dynamics and handling them. Facilitating summarisation and evaluation of both the process and the supervisees'/coachees' professional development.
Evaluation	Knowledge about • Evaluation methodology, various methods and tools. • Process factors that influence learning outcomes (e.g. a strong working alliance).	Evaluating outcomes by • Transferring questions and issues into goals, desired outcomes and evaluation criteria with supervisee(s)/coachee(s) and the contractual partner. • Gathering and interpreting information about the development regarding the evaluation criteria on an individual or group level.	Establishing criteria for evaluation and co-creating opportunities for engaging in evaluation with supervisee(s)/coachee(s) and contractual partner. Choosing appropriate methods and periods for evaluation. Providing comprehensive written documentation. Using evaluation during the process to enhance further development. Discussing the evaluation results with parties involved as a form of feedback and input for further development and learning.
		Evaluating of process and working alliance by • Monitoring, assessing and reflecting on the process and the working relationship. • Requesting feedback on the process and working alliance.	Discussing the process and working relationship with the parties. Asking for feedback on both the process and the working alliance and showing how it is received and used.

Kompetenz	Kenntnisse	Fähigkeiten	Performance
		Umgang mit Zirkularität	Bezieht die Wirkungen des Beobachters einer Aktion auf diese Aktion mit ein. Beobachtet die Auswirkungen des eigenen Handelns. Interveniert auf Basis dieser Beobachtungen.
		Beendigung der Arbeitsbeziehung durch: • Planung und Vorbereitung der Beendigung einer Supervision/Coaching-Beziehung. • Bearbeiten von Fragen, die bei Beendigung einer Arbeitsbeziehung aufkommen.	Identifiziert Ausdrucksformen und Muster von Trennungsdynamiken und ist in der Lage, mit ihnen umzugehen. Ermöglicht die Zusammenfassung und Bewertung sowohl des Prozesses wie auch der professionellen Entwicklung der SupervisandInnen/Coachees.
Evaluieren	Wissen um: • Methodologie sowie verschiedene Methoden und Werkzeuge der Evaluation • Prozessfaktoren, die Lernergebnisse beeinflussen (z. B. ein starkes Arbeitsbündnis)	Evaluieren der Ergebnisse durch: • Umformulieren von Fragen und Themen in Ziele, gewünschte Ergebnisse und Kriterien für die Evaluation gemeinsam mit SupervisandInnen/Coachees und Auftraggebern. • Ermitteln und Auswerten von Informationen über die Entwicklung gemäß der Kriterien sowohl für Personen wie auch auf Gruppenebene.	Co-kreiert Kriterien für die Evaluation und schafft Gelegenheiten zur Evaluation sowohl mit SupervisandInnen/Coachees wie auch Auftraggebern. Wählt geeignete Methoden und Momente für die Evaluation. Stellt angemessene schriftliche Dokumentationen zur Verfügung. Nutzt Evaluation während des Prozesses zur Entwicklungsförderung. Diskutiert die Ergebnisse der Evaluation mit den Beteiligten als eine Form von Feedback und als Impuls für weitere Entwicklung und weiteres Lernen.
		Evaluieren des Prozesses sowie der Arbeitsbeziehung durch: • Ständiges Beobachten, Überprüfen und Reflektieren des Prozesses und der Arbeitsbeziehung. • Erfragen von Feedback über den Prozess und die Arbeitsbeziehung.	Diskutiert den Prozess und die Arbeitsbeziehung mit den Beteiligten. Erfragt Feedback über den Prozess und die Arbeitsbeziehung und zeigt so, wie es akzeptiert und genutzt werden kann.

2. Facilitating Outcomes

Competence	Knowledge	Skills	Performance
Facilitating Professional Development	Basic knowledge about the supervisees'/coachees' function, professional standards and their implications.	Focussing on the professional standards relevant for the supervisees'/coachees' function. Providing tools for gathering information about the effectiveness of a supervisees'/coachees' professional performance. Mastering different methods and tools for fostering creativity.	Keeping the perspective on person, work and organisation while working with supervisees/coachees on specific issues. Applying different methods and tools for fostering creative processes. Supporting supervisees/coachees in learning how to use resources and processes independently. Exploring ethical issues in a non-normative way.
	Basic knowledge of the supervisees'/coachees' organisational field.	Focussing on procedures and dynamics in the supervisees'/coachees' organisation.	Keeping up to date with developments in the professional field of the supervisees/coachees. Challenging the underlying rationale and supporting the supervisees/coachees in finding alternative perspectives.
	Knowledge about opportunities and limitation for personal development within supervision/coaching. Basic knowledge of burnout and mental health disorders.	Recognising opportunities and limitations for personal development within supervision/coaching. Keeping limits against the seductive appeal of forcing personal development. Assessing whether supervisee's/coachee's needs can be covered by supervision/coaching.	Monitoring the limits of the supervisees'/coachees' abilities. Stimulating reflection on the supervisees'/coachees' abilities. Referring a supervisee/coachee to another professional, if necessary. Maintaining a professional network.
Facilitating Change	Basic knowledge of definitions of change in learning theories and theories of organisational development.	Focussing on possible changes concerning a supervisee/coachee/a team/an organisation within the process of supervision/coaching. Stimulating development of new insights and perspectives of action, while keeping the balance between preservation and change. Using tools for handling constraints and resistance against change.	Assessing whether a change of perspective or a change of attitude or behaviour is indicated. Fostering a more complex understanding of a professional issue in context. Supporting the finding of opportunities for professional action on the personal and/or system level. Supporting the finding of a solution on the personal or system level. Providing specific tools for handling barriers, constraints and resistance.

2. Entwicklung fördern

Kompetenz	Kenntnisse	Fähigkeiten	Performance
Berufliche Entwicklung fördern	Grundkenntnisse über die Funktion der SupervisandInnen/Coachees, sowie deren professionelle Standards und deren Implikationen.	Fokussieren auf für SupervisandInnen/Coachees relevante professionelle Standards. Über Werkzeug verfügen, um Information zur Wirksamkeit des professionellen Verhaltens von SupervisandInnen/Coachees zu generieren. Methoden zur Kreativitätsförderung beherrschen.	Hält die Perspektive auf die Interaktion von Person, Arbeit und Organisation in der Arbeit mit SupervisandInnen/Coachees durchgängig bei verschiedensten Themen. Wendet differenzierte Methoden und Werkzeuge an, um kreative Prozesse zu fördern. Unterstützt SupervisandInnen/Coachees dabei, Ressourcen und Prozesse selbst nützen zu lernen. Untersucht ethische Fragen in nicht-normativer Weise.
	Grundkenntnisse des organisationalen Umfeldes der SupervisandInnen/Coachees.	Fokussieren auf Abläufe und Dynamiken in der Organisation der SupervisandInnen/Coachees.	Bleibt in Kontakt mit Entwicklungen im Berufsfeld. Hinterfragt Rationalisierungen und unterstützt die SupervisandInnen/Coachees bei der Suche nach alternativen Perspektiven.
	Wissen um Möglichkeiten und Grenzen persönlicher Entwicklung im Rahmen von Supervision/Coaching. Grundkenntnisse über Burnout und psychische Erkrankungen.	Erkennen von Chancen & Grenzen für persönliche Entwicklung im Rahmen von Supervision/Coaching. Der Verführung widerstehen, Persönlichkeitsentwicklung zu forcieren. Beurteilen, ob Supervision/Coaching den Erfordernissen der SupervisandInnen/Coachees entspricht.	Bezieht die Grenzen der Fähigkeiten von SupervisandInnen/Coachees mit ein. Stimuliert die Reflexion von SupervisandInnen/Coachees über die eigenen Fähigkeiten. Verweist SupervisandInnen/Coachees an eine/n andere/n professionellen BeraterIn, falls erforderlich. Verfügt über ein professionelles Netzwerk.
Veränderung ermöglichen	Kenntnisse der Definitionen von Veränderung in Lerntheorien und Theorien der Organisationsentwicklung.	Fokussieren auf mögliche Veränderungen einer SupervisandIn/eines Teams/einer Organisation innerhalb eines Supervisions-/Coaching-Prozesses. Entwicklung neuer Erkenntnisse und Handlungsperspektiven stimulieren, unter Wahrung der Balance zwischen Bewahrung und Wandel. Werkzeuge nutzen, um Barrieren, Einschränkungen und Widerstand gegen Veränderung zu handhaben.	Überprüft, ob eine Änderung der Perspektive, oder eine Änderung der Haltung bzw. des Verhaltens angezeigt ist. Fördert ein komplexeres Verständnis von einer professionellen Aufgabe und von deren Umfeld. Unterstützt die Suche nach Lösungen auf der persönlichen wie auch der System-Ebene. Unterstützt die Suche nach einer Lösung auf der persönlichen oder System-Ebene. Verwendet spezifische Werkzeuge im Umgang mit Barrieren, Einschränkungen und Widerstand.

Competence	Knowledge	Skills	Performance
Facilitating Learning	Knowledge about learning theories and neuroscience.	Supporting and evoking learning processes. Dealing with different learning styles of supervisees/coachees.	Promoting the embracing of new ways of learning. Monitoring supervisees'/coaches` stages of learning, professional growth and reflectivity. Stimulating reflection about the supervisees'/coachees' learning styles. Handling the dynamics of learning processes within a contracted framework and a supervision/coaching relationship.

3. Performing Advanced Communication

Competence	Knowledge	Skills	Performance
Using One's Own Communication Style Professionally	Knowledge about • communication theories and traditions (e.g. phenomenological, cybernetic, sociological, critical). • the impact of a supervisor's/coach's non-verbal and verbal communication style on any supervisory relationship. • issues of power in communication processes.	Using theoretical knowledge as a framework for assessment of one's own communication style and its impact on the relationship. Reflecting upon one's own communication style and identifying deficiencies in communication knowledge, skills, and attitudes. Self-monitoring changes of one's own communication patterns.	Adjusting her/his own communication style to the needs and vulnerabilities of supervisees/coachees. Handling and balancing the power relationship in communication during supervision/ coaching. Observing when and how communication patterns change. Using her/his personal communication style as a tool for promoting the supervision/coaching process.Recognising early signs of discrepancy between own communication style and the needs of supervisees/coachees.

Kompetenz	Kenntnisse	Fähigkeiten	Performance
Lernen fördern	Kenntnisse von Lerntheorien und Neurowissenschaften.	Unterstützen und evozieren von Lernprozessen. Umgang mit verschiedenen Lernstilen der SupervisandInnen/Coachees.	Unterstützt die Öffnung für neue Formen des Lernens. Beobachtet die Phasen des Lernens, des beruflichen Wachstums und der Reflexivität der SupervisandInnen/Coachees. Stimuliert die Reflexion über die Lernstile der SupervisandInnen/Coachees. Handhabt die Dynamik eines Lernprozesses innerhalb eines vertraglich vereinbarten Rahmens und einer Supervisions-/Coaching-Beziehung.

3. Komplexe Kommunikation steuern

Kompetenz	Kenntnisse	Fähigkeiten	Performance
Den eigenen Kommunikationsstil professionell nutzen	Wissen um: • Kommunikationstheorien (z.B. phänomenologische, kybernetische, soziologische, kritische). • die Auswirkungen des nonverbalen und verbalen Kommunikationsstils von SupervisorInnen/Coaches auf jede Supervisions-/Coaching-Beziehung. • Machtfragen in Kommunikationsprozessen.	Nutzen theoretischen Wissens als Rahmen für die Überprüfung des eigenen Kommunikationsstils und seiner Auswirkungen auf die Supervisions-/Coaching-Beziehung. Reflektieren des eigenen Kommunikationsstils und Erkennen von Schwachstellen in Wissen, Fertigkeiten und Haltungen. Selbstbeobachtung von Veränderungen eigener Kommunikationsmuster.	Passt den eigenen Kommunikationsstil den Bedürfnissen und Verletzlichkeiten der SupervisandInnen/Coachees an. Handhabt Machtbeziehungen in der Kommunikation während des Supervisions-/Coaching-Prozesses und balanciert sie aus. Beobachtet, wann und wie sich Kommunikationsmuster ändern. Verwendet ihren/seinen persönlichen Kommunikationsstil als Werkzeug, um den Supervisions-/Coaching-Prozess voranzutreiben. Registriert frühe Anzeichen einer Diskrepanz zwischen dem eigenen Kommunikationsstil und den Bedürfnissen der SupervisandInnen/Coachees.

Competence	Knowledge	Skills	Performance
Managing the Communication Process	Knowledge about • Various communication skills and their classifications. • The relation between communication processes and context. • Aspects and function of communication in supervision/coaching processes. • The difference between basic and advanced, complex communication skills. • Dialogue as a way of co-constructing meanings in communication.	Observing and guiding the communication process. Recognising the supervisees'/coachees' communication styles and skills. Using **basic** and **complex** communication skills (e.g. feedback, confrontation) purposely, appropriately and timely (e.g. observing, listening, asking questions) to facilitate the supervisees'/coaches' professional development. Mastering meta-communication.	Modelling and leading the supervision/coaching communication process efficiently. Supporting supervisees'/coachees' in becoming aware of their own communication skills and styles. Supporting supervisees/coachees in analysing and adapting own communication styles and patterns. Integrating information arising from verbalised and non-verbalised aspects of any communication between the supervisor/coach and the supervisees/coachees. Using dialogue as a tool for co-creation of implications relevant for professional behaviour. Reacting purposely, appropriately and timely to both the content-related and relational messages of the supervisees/coachees. Meta-communicating about the communication process in a supervision/coaching relationship.
Managing the Person – Work – Organisation – Communication	Knowledge about • Function, characteristics and barriers of efficient communication within organisations. • Formal and informal communication channels in organisations.	Analysing formal and informal communication processes within organisations. Analysing communication within person – work – organisation interaction.	Handling communication issues focussing on the interaction of person – work – organisation. Supporting supervisees/coachees in analysing their own communication styles and patterns within their organisational context. Supporting supervisees/coachees in applying their communication skills within their working context.

Kompetenz	Kenntnisse	Fähigkeiten	Performance
Kommunikationsprozesse gestalten	Wissen um: • Kommunikationsstile und deren Klassifizierungen. • die Beziehung zwischen Kommunikationsprozessen und Kontext. • Aspekte und Funktion der Kommunikation im Supervisions-/Coaching-Prozess. • den Unterschied zwischen grundlegenden, fortgeschrittenen und komplexen Kommunikationsfähigkeiten. • Dialog als eine Möglichkeit, Bedeutung in der Kommunikation zu ko-konstruieren.	Beobachten und Anleiten des Kommunikationsprozesses. Wahrnehmen und Erkennen der Kommunikationsstile & -fertigkeiten der SupervisandInnen/Coachees. Gezielter, angemessener und zeitadäquater Einsatz **grundlegender** (z.B. beobachten, zuhören, Fragen stellen) und **komplexer** (z.B. Feedback, Konfrontation) Kommunikationsfähigkeiten, um die berufliche Entwicklung der SupervisandInnen/Coachees zu fördern. Meta-Kommunikation beherrschen.	Gestaltet und führt den Kommunikationsprozess effizient. Unterstützt SupervisandInnen/Coachees dabei, sich ihrer eigenen Kommunikationsstile und -muster bewusst zu werden. Unterstützt SupervisandInnen/Coachees beim Analysieren und Anpassen ihrer eigenen Kommunikationsstile und -muster. Integriert Informationen aus verbalen und nonverbalen Aspekten der Kommunikation zwischen SupervisorIn/Coach und SupervisandInnen/Coachees. Verwendet den Dialog als Werkzeug, um für professionelles Verhalten relevante Bedeutungen zu ko-konstruieren. Reagiert gezielt, angemessen und zeitadäquat sowohl auf inhaltliche wie auch relationale Botschaften der SupervisandInnen/Coachees. Meta-kommuniziert über den Kommunikationsprozess in der Supervisions-/Coaching-Beziehung.
Die Kommunikation von Person – Arbeit – Organisation gestalten	Wissen um: • Funktion, Merkmale und Barrieren effizienter Kommunikation in Organisationen. • Formelle und informelle Kommunikationskanäle in Organisationen.	Analysieren formeller und informeller Kommunikationsprozesse in Organisationen. Analysieren der Kommunikation in der Interaktion von Person – Arbeit – Organisation.	Gestaltet die Kommunikation mit Fokus auf die Interaktion von Person-Arbeit-Organisation. Unterstützt SupervisandInnen/Coachees bei der Analyse eigener Kommunikationsstile und -muster in ihrem organisationalen Kontext. Unterstützt SupervisandInnen/Coachees dabei, ihre Kommunikationsfähigkeiten innerhalb ihres Arbeitskontexts gezielt einzusetzen.

Competence	Knowledge	Skills	Performance
Managing Tensions, Disruptions and Conflicts	Knowledge about • Conflict theories. • Conflict management and related communication patterns.	Recognising tensions and conflicts at an early stage. Handling the grade of escalation within a conflict. Bringing tension and conflict into communication. Recognising conflict patterns, both on a personal level and within person – work – organisation interaction.	Anticipating and dealing with tensions and conflicts. Recognising the grade of escalation of a conflict and intervening accordingly. Dealing with differences through dialogue. Handling barriers, disagreements and resistance sensitively, if necessary in a confronting manner. Keeping an all-party stance during all phases of the conflict. Facilitating constructive and creative conflict solutions, both on a personal level and by person – work – organisation interaction. Fostering the supervisees'/coachees' awareness of sources and related communication patterns while working on tensions and conflicts.

4. Handling Diversity

Competence	Knowledge	Skills	Performance
Diversity Awareness	Knowledge about • how values and assumptions guide human action generally. • own values and assumptions.	Sensitivity for differences and their impact.	Constantly reflecting on one's own values and action-guiding assumptions, especially in comparison to others. Assessing the supervisees'/coachees' underlying socio-cultural values and action-guiding assumptions.
	Knowledge of socio-cultural attribution practices and their effects on supervision/coaching processes.	Ability to tackle sociocultural attribution practices and their effects.	Knowledge and mastering of interventions that question retracted perspectives and behaviours. Challenging stereotyping attributions in personal and professional interactions.

Kompetenz	Kenntnisse	Fähigkeiten	Performance
Spannungen, Brüche und Konflikte halten und bearbeiten	Wissen um: • Konflikt-Theorien • Konfliktmanagement und entsprechende Kommunikationsmuster.	Spannungen und Konflikte frühzeitig erkennen. Handhaben der Eskalationsstufe eines Konflikts. Spannungen und Konflikte in Kommunikation bringen. Konfliktmuster erkennen, sowohl auf einer persönlichen Ebene als auch in der Interaktion von Person – Arbeit – Organisation.	Rechnet mit Spannungen und Konflikten und befasst sich mit ihnen. Erkennt den Grad der Eskalation eines Konflikts und interveniert entsprechend. Geht mit Differenzen in dialogischer Weise um. Behandelt Barrieren, Brüche und Widerstand sensibel, wenn nötig konfrontierend. Nimmt in allen Phasen des Konflikts eine allparteiliche Haltung ein. Erleichtert konstruktive und kreative Konfliktlösungen, sowohl persönlich als auch in der Interaktion von Person – Arbeit – Organisation. Fördert ein Bewusstsein der SupervisandInnen/Coachees für Ressourcen und damit verbundene Kommunikationsmuster während der Arbeit an Spannungen und Konflikten.

4. Umgang mit Vielfalt

Kompetenz	Kenntnisse	Fähigkeiten	Performance
Diversity-Bewusstsein	Wissen um: • Den Einfluss von Werten und handlungsleitenden Annahmen auf menschliche Interaktion. • Eigene Werte und handlungsleitende Annahmen.	Sensibilität für Unterschiede und ihre Auswirkungen.	Kennt und reflektiert eigene Werte, Kommunikationsstile und handlungsleitende Annahmen; insbesondere in Gegenüberstellung zu anderen. Beobachtet kritisch die Kommunikationsstile und handlungsleitenden Annahmen der SupervisandInnen/Coachees.
	Wissen um gesellschaftliche Zuschreibungspraxen und ihre Wirkungen in Supervisions-/Coaching-Prozessen.	Fähigkeit, mit Zuschreibungspraxen und deren Auswirkungen konstruktiv umzugehen.	Kennt und beherrscht Interventionen, die festgefahrene Perspektiven und Verhaltensweisen in Frage stellen. Stellt stereotype Zuschreibungen in persönlichen wie professionellen Interaktionen in Frage.

Competence	Knowledge	Skills	Performance
Managing Power, Hierarchy and Discrimination	Knowledge about • gender theories. • cultural theories. • intersectionality.	Knowing how stereotyping and discrimination are (re-)produced during communication. Opening up new scopes of action.	Recognising stereotyping and linking it to concrete behaviour. Addressing processes of power and the distribution of resources in a way that enhances the supervisees'/coachees' abilities to deal with them. Realising when someone is at risk of being excluded and using counteractive interventions. Fostering gender and diversity competence in the supervisees/coachees.
	Basic knowledge about the impact of bilingualism/second language.	Dealing with the effects of bilingualism on supervision/coaching processes.	Adapting flexibly to different language levels and speaking styles.

Kompetenz	Kenntnisse	Fähigkeiten	Performance
Macht, Hierarchie und Diskriminierung handhaben	Wissen um: • Gender-Theorien • Kulturtheorien • Intersektionalität	Wissen, wie Stereotypisierung und Diskriminierung sich in der Kommunikation (re-) produzieren. Eröffnen neuer Handlungsspielräume.	Erkennt Rollenklischees und verknüpft sie mit konkretem Verhalten. Spricht Prozesse der Macht- und Ressourcenverteilung so an, dass die SupervisandInnen/Coachees neue Handlungsspielräume im Umgang mit ihnen entwickeln können. Erkennt Außenseiterentwicklungen und setzt Interventionen, die dem entgegenwirken. Fördert die Gender- und Diversity-Kompetenz der SupervisandInnen/Coachees.
	Grundkenntnisse der Auswirkungen von Zwei- bzw. Zweitsprachigkeit.	Kennt die Wirkungen von Zweisprachigkeit auf Beratungsprozesse.	Kann sprachlich flexibel auf unterschiedliche Sprachniveaus und Sprechstile eingehen.

5. Mastering Settings, Techniques and Methods

Competence	Knowledge	Skills	Performance
Performing in Different Settings	Knowledge about • characteristics of different settings, • their implications, and • how to handle them. Knowledge about formats of professional counselling (psychotherapy, organisation development, organisational consulting etc.).	Setting boundaries. Cooperating with other formats. Building dyadic processes. Building group processes. Building team processes. Building organisational processes. Building blended learning.	Analysing whether the supervisees'/teams'/organisations' needs can be met by supervision/coaching and then recommending the appropriate format. Neither ignoring nor focussing on issues not to be addressed in the supervision process.
		Performing in dyadic settings	Handling the difference between dyadic and triangular and quadrilateral contracts and their implications on the supervision process. Responding to the supervisees'/coachees' actual situation without losing sight of goals and needs. Reviewing an ongoing process, to see whether the chosen setting still corresponds to the contracted goals.
		Performing in group settings	Knowing and dealing with the characteristics of group processes. Working with the specific group process. Using the group process to achieve the contracted goals.
		Performing in team settings	Knowing and dealing with the characteristics of teams and team processes. Knowing and dealing with the tasks of teams within an organisation and considering them. Deciding on team supervision with or without a team leader according to the contracted goals.
		Performing in an organisational context	Integrating organisational aspects into the process, especially those issues that most frequently arise, such as authority, subservience and competition.

5. Handwerkszeug, Techniken und Methoden gezielt einsetzen

Kompetenz	Kenntnisse	Fähigkeiten	Performance
Gestalten unterschied-licher Settings	Wissen um: • Merkmale der verschiedenen Settings, • deren Auswirkungen und • wie in ihnen gearbeitet werden muss. Wissen um andere Formate professioneller Beratung (Psychotherapie, Organisationsentwicklung, Organisationsberatung, …)	Grenzen setzen. Mit anderen Formaten kooperieren. Gestaltung von: Dyadischen Prozessen Gruppen-Prozessen Team-Prozessen Organisations-Prozessen Blended Learning.	Analysiert, ob die Bedürfnisse von SupervisandInnen/Teams/Organisationen durch Supervision/Coaching erreicht werden können und empfiehlt das passende Format. Hält Anliegen, die nicht in Supervision/Coaching bearbeitet werden können, in Kommunikation, ohne sie zu ignorieren oder sich in ihnen zu verfangen.
		Dyadische Prozesse gestalten	Handhabt den Unterschied zwischen dyadischen, Dreiecks- und Vierecks-Verträgen und deren Auswirkungen auf die Supervision. Reagiert auf die aktuelle Situation der SupervisandInnen/Coachees, ohne den Zusammenhang von Zielen und Bedürfnissen aus dem Blick zu verlieren. Überprüft im laufenden Prozess, ob das gewählte Setting noch zu den vertraglich vereinbarten Zielen passt.
		Gruppen-Prozesse gestalten	Kennt und handhabt Merkmale von Gruppenprozessen. Arbeitet mit dem Gruppenprozess. Verwendet den Gruppenprozess, um die vertraglich vereinbarten Ziele zu erreichen.
		Team-Prozesse gestalten	Kennt und handhabt Merkmale von Teams und Teamprozessen. Kennt und handhabt die Aufgaben eines Teams innerhalb einer Organisation und bezieht sie mit ein. Entscheidet entsprechend der vertraglich festgelegten Ziele, ob die Team-Supervision mit oder ohne Teamleitung stattfindet.
		Organisations-Prozesse gestalten.	Integriert organisationale Komponenten in den Prozess, vor allem jene Themen, die am häufigsten auftreten wie Autorität, Unterordnung und Konkurrenz.

Competence	Knowledge	Skills	Performance
		Performing blended learning	Using new media and face-to-face settings in a purposeful way.
Using Methods and Techniques	Knowledge about various methods and techniques. Knowledge about theories of intervention.	Mastering a set of methods and techniques. Having a clear and theory-based concept of how to use these methods.	Using methods and techniques in specific contexts. Intervening by referring to a concept applied both theory-based and individually to specific issues and moments.
		Giving professional feedback	Providing information to the other person about one's impression of her/his behaviour. Adapting the feedback rules flexibly to the needs of a supervisee/coachee or to a situation. Reinforcing and challenging a supervisee's/coachee's thinking and behaviour. Stimulating the collaborative process in group or team settings by introducing feedback.
		Focussing problems	Recognising when a current problem proves to be chaotic, consequently producing anxiety. Supporting the supervisees/coachees to take a step back from the problem to view it from a new perspective. Supporting the supervisees/coachees to proceed from words and insights to new and unfamiliar action.
		Moderating the process of supervision/coaching	Purposefully using all methods with regard to structuring the process to achieve the contracted goals.

Kompetenz	Kenntnisse	Fähigkeiten	Performance
		Gestalten von Blended Learning.	Nutzt neue Medien und Face-to-Face-Settings sinnvoll und gezielt.
Methoden und Techniken einsetzen	Wissen um: • verschiedenste Methoden und Techniken. • Theorien oder Intervention.	Beherrschen vielfältiger Methoden und Techniken. Verfügen über ein klares und theoriebasiertes Konzept für den Einsatz dieser Methoden.	Verwendet Methoden und Techniken kontextspezifisch. Interveniert mit Rückbezug auf ein Konzept, das sowohl theoriebasiert ist, als auch individuell angepasst an spezifische Themen und Situationen.
		Professionell Feedback geben	Teilt einer anderen Person den eigenen Eindruck von ihrem/seinem Verhalten mit. Passt die Feedback-Regeln flexibel an die Bedürfnisse von SupervisandInnen/Coachees oder an eine Situation an. Baut auf dem Denken und Handeln von SupervisandInnen/Coachees auf und stellt es gegebenfalls auch in Frage. Stimuliert Zusammenarbeit in Gruppensettings durch die Einführung von Feedback.
		Probleme fokussieren	Erkennt, wenn sich ein aktuelles Problem als chaotisch erweist und folglich Angst erzeugt. Unterstützt die SupervisandInnen/Coachees dabei, einen Schritt zurückzutreten und das Problem aus einer neuen Perspektive zu betrachten. Unterstützt die SupervisandInnen, um von Worten und Einsichten zu neuen und ungewohnten Handlungen zu gelangen.
		Den Supervisions-/Coaching-Prozess moderieren	Nutzt gezielt alle Methoden zur Strukturierung des Prozesses und um die vertraglich vereinbarten Ziele zu erreichen.

Competence	Knowledge	Skills	Performance
		Stimulating reflection	Stimulating articulation of a supervisee's/coachee's experiences, thoughts and beliefs. Deciding whether to reflect on the contents, on the process or on the modes of reflecting (meta-reflection). Encouraging the supervisees/coachees to consider their personal emotional states and behavioural aspects. Supporting the supervisees/coachees in drawing their own conclusions about changes necessary to achieve the desired results in the future.
		Using empathy	Recognising the emotional state of supervisees. Separating one's own emotional response as supervisor/coach from those of the supervisees/coachees. Handling (counter)transference and one's own preoccupations professionally.
		Applying professional dialogue	Expressing respect for the way an individual experiences reality. Expressing genuine curiosity and facilitating mutual understanding. Using creative techniques to facilitate the supervisees'/coachees' comprehension of the situations in which they find themselves.

Kompetenz	Kenntnisse	Fähigkeiten	Performance
		Reflexion stimulieren	Stimuliert die Artikulation von Erfahrungen, Gedanken und Überzeugungen der SupervisandInnen/Coachees. Entscheidet, ob der Inhalt, der Prozess oder die Weise der Reflexion (Meta-Reflexion) reflektiert werden soll. Unterstützt die SupervisandInnen/Coachees, ihre persönliche emotionale Verfassung und ihr Verhalten zu untersuchen. Unterstützt die SupervisandInnen/Coachees in ihren eigenen Schlussfolgerungen über Änderungen, die zum Erreichen gewünschter Ergebnisse in der Zukunft notwendig wären.
		Arbeiten mit Empathie	Erkennt den emotionalen Zustand von SupervisandInnen/Coachees. Trennt die eigene emotionale Reaktion als SupervisorIn/Coach von dem, was die SupervisandInnen/Coaches einbringen. Handhabt (Gegen-)Übertragung und eigene Anliegen professionell.
		Professionellen Dialog gestalten	Zeigt Respekt für die Art und Weise, in der jeder Mensch seine eigene Realität erfährt. Drückt genuine Neugier aus und ermöglicht gegenseitige Verständigung. Nützt kreative Techniken, um das Verständnis der SupervisandInnen/Coaches für die Situation, in der sie sich befinden, zu fördern.

Validating Competences
The ECVision Reference Table ECTS-ECVET

Marina Ajdukovic
Lilja Cajvert
Michaela Judy
Hubert Kuhn

Kompetenzen validieren
Die ECVision Referenztabelle ECTS-ECVET

Marina Ajdukovic
Lilja Cajvert
Michaela Judy
Hubert Kuhn

A Model for Accreditation and Validation of Learning Outcomes in Education and Training of Supervision & Coaching in Europe, comparing the following continuous education programmes for Supervision and Coaching:

"Coaching & Supervision", provided by TOPS München-Berlin e.V., accredited by DGSv (German Association for Supervision).

"Systemic Supervision & Coaching", provided by ASYS Wien (Association for Systemic Social Work, Counselling and Supervision), accredited by ÖVS (Austrian Organisation for Supervision).

"Postgraduate Specialist University Study Program in Supervision in Psychosocial Work" University of Zagreb, accredited in ECTS by University of Zagreb.

Table 3: ECVET Learning Units TOPS: Training Course "Coaching & Supervision"

TOPS München-Berlin e.V.

Unit of learning outcomes		Contracting	Diagnosis, process, communication, conflict	Clarification of function & role	Selfdevelopment/ selfawareness	Organisation, Leadership, working environment	Group- & Team-dynamics	Methods	Learning supervision	Educational supervision, Intervision	Theses	Total
LEARNING OUTCOMES	Professional Attitude	0,6		2,6	3,2			1,0	3,5	2,3	3,2	16
	Ethics					0,6			3,5	2,3	3,2	10
	Quality Development			0,6	0,6	0,6			3,5	2,3	3,2	11
	Perspective on Person, Work & Organisation	0,6		1,0		3,8			3,5	2,3	3,2	15
	Building a Professional Relationship	3,8	1,6	1,0	1,3		0,3	1,0	3,5	2,3	3,2	18
	Facilitating Outcomes	0,6	1,6	0,6		0,4	0,3		3,5	2,3	3,2	13
	Performing Advanced Communication		1,6				3,8		3,5	2,3	3,2	14
	Handling Diversity				0,6		0,8		3,5	2,3	3,2	10
	Mastering Settings, Techniques & Methods						0,8	3,8	3,5	2,3	3,2	13
		5,76	4,8	5,8	5,8	5,6	6,0	5,8	31,2	20,6	28,8	120

Ein Modell zur Akkreditierung und Validierung von Lernergebnissen in Supervisions- & Coaching-Ausbildungen in Europa. Die Referenztabellen vergleichen die folgenden Ausbildungen für Supervision und Coaching:

„Coaching & Supervision" von TOPS München-Berlin e.V., akkreditiert von der DGSv (Deutsche Gesellschaft für Supervision).

„Systemische Supervision & Coaching" von ASYS Wien (Arbeitskreis für Systemische Sozialarbeit, Beratung und Supervision), akkreditiert von der ÖVS (Österreichische Gesellschaft für Supervision & Coaching).

„Postgraduales Studienprogramm für Supervision in der psychosozialen Arbeit", Universität Zagreb, akkreditiert in ECTS von der Universität Zagreb.

Tabelle 3: ECVET Einheiten von Lernergebnissen – TOPS München-Berlin e.V.

Ausbildung zum Supervisor/zur Supervisorin/zum Coach (DGSv akkreditiert)

Einheiten von Lernergebnissen	Auftragsklärung & Kontrakt	Diagnoseprozess, Kommunikation, Konflikt	Klärung von Funktion und Rolle	Persönlichkeitsentwicklung/Selbsterfahrung	Organisation, Führung, Feld, Arbeitswelt	Gruppen- & Teamdynamik	Methoden	Lern-SV	Lehr-SV, Intervision	Abschlussarbeit	Gesamt
Professionelle Haltung	0,6		2,6	3,2		1,0		3,5	2,3	3,2	16
Ethik					0,6			3,5	2,3	3,2	10
Qualitätsentwicklung			0,6	0,6	0,6			3,5	2,3	3,2	11
Perspektive auf Person, Arbeit und Organisation	0,6		1,0		3,8			3,5	2,3	3,2	14
Arbeitsbeziehung gestalten	3,8	1,6	1,0	1,3		0,3	1,0	3,5	2,3	3,2	18
Entwicklung fördern	0,6	1,6	0,6		0,4	0,3		3,5	2,3	3,2	13
Komplexe Kommunikation steuern		1,6				3,8		3,5	2,3	3,2	14
Umgang mit Vielfalt				0,6		0,8		3,5	2,3	3,2	10
Techniken und Methoden gezielt einsetzen						0,8	0,8	3,5	2,3	3,2	13
	5,76	4,8	5,8	5,8	5,6	5,8	5,8	31,2	20,6	28,8	120

(LERNERGEBNISSE)

Table 4: ECVET Learning Units – ASYS (Association for Systemic Social Work, Counselling and Supervision)

Training Course "Systemic Supervision & Coaching (ÖVS)"

	Unit of learning outcomes	Professional Self Awareness	Mastering Organisational Issues	Intervening in social processes	Action guiding theory	Comprehension of role & function	Learning supervision	Educational supervision	Peergroup & Intervision	Thesis	Total
LEARNING OUTCOMES	Professional Attitude	3,8	1,3	1,4	2,6	1,0	1,6	2,2	1,9	4,9	21
	Ethics	0,9		0,6	0,6	0,6	1,0	0,6	0,6	2,8	8
	Quality Development	1,3		1,3		0,6	1,0	1,9	1,3	2,8	10
	Perspective on Person, Work & Organisation	1,3	3,2	1,3	0,6	0,6	1,0	1,0	1,3	4,2	15
	Building a Professional Relationship	3,8	2,6	1,9	2,1	0,6	1,0	1,6	1,0	2,8	18
	Facilitating Outcomes	1,3		0,6	0,6	0,6	1,0	0,6	1,0	2,8	8
	Performing Advanced Communication	3,2		2,6	2,2	0,6	1,9	0,6	1,0	3,9	15
	Handling Diversity	1,3	0,9	0,6		0,6	1,0	0,6	1,4	2,8	9
	Mastering Settings, Techniques & Methods		1,3	3,8		0,6	1,9	1,9	1,9	4,5	16
	Total	**17**	**9**	**14**	**9**	**6**	**11**	**11**	**11**	**32**	**120**

Tabelle 4: ECVET Einheiten von Lernergebnissen – ASYS – Arbeitskreis für Systemische Sozialarbeit, Beratung und Supervision

Lehrgang Systemische Supervision & Coaching – ASYS (ÖVS-akkreditiert)

	Einheiten von Lernergebnissen	Professionelle Identität	Denken & Handeln in organisatorischen Strukturen	Intervenieren in sozialen Prozessen	Handlungsleitende Theorie	Supervisorisches Funktionsverständnis	Lern-SV	Lehr-SV	Peergroup & Intervision	Abschlussarbeit	Gesamt
LERNERGEBNISSE	Professionelle Haltung	3,8	1,3	1,4	2,6	1,0	1,6	2,2	1,9	4,9	21
	Ethik	0,9		0,6	0,6	0,6	1,0	0,6	0,6	2,8	8
	Qualitäts-entwicklung	1,3		1,3		0,6	1,0	1,9	1,3	2,8	10
	Perspektive auf Person, Arbeit & Organisation	1,3	3,2	1,3	0,6	0,6	1,0	1,0	1,3	4,2	15
	Arbeitsbeziehung gestalten	3,8	2,6	1,9	2,1	0,6	1,0	1,6	1,0	2,8	18
	Entwicklung fördern	1,3		0,6	0,6	0,6	1,0	0,6	1,0	2,8	8
	Komplexe Kommunikation steuern	3,2		2,6	2,2	0,6	1,9	0,6	1,0	3,9	15
	Umgang mit Vielfalt	1,3	0,9	0,6		0,6	1,0	0,6	1,4	2,8	9
	Techniken und Methoden gezielt einsetzen		1,3	3,8		0,6	1,9	1,9	1,9	4,5	16
	Gesamt	**17**	**9**	**14**	**9**	**6**	**11**	**11**	**11**	**32**	**120**

Table 5: Reference Table ECVET

using the following training programmes for Supervision & Coaching:
ASYS (Arbeitskreis für systemische Sozialarbeit, Beratung & Supervision)
Training Course „Coaching & Supervision", TOPS München-Berlin e.V.

LEARNING ACTIVITIES		TOPS München-Berlin e.V.	ASYS (Arbeitskreis für systemische Sozialarbeit, Beratung & Supervision)	Difference
LEARNING OUTCOMES	Professional Attitude	16	21	5
	Ethics	10	8	2
	Quality Development	11	10	1
	Perspective on Person, Work & Organisation	15	15	0
	Building a Professional Relationship	18	18	0
	Facilitating Outcomes	13	8	4
	Performing Advanced Communication	14	15	1
	Handling Diversity	10	9	1
	Mastering Settings, Techniques & Methods	13	16	3
	ECTS	**120**	**120**	

Tabelle 5: Referenztabelle ECVET

Auf Basis der folgenden Ausbildungen für Supervision & Coaching:
„Systemische Supervision & Coaching", ASYS, Wien
„Coaching & Supervision", TOPS München-Berlin e.V.

LERNAKTIVITÄTEN		TOPS München-Berlin e.V.	ASYS (Arbeitskreis für systemische Sozialarbeit, Beratung & Supervision)	Differenzen
LERNERGEBNISSE	Professionelle Haltung	16	21	4
	Ethik	10	8	2
	Qualitätsentwicklung	11	10	1
	Perspektive auf Person, Arbeit & Organisation	15	15	0
	Arbeitsbeziehung gestalten	18	18	0
	Entwicklung fördern	13	18	4
	Komplexe Kommunikation steuern	14	15	1
	Umgang mit Vielfalt	10	9	1
	Techniken und Methoden gezielt einsetzen	13	16	3
	ECTS	**120**	**120**	

Table 6: ECTS Accreditation

Postgraduate Specialist University Study Program in Supervision in Psychsocial Work, University of Zagreb

	LEARNING ACTIVITIES	Introduction to Individual and Group Supervision	Communication Processes in Supervision	Counselling Skills	Elective courses (3 courses)	Supervision of Direct Psychosocial Work	Evaluation Research in Psychosocial Work	Supervision Pro-cesses, methods and competencies	Leading Group Supervision	Meta-supervision	Team Supervision	Organisational Supervision and Org. Development	Thesis	Total ECTS
LEARNING OUTCOMES	Professional Attitude	1	1	1	2	1	1	1	2	2	1	1	12	26
	Ethics	0.5		0.5	1	1	1	1	1	1	0.5	0.5	2	10
	Quality Development				1	0.5	2	1	1	1	0.5	0.5		7.5
	Perspective on Person, Work & Organisation	1			2	0.5			2	2		1.5	2	11
	Building a Professional Relationship	1		1		1			2	2				7
	Facilitating Outcomes			1	2	1	1		2	2			2	11
	Performing Advanced Communication	1	2	1	2	1		1	2	2	1		2	15
	Handling Diversity	1	1	1	2	1		1	2	2	1	0.5		12.5
	Mastering Settings, Techniques & Methods	1.5	1	1,5	3	1		2	4	4	1	1		20
Total ECTS		7	5	7	15	8	5	7	18	18	5	5	20	120

Tabelle 6: ECTS Akkreditierung

Postgraduales spezialisiertes Universitätsstudienprogramm für Supervision in der psychosozialen Arbeit, Universität Zagreb

LERN-AKTIVITÄTEN	Einführung in Einzel- & Gruppen-Supervision	Kommunikationsprozesse in der Supervision	Beratungsfertigkeiten	Wahlseminare (3 Seminare)	Supervision psychosozialer Arbeit	Evaluation & Forschung in psychosozialer Arbeit	Supervisionsprozesse, Methoden und Kompetenzen	Lern-SV Gruppe & Einzel	Lehr-SV Einzel	Lehr-SV Team	Organisations-Supervision und Org. Entwicklung	Abschlussarbeit	Gesamt ECTS
Professionelle Haltung	1	1	1	2	1	1	1	2	2	1	1	12	26
Ethik	0.5		0.5	1	1	1	1	1	1	0.5	0.5	2	10
Qualitätsentwicklung				1	0.5	2	1	1	1	0.5	0.5		7.5
Perspektive auf Person, Arbeit & Organisation	1			2	0.5		2	2			1.5	2	11
Arbeitsbeziehung gestalten	1		1		1			2	2				7
Entwicklung fördern			1	2	1	1		2	2			2	11
Komplexe Kommunikation steuern	1	2	1	2	1		1	2	2	1		2	15
Umgang mit Vielfalt	1	1	1	2	1		1	2	2	1	0.5		12.5
Techniken und Methoden gezielt einsetzen	1.5	1	1,5	3	1		2	4	4	1	1		20
Gesamt ECTS	7	5	7	15	8	5	7	18	18	5	5	20	120

LERNERGEBNISSE

Table 7: Reference Table ECTS – ECVET using the following training programmes for Supervision & Coaching

Postgraduate University Study Program in Supervision in Psychosocial Work, Univ. of Zagreb (ECTS),

Training Course „Coaching & Supervision", TOPS München-Berlin e.V. (ECVET)

LEARNING ACTIVITIES / LEARNING OUTCOMES	Introduction to Individual and Group Supervision	Communication Processes in Supervision	Counselling Skills	Elective Courses	Supervision of Direct Psychosocial Work	Evaluation Research in Psychosocial Work	Individual and Group Supervision Processes	Leading Group Supervision	Meta-supervision	Team Supervision	Organisational Supervision and Org. Development	Thesis	Total ECVET
Professional Attitude	x	x	x	x	x	x	x	x	x	x	x	x	16
Ethics						x		x	x			x	10
Quality Development	x					x		x	x			x	11
Perspective on Person, Work & Organisation			x		x	x		x	x	x	x	x	15
Building a Professional Relationship	x	x	x	x	x	x	x	x	x	x	x	x	19
Facilitating Outcomes			x	x	x	x	x	x	x	x	x	x	12
Performing Advanced Communication		x	x	x	x		x	x	x	x	x	x	14
Handling Diversity			x				x	x	x	x	x	x	11
Mastering Settings, Techniques & Methods	x	x	x	x	x	x	x	x	x	x	x	x	12
Total ECTS	7	5	7	15	8	5	7	18	18	5	5	20	120

Tabelle 7: Referenztabelle ECTS – ECVET auf Basis der Ausbildungsprogramme für Supervision & Coaching

Postgraduales spezialisiertes Universitätsstudienprogramm für Supervision in der psychosozialen Arbeit, Univ. Zagreb (ECTS),
Lehrgang „Coaching & Supervision", TOPS München-Berlin e.V. (ECVET)

	LERN-AKTIVITÄTEN	Einführung in Einzel- & Gruppen-Supervision	Kommunikationsprozesse in der Supervision	Beratungsfertigkeiten	Wahlseminare (3 Seminare)	Supervision psychosozialer Arbeit	Evaluation & Forschung in psychosozialer Arbeit	Supervisionsprozesse, Methoden und Kompetenzen	Lehr-SV Gruppe & Einzel	Lehr-SV Einzel	Lehr-SV Team	Organisations-Supervision und Org. Entwicklung	Abschlussarbeit	Gesamt ECVET
LERNERGEBNISSE	Professionelle Haltung	x	x	x	x	x	x	x	x	x	x	x	x	16
	Ethik						x		x	x			x	10
	Qualitäts-entwicklung	x					x		x	x			x	11
	Perspektive auf Person, Arbeit & Organisation			x		x	x		x	x	x	x	x	15
	Arbeits-beziehung gestalten	x	x	x	x	x	x	x	x	x	x	x	x	19
	Entwicklung fördern			x	x	x	x	x	x	x	x	x	x	12
	Komplexe Kommunikation steuern		x	x	x	x		x	x	x	x	x	x	14
	Umgang mit Vielfalt			x				x	x	x	x	x	x	11
	Techniken und Methoden gezielt einsetzen	x	x	x	x	x	x	x	x	x	x	x	x	12
	Gesamt ECTS	7	5	7	15	8	5	7	18	18	5	5	20	120

Reference list

Resources used for the ECVision glossary

Abdul-Hussain, S. (2012). Genderkompetenz in Supervision und Coaching, VS Verlag Wiesbaden.

Ajduković, M. & Cajvert. L. (2004). Supervizija u psihosocijalnom radu./Supervision in psychosocial work. Zagreb: Društvo za psihološku pomoć. (University textbook, pp. 383).

Ajduković, M., Cajvert, Lj., Kobolt, Žižak, A. (2012). Obilježja metasupervizora iz perspektive supervizanta i metasupervizora. 3. Hrvatska konferencija o superviziji. Postignuća i izazovi razvoja supervizije. Opatija, 18. do 20. travanja 2012. Knjiga sažetaka, 26.

Ajduković, M., Urbanc, K. (2010). Supervision as a safety net. In: Van Hess, G., Geissler-Pilitz, B. (Eds.) Supervision meets education. Supervision in the Bachelor of Social Work in Europe. Maastricht: CERST Research Centre Social Integration, Faculty of Social Studies/Zuyd University of Applied Science, 114–133.

Ambruš-Kiš, R., Cimperman, R., Fajdetić, M., Kazija, M., Listeš, S., Marunčić, S., Miletić, L., Milić, V., Ništ, M., Ozorlić-Dominić, R., Petljak-Jakunić, B., Požnjak-Malobabić, A., Skelac & M., Vidović, T. (2009). Integrativna supervizija u odgoju i obrazovanju./Integrative supervision in educational system. Zagreb: Agencija za odgoj i obrazovanje.

Andersen, T. (1996). Das Reflektierende Team. Dialoge und Dialoge über die Dialoge. Dortmund: Verlag Modernes Lernen.

Bastaić, Lj. (2007). Supervizija i interpersonalna neurobiologija- kako supervizijski odnos mijenja supervizora i supervizanta/Supervision and interpersonal neurobiology- how the supervisory relationship changes the supervisor and supervisees. Ljetopis socijalnog rada/Annual of Social Work, 14 (2), 453–463.

Belardi, N.(2009). Supervision. Grundlagen, Techniken, Perspektiven. München: C.H. Beck, 3. Ed.

Berg, E M, (2004/2012). Coaching – att hjälpa ledare och medarbetare att lyckas. 2a uppl. Lund: Studentlitteratur.

Bergknapp, A. (2009). Supervision und Organisation – Zur Logik von Beratungssystemen. Wien: Facultas.wuv.

Bernler, G & Johnsson, L. (1985/2000). Handledning i psykosocialt arbete. Stockholm: Natur och Kultur.

Verwendete Literatur

Abdul-Hussain, S. (2012). Genderkompetenz in Supervision und Coaching, VS Verlag Wiesbaden.

Ajduković, M. & Cajvert. L. (2004). Supervizija u psihosocijalnom radu./Supervision in psychosocial work. (University textbook, pp. 383). Zagreb: Društvo za psihološku pomoć.

Ajduković, M., Cajvert, Lj., Kobolt, Žižak, A. (2012). Obilježja metasupervizora iz perspektive supervizanta i metasupervizora. 3. Hrvatska konferencija o superviziji. Postignuća i izazovi razvoja supervizije. Opatija, 18. do 20. travanja 2012. Knjiga sažetaka, 26.

Ajduković, M., Urbanc, K. (2010). Supervision as a safety net. In: Van Hess, G., Geissler-Pilitz, B. (Eds.) Supervision meets education. Supervision in the Bachelor of Social Work in Europe. Maastricht: CERST Research Centre Social Integration, Faculty of Social Studies/Zuyd University of Applied Science, 114–133.

Ambruš-Kiš, R., Cimperman, R., Fajdetić, M., Kazija, M., Listeš, S., Marunčić, S., Miletić, L., Milić, V., Ništ, M., Ozorlić-Dominić, R., Petljak-Jakunić, B., Požnjak-Malobabić, A., Skelac & M., Vidović, T. (2009). Integrativna supervizija u odgoju i obrazovanju./Integrative supervision in educational system. Zagreb: Agencija za odgoj i obrazovanje.

Andersen, T. (1996). Das Reflektierende Team. Dialoge und Dialoge über die Dialoge. Dortmund: Verlag Modernes Lernen.

Bastaić, Lj. (2007). Supervizija i interpersonalna neurobiologija- kako supervizijski odnos mijenja supervizora i supervizanta/Supervision and interpersonal neurobiology- how the supervisory relationship changes the supervisor and supervisees. Ljetopis socijalnog rada/Annual of Social Work, 14 (2), 453–463.

Belardi, N.(2009). Supervision. Grundlagen, Techniken, Perspektiven, München: C.H. Beck, 3. Ed.

Berg, E. M. (2004/2012). Coaching – att hjälpa ledare och medarbetare att lyckas. 2a uppl. Lund: Studentlitteratur.

Bergknapp, A. (2009). Supervision und Organisation – Zur Logik von Beratungssystemen. Wien: Facultas.wuv.

Bernler, G. & Johnsson, L. (1985/2000). Handledning i psykosocialt arbete. Stockholm: Natur och Kultur.

Bezić, I. (2007). Supervizija kao način razvijanja samopouzdanja i sposobnosti podnošenja konfrontacije/Supervision as a way to develop self-confidence and the

Bezić, I. (2007). Supervizija kao na in razvijanja samopouzdanja i sposobnosti podnošenja konfrontacije/Supervision as a way to develop self-confidence and the ability to cope with confrontation.Ljetopis socijalnog rada/Annual of Social Work, 14 (2), 443–452.

Boalt Boéthius, S. & Ögren, M-L. (2000). Grupphandledning Den lilla gruppen som forum för lärande. Lund: Studentlitteratur.

Boalt Boéthius, S. & Ögren, M-L. (2012). Möjligheter och utmaningar i grupphandledning. Teori och verklighet. Lund: Studentlitteratur.

Cajvert, L. (2009). Nesvjesni procesi u superviziji terapijskog rada. In: Ajdukovic, M. (Ed.) Reflection about supervision: International perspective. Zagreb: Faculty of Law. Department of Social Work, 67–89.

Cajvert, L. (1998). Behandlarens kreativa rum. Om handledning. Lund: Studentlitteratur.

Curriculum Chr. Rauen Coaching, http://www.rauen.de/christopher-rauen.htm, 30.05.2012

Curriculum Katholische Stiftungsfachhochschule Munich, http://www.ksfh.de/weiter bildung, 30.05.2012

Curriculum Tops Munich-Berlin e.V.,www.tops-ev.de; 30.05.2012

Curriculum Trainingsprogramma Coaching Alba Academie (2013)

Curriculum Trainingsprogramma Coaching Hanze Hogeschool Groningen (2013)

Curriculum Trainingsprogramma Supervisiekunde Hanze hogeschool Groningen (2008)

Curriculum, Lehrgang: Systemische Supervision (2013), Arbeitskreis für Systemische Sozialarbeit, Beratung und Supervision (ASYS).

Čačinovič Vogrinčič. G. (2009). Supervizija u socijalnom radu: su-stvaranje supervizije kroz suradni odnos. In: Ajdukovic, M. (Ed.), (2012). Refleksije o superviziji: Međunarodna perspektiva/Reflection about supervision: International perspective. Zagreb: Faculty of Law. Department of Social Work, 67–89.

DBVC, http://www.dbvc.de, 30.05.2012

DGSF, www.dgsf.de, 30.05.2012

DGSv, www.dgsv.de, 30.05.2012

Doppler, K., Lauterburg, Ch. (2007). Change Management. Campus.

DVC, http://www.coachingverband.org, 30.05.2012

Edding, C./Schattenhofer, K. (Hg) (2009). Handbuch: Alles über Gruppen. Weinheim/ Basel.

Fatzer, G., Rappe-Geiseke, K., Looss, W. (1999). Qualität und Leistung von Beratung (Supervision, Coaching, Organisationsentwicklung). Edition Humanistische Psychologie.

Fagerström, K., Karvinen-Niinikoski, S. (2013). What makes social work "systemic"? In: STEP-Manual.

Geissler, Karlheinz, A. (1996). Szupervízió a modernben – modern szupervízió. In: Norbert Lippenheimer (szerk.): Tanulmányok a szupervízió köréből. Supervisio Hungarica.

Gjerde, S. (2007/2012). Coaching vad – varför – hur. Lund: Studentlitteraturen.

ability to cope with confrontation.Ljetopis socijalnog rada/Annual of Social Work, 14 (2), 443–452.

Boalt Boéthius, S. & Ögren, M-L. (2000). Grupphandledning Den lilla gruppen som forum för lärande. Lund: Studentlitteratur.

Boalt Boéthius, S. & Ögren, M-L. (2012). Möjligheter och utmaningar i grupphandledning. Teori och verklighet. Lund: Studentlitteratur.

Cajvert, L. (2009). Nesvjesni procesi u superviziji terapijskog rada. In: Ajdukovic, M. (Ed.) Reflection about supervision: International perspective. Zagreb: Faculty of Law. Department of Social Work, 67–89.

Cajvert, L. (1998). Behandlarens kreativa rum. Om handledning. Lund: Studentlitteratur.

Čačinovič Vogrinčič. G. (2009). Supervizija u socijalnom radu: su-stvaranje supervizije kroz suradni odnos. In: Ajdukovic, M. (Ed.), (2012) Refleksije o superviziji: Medunarodna perspektiva/Reflection about supervision: International perspective. Zagreb: Faculty of Law. Department of Social Work, 67–89.

CEDEFOP: Using Learning Outcomes; European Qualifications Framework Series: Note 4; http://www.cedefop.europa.eu/en/news-and-press/news/using-learning-outcomes, (Juni 2016).

Doppler, K., Lauterburg, Ch. (2007). Change Management. Frankfurt: Campus.

Edding, C., Schattenhofer, K. (Ed) (2009). Handbuch: Alles über Gruppen, Weinheim/Basel.

Fatzer, G., Rappe-Geiseke, K., Looss, W. (1999). Qualität und Leistung von Beratung (Supervision, Coaching, Organisationsentwicklung). Edition Humanistische Psychologie.

Fagerström, K., Karvinen-Niinikoski, S. (2013). What makes social work "systemic"? In: STEP-Manual,

Geissler, Karlheinz, A. (1996). Szupervízió a modernben – modern szupervízió. In: Norbert Lippenheimer (szerk.): Tanulmányok a szupervízió köréből. Supervisio Hungarica.

Gjerde, S. (2007/2012). Coaching vad – varför – hur. Lund: Studentlitteraturen.

Göncz, K. (2003): ELTE TTK szupervizor szakirányú továbbképzésének szakindítási kérelme.

Gordan, K. (1992). Psykoterapihandledning inom utbildning, i kliniskt arbete och på institution. Stockholm: Stockholm: Natur och Kultur.

Gotthardt-Lorenz, A. (2000). Die Methode Supervision – eine Skizze. In Pühl, H. (Hrsg.), Supervision und Organisationsentwicklung. (S. 55–69). Opladen: Leske und Budrich.

Gotthardt-Lorenz, A. (2009). Organisationssupervision – Raum für wachsende Anforderungen. In Pühl, H. (Hrsg.), Supervision und Organisationsentwicklung. Wiesbaden: VS Verlag.

Gotthardt-Lorenz, A.; Hausinger, B.; Sauer, J. (2009). Die supervisorische Forschungskompetenz. In Pühl, H. (Hrsg.), Handbuch der Supervision 3. Berlin: Ulrich Leutner Verlag.

Gotthardt-Lorenz, A. (1994 und 2000). „Organisationssupervision", Rollen und In-

Göncz, K. (2003). ELTE TTK szupervizor szakirányú továbbképzésének szakindítási kérelme.

Gordan, K. (1992). Psykoterapihandledning inom utbildning, i kliniskt arbete och på institution. Stockholm: Natur och Kultur. Stockholm.

Gotthardt-Lorenz, A. (2000). Die Methode Supervision – eine Skizze. In Pühl, H. (Hrsg.), Supervision und Organisationsentwicklung. (S. 55–69). Opladen: Leske und Budrich.

Gotthardt-Lorenz, A. (2009). Organisationssupervision – Raum für wachsende Anforderungen. In Pühl, H. (Hrsg.), Supervision und Organisationsentwicklung. Wiesbaden: VS Verlag.

Gotthardt-Lorenz, A.; Hausinger, B.; Sauer, J. (2009). Die supervisorische Forschungskompetenz. In Pühl, H. (Hrsg.), Handbuch der Supervision 3. Berlin: Ulrich Leutner Verlag.

Gotthardt, Lorenz, A. (1994 und 2000). „Organisationssupervision", Rollen und Interventionen. In Pühl, H. (Hrsg.), Handbuch der Supervision 2 (S. 365–379). Berlin: Edition Marhold.

Greif, S. (2008). Coaching und ergebnisorientierte Selbstreflexion: Theorie, Forschung und Praxis des Einzel- und Gruppencoachings. Göttingen: Hogrefe.

Grundel, U. (red) Arvas, A.. Resa in i ett samtal. Coaching på gestaltiskt vis.

Haan, E. de (2004). Coachen met collega's. Assen: Van Gorkum.

Haan, E. de (2008). Relational coaching. Chichester West Sussex: John Wiley & Sons.

Hamreby, M. (2004). Tankar om det sårbara förståndet och att försöka bevara förståndet. I Wrangsjö, B. (red). (2004). Utforska tillsammans. Handledande förhållningssätt. Stockholm: Mareld.

Hartmann, G. & Judy, M. (2005) (Hg.). Unterschiede machen. Managing Gender & Diversity in Organisationen und Gesellschaft. Edition Volkshochschule.

Hausinger, B. (2007). Zur Wirkungsforschung in der Supervision. In: Supervision, 1.2007, S. 50–54.

Hausinger, B. (2008). Wirken und Nutzen von Supervision. Verzeichnis von Evaluationen und wissenschaftlicher Arbeiten. Hrsg: DGSv. 2. überarbeitete Auflage, Kassel university press.

Hilmarsson, H. T. (2012). Coachingtrappan, en handbok i att coacha och motivera resultat. Lund: Studentlitteratur.

Hofsten, G. & Sundberg, E. M. (2004). Handledning – ett möte mellan professionella. I Wrangsjö, B. (red). (2004). Utforska tillsammans. Handledande förhållningssätt. Stockholm: Mareld.

Höjer, S. & Beijer, E. & Wissö, T. (2007). Varför handledning? Handledning som professionellt projekt och organisatoriskt verktyg inom handikappomsorg och individ och familjeomsorg. Göteborg: FoU/Väst Rapport 1:2007.

http://coachszemle.hu/media/Lapszamok/MC_2013_1.pdf, March 2, 2013

http://szupervizio.webs.com, Feb 20, 2013

http://www.coachutbildning.se/Coachetik.html

http://www.emccouncil.org/May 16, 2013

terventionen. In Pühl, H. (Hrsg.), Handbuch der Supervision 2 (S. 365–379). Berlin: Edition Marhold.

Greif, S. (2008). Coaching und ergebnisorientierte Selbstreflexion: Theorie, Forschung und Praxis des Einzel- und Gruppencoachings, Göttingen: Hogrefe.

Grundel, U., Arvas, A. (ed), (2008). Resa in i ett samtal. Coachning på gestaltiskt vis. Stockholm: Mareld

Haan, E. de (2004). Coachen met collega's. Assen: Van Gorkum.

Haan, E. de (2008). Relational coaching. Chichester West Sussex: John Wiley & Sons.

Hamreby, M. (2004). Tankar om det sårbara förståndet och att försöka bevara förståndet. I Wrangsjö, B. (ed). (2004). Utforska tillsammans. Handledande förhållningssätt. Stockholm: Mareld.

Hausinger, B. (2007). Zur Wirkungsforschung in der Supervision. In: Supervision, 1.2007: S. 50–54.

Hausinger, B. (2008). Wirken und Nutzen von Supervision. Verzeichnis von Evaluationen und wissenschaftlicher Arbeiten. Hrsg: DGSv. 2. überarbeitete Auflage: Kassel university press.

Hilmarsson, H. T. (2012). Coachingtrappan, en handbok i att coacha och motivera resultat. Lund: Studentlitteratur.

Hofsten, G. & Sundberg, E. M. (2004). Handledning – ett möte mellan professionella. I Wrangsjö, B. (ed). (2004). Utforska tillsammans. Handledande förhållningssätt. Stockholm: Mareld.

Höjer, S., Beijer, E., Wissö, T. (2007). Varför handledning? Handledning som professionellt projekt och organisatoriskt verktyg inom handikappomsorg och individ och familjeomsorg. Göteborg: FoU/Väst Rapport.

Judy, M. (2004). Tango tanzen. Psychoanalytische und systemische Konzepte zu Übertragung & Gegenübertragung. In: Brush up your Tools. Wien: Studienverlag.

Kennedy, D., Hyland, A. Ryan, N. (2006). Writing and Using Learning Outcomes: A Practical Guide. http://www.tcd.ie/teaching-learning/academic-development/assets/pdf/ Kennedy_Writing_and_Using_Learning_Outcomes.pdf), (Juni 2016).

Knopf, W. (2008). Life Long Learning: Eine politische und praktische Chance für Supervision und Coaching. BSO Journal (2008)1: 21–22. Bern.

Knopf, W., Walther, I. (Ed.)(2010). Beratung mit Hirn. Neurowissenschaftliche Erkenntnisse für die Praxis von Supervision und Coaching. Wien: Facultas.

Knopf, W., De Roos, S. (2009). The Advancement of Supervisory Learning. Science, Profession or Practical Wisdom. A dialogue between Wolfgang Knopf and Sijtze de Roos. Supervision (2009)1:23–28. Weinheim: Beltz.

Kobolt, A., Žižak, A. (2007). Timski rad i supervizija timova/Teamwork and supervision of teams. Ljetopis socialnog rada/Annual of Social Work, 14 (2), 367–386.

Korman, J. (2002). Lösningsfokus i handledning. I Söderquist, M. (ed.) (2002) Möjligheter handledning och konsultation i systemteoretiskt perspektiv. Stockholm. Mareld.

Kouwenhoven, M. (2007). Het handboek strategisch coachen. Amsterdam: Boom Nelissen.

Lingsma, M. (2005). Aan de slag met teamcoaching. Soest: Uitgeverij Nelissen.

http://www.szupervizio.eoldal.hu, Feb 20, 2013

https://nl.wikipedia.org/wiki/Coaching May 16, 2013

Judy, M. (2004). Tango tanzen. Psychoanalytische und systemische Konzepte zu Übertragung & Gegenübertragung. In: Brush up your Tools 1/2014.

Knopf, W. (2008). Life Long Learning: Eine politische und praktische Chance für Supervision und Coaching. BSO Journal (2008)1: 21.–22. Bern.

Knopf, W./Walther, I. (Hg.)(2010). Beratung mit Hirn. Neurowissenschaftliche Erkenntnisse für die Praxis von Supervision und Coaching. Wien: Facultas.

Knopf, W./Roos, S. de (2009). The Advancement of Supervisory Learning. Science, Profession or Practical Wisdom. A dialogue between Wolfgang Knopf and Sijtze de Roos. Supervision (2009)1: 23–28. Weinheim: Beltz.

Kobolt, A., Žižak, A. (2007). Timski rad i supervizija timova/Teamwork and supervision of teams.Ljetopis socijalnog rada/Annual of Social Work, 14 (2), 367–386.

Korman, J. (2002). Lösningsfokus i handledning. I Söderquist, M. (red) (2002) Möjligheter handledning och konsultation i systemteoretiskt perspektiv. Stockholm. Mareld.

Kouwenhoven, M. (2007). Het handboek strategisch coachen. Amsterdam: Boom Nelissen.

Lingsma, M. (2005). Aan de slag met teamcoaching. Soest: Uitgeverij Nelissen.

Luif I. (Hrsg.), Supervision in Österreich. Wien: Orac.

Matić, V. (2011). Razvoj odnosa u superviziji psihosocijalnog rada/Developing a relationship in supervision of psychosocial work.Ljetopis socijalnog rada/Annual of Social Work, 18 (2), 217–244.

Michels, H. & Looss, W. (2006). Unter vier Augen. Coaching für Manager. EHP – Organisation.

Migge, B. (2005). Handbuch Coaching und Beratung, Weinheim: Beltz.

Milowiz, W. (2009). Teufelskreis und Lebensweg – Systemisch denken im sozialen Feld. Goettingen: Vandehoeck & Ruprecht.

Mohr, G. (2006). Systemische Organisationsanalyse. EHP (2009).

Möller, H. (2001). Was ist gute Supervision? Stuttgart: Klett-Cotta.

Möller, H., Hausinger, B. (2009). Quo Vadis Beratungswissenschaft? Wiesbaden: VS Verlag für Sozialwissenschaften.

Moltke, H. V., och Molly, A. (red). (2011). Systemisk coaching en grundbok. Lund: Studentlitteratur.

Münch, W. (2011). Tiefenhermeneutische Beratung und Supervision: Konzeptualisierung und Praxisreflexion, Brandes und Apses.

Näslund, J. & Ögren, M-L. (ed) (2010). Grupphandledning. Forskning och erfarenheter från olika verksamhetsområden. Lund. Studentlitteratur.

Neuberger, O. (2006). Mikropolitik und Moral in Organisationen. Herausforderung der Ordnung, Stuttgart: UTB.

Olson, H. & Arnoldsson, Ch. (2010). Samtal kring handledning. Erfarenheter och reflektioner. Lund: Studentlitteratur.

Pechtl, W. (1995). Zwischen Organismus und Organisation, Wegweiser und Modelle

Luif, I. (Hrsg.), (1997). Supervision in Österreich. Wien: Orac.

Matić, V. (2011). Razvoj odnosa u superviziji psihosocijalnog rada/Developing a relationship in supervision of psychosocial work.Ljetopis socijalnog rada/Annual of Social Work, 18 (2), 217–244.

Michels, H. und Looss, W. (2006). Unter vier Augen. Coaching für Manager. EHP – Organisation.

Migge, B. (2005). Handbuch Coaching und Beratung, Weinheim: Beltz.

Milowiz, W. (2009). Teufelskreis und Lebensweg – Systemisch denken im sozialen Feld. Göttingen: Vandenhoeck & Ruprecht.

Mohr, G. (2006). Systemische Organisationsanalyse. Köln: Edition Humanistische Psychologie.

Möller, H. (2001). Was ist gute Supervision? Stuttgart: Klett-Cotta.

Möller, H., Hausinger, B. (2009). Quo Vadis Beratungswissenschaft? VS Verlag für Sozialwissenschaften Moltke.

Molly, A. (ed). (2011). Systemisk coaching en grundbok. Lund: Studentlitteratur.

Münch, W. (2011). Tiefenhermeneutische Beratung und Supervision: Konzeptualisierung und Praxisreflexion. Frankfurt/Main: Brandes und Apsel.

Näslund, J., Ögren, M-L. (ed) (2010). Grupphandledning. Forskning och erfarenheter från olika verksamhetsområden. Lund. Studentlitteratur.

Neuberger, O. (2006). Mikropolitik und Moral in Organisationen. Herausforderung der Ordnung, UTB.

Olson, H., Arnoldsson, Ch. (2010). Samtal kring handledning. Erfarenheter och reflektioner. Lund: Studentlitteratur.

Pechtl, W. (1995). Zwischen Organismus und Organisation, Wegweiser und Modelle für Berater und Führungskräfte, Wien: Veritas.

Pertoft, M., Larsen, B. (2003). Grupphandledning med yrkesverksamma i människovård. Stockholm: Liber.

Petitt, B. (2002). Reflektion. I Söderquist, M. (ed). (2002). Möjligheter handledning och konsultation i systemteoretiskt perspektiv: Stockholm. Mareld.

Petzold, H. (2005). Supervision in der Altenarbeit. Paderborn: Junfermann.

Petzold, H. (2005). „Beratung" als Disziplin und Praxeologie zum Umgang mit subjektiven Theorien. In: Beratung Aktuell (2005) 1: 4–21.

Petzold, H.(1998). Integrative Supervision, Meta-Consulting, Organisationsentwicklung: Ein Handbuch für Modelle und Methoden reflexiver Praxis, Paderborn: Junfermann.

Pol, I.G.M. van (2012). Coachen als professie. Den Haag: Boom Lemma Uitgevers.

Praag-van Asperen, H.M. van, Praag, Ph.H. van (2000). Handboek supervisie en intervisie. Leusden: De Tijdstroom.

Pühl, H. (2012). Handbuch der Supervision 3. Berlin: Wissenschaftsverlag Spiess.

Pühl, H. (Ed.) (2012). Supervision und Organisationsentwicklung. Handbuch 3. Opladen: Leske u. Budrich.

Rappe-Giesecke, K. (2009). Supervision für Gruppen und Teams, Heidelberg: Springer, 4. ed.

Rappe-Giesecke, K. (1999). Supervision – Veränderung durch soziale Selbstreflexion.

für Berater und Führungskräfte, Veritas, 1995, zit. nach Tippe/Jakob, oe263, 2012, unveröffentlichtes Manuskript.

Pertoft, M. & Larsen, B. (2003). Grupphandledning med yrkesverksamma i människovård. Stockholm: Liber.

Petitt, B. (2002). Reflektion. I Söderquist, M. (red). (2002). Möjligheter handledning och konsultation i systemteoretiskt perspektiv: Stockholm. Mareld.

Petzold, H. (2005). Supervision in der Altenarbeit. Junfermann, Paderborn.

Petzold, H. (2005). „Beratung" als Disziplin und Praxeologie zum Umgang mit subjektiven Theorien.

Petzold, H. (1998). Integrative Supervision, Meta-Consulting, Organisationsentwicklung: Ein Handbuch für Modelle und Methoden reflexiver Praxis, Junfermann Paderborn.

Pol, I.G.M. van (2012). Coachen als professie. Den Haag: Boom Lemma Uitgevers.

Praag-van Asperen, H.M. van en Praag, Ph.H. van (2000). Handboek supervisie en intervisie. Leusden: De Tijdstroom.

Pühl, H. (2012). Handbuch der Supervision 3. Berlin: Wissenschaftsverlag Spiess.

Pühl, H. (Hg.) (2012). Supervision und Organisationsentwicklung. Handbuch, 3. Opladen: Leske u. Budrich.

Rappe-Giesecke, K. (2009). Supervision für Gruppen und Teams, Heidelberg: Springer, 4. ed.

Rappe-Gieseke, K. (1999). Supervision – Veränderung durch soziale Selbstreflexion. In: Fatzer, Gerhard u.a.: Qualität und Leistung von Beratung (Supervision,Coaching, Organisationsentwicklung). Edition Humanistische Psychologie.

Rittershausen, K. (2010). Coaching, empowerment and health A literature review Examensarbete i Folkhälsovetenskap, C- nivå, 15 hp VT 2010 Högskolan i Skövde: Institutionen för vård och natur.

Sárvári, Gy. (1996). Az európai és az angolszász szupervíziós gyakorlat néhány eltérése a szupervízió folyamattanulásának tükrében. In: Louis van Kessel, Sárvári György (szerk.): Tanulmányok a szupervízió köréből. Supervisio Hungarica.

Schattenhofer, K. (2009). Was ist eine Gruppe? Verschiedene Sichtweisen und Unterscheidungen, in: Edding/Schattenhofer (Hg) (2009). Handbuch: Alles über Gruppen, Weinheim/Basel.

Siegers, F. (2002). Handboek supervisiekunde. Houten/Mechelen: Bohn Stafleu Van Loghum.

Söderquist, M. (red). (2002). Möjligheter handledning och konsultation i systemteoretiskt perspektiv. Stockholm: Mareld.

Ståhl, F. (2004). Det personliga ställningstagandet. I Wrangsjö, B. (red). (2004). Utforska tillsammans. Handledande förhållningssätt. Stockholm: Mareld.

Steinhardt, K. (2005). Psychoanalytisch orientierte Supervision. Auf dem Weg zu einer Profession? Zur historischen, professionstheoretischen und empirischen Fundierung von psychoanalytisch orientierter Supervision, Psychosozialer Verlag Gießen.

Stiwne, D. (red). (1993). Perspektiv på handledning i psykoterapi och avgränsande områden. Stockholm: Natur & Kultur.

Stumpf, S./Thomas, A. (Hrsg.) (2003). Teamarbeit und Teamentwicklung, Hogrefe.

In: Fatzer, Gerhard u. a.: Qualität und Leistung von Beratung (Supervision, Coaching, Organisationsentwicklung). Köln: Edition Humanistische Psychologie.

Rittershausen, K. (2010). Coaching, empowerment and health A literature review Examensarbete i Folkhälsovetenskap, C- nivå, 15 hp VT 2010 Högskolan i Skövde: Institutionen för vård och natur.

Sárvári, Gy. (1996). Az európai és az angolszász szupervíziós gyakorlat néhány eltérése a szupervízió folyamattanulásának tükrében. In: Louis van Kessel, Sárvári György (szerk.): Tanulmányok a szupervízió köréből. Supervisio Hungarica.

Schattenhofer, K. (2009). Was ist eine Gruppe? Verschiedene Sichtweisen und Unterscheidungen, in: Edding/Schattenhofer (ed) (2009). Handbuch: Alles über Gruppen, Weinheim/Basel.

Schlippe, A. von, Schweitzer, J. (2006). Lehrbuch der systemischen Therapie und Beratung. Göttingen: Vandenhoeck & Ruprecht.

Schwing, R., Fryszer, A. (2012). Systemisches Handwerk. Werkzeug für die Praxis. Göttingen: Vandenhoeck & Ruprecht.

Siegers, F. (2002). Handboek supervisiekunde. Houten/Mechelen: Bohn Stafleu Van Loghum.

Söderquist, M. (ed). (2002). Möjligheter handledning och konsultation i systemteoretiskt perspektiv. Stockholm: Mareld.

Ståhl, F. (2004). Det personliga ställningstagandet. I Wrangsjö, B. (ed). (2004). Utforska tillsammans. Handledande förhållningssätt. Stockholm: Mareld.

Steinhardt, K. (2005). Psychoanalytisch orientierte Supervision. Auf dem Weg zu einer Profession? Zur historischen, professionstheoretischen und empirischen Fundierung von psychoanalytisch orientierter Supervision, Gießen: Psychosozialer Verlag.

Stiwne, D. (ed). (1993). Perspektiv på handledning i psykoterapi och avgränsande områden. Stockholm: Natur & Kultur.

Stumpf, S., Thomas, A. (Hrsg.) (2003). Teamarbeit und Teamentwicklung. Göttingen: Hogrefe.

Tatschl, S. (2009). Reflektiranje – ključna kompetencija u superviziji. In: Ajdukovic, M. (Ed.) Reflection about supervision: International perspective. Zagreb: Faculty of Law. Department of Social Work, 49–66.

Tatschl, S. (1997). Organisationssupervision und Organisationskompetenz als Antwort auf Herausforderungen des Wandels von Sozialen Organisationen. In: Luif I. (Hrsg.), Supervision in Österreich. Wien: Orac.

Tippe, A. (2008). Veränderung stabilisieren. Strategische Teamentwicklung als Führungsaufgabe zur Stabilisierung von Organisationsentwicklungsprozessen. Heidelberg: Carl-Auer-Verlag.

Tomić, V. (2011). Razine odgovornosti u supervizijskim odnosima/Levels of responsibilities in supervision relationships. Ljetopis socijalnog rada, Annual of Social Work, 18 (2), 245–280.

Tuđa Družinec, Lj. (2011). Utjecaj profesionalnog iskustva supervizora i konteksta na supervizijski proces u pomažućim profesijama/Influence of professional experience of supervisor and context to the supervision process to helping professions. Ljetopis socijalnog rada/Annual of Social Work, 18 (2), 333–363.

Tatschl, S (2009). Reflektiranje – klju na kompetencija u superviziji. In: Ajdukovic, M. (Ed.) Reflection about supervision: International perspective. Zagreb: Faculty of Law. Department of Social Work, 49–66.

Tatschl, S. (1997). Organisationssupervision und Organisationskompetenz als Antwort auf Herausforderungen des Wandels von Sozialen Organisationen. In: Luif I. (Hrsg.), Supervision in Österreich. Wien: Orac.

Tippe, A. (2008). Veränderung stabilisieren. Strategische Teamentwicklung als Führungsaufgabe zur Stabilisierung von Organisationsentwicklungsprozessen. Heidelberg: Carl-Auer-Verlag.

Tomić, V. (2011). Razine odgovornosti u supervizijskim odnosima/Levels of responsibilities in supervision relationships. Ljetopis socijalnog rada/Annual of Social Work, 18 (2), 245–280.

Tuđa Družinec, Lj. (2011). Utjecaj profesionalnog iskustva supervizora i konteksta na supervizijski proces u pomažu im profesijama/Influence of professional experience of supervisor and context to the supervision process to helping professions.Ljetopis socijalnog rada/Annual of Social Work, 18 (2), 333–363.

Tveiten, S. (2010). Yrkesmässig handledning – mer än ord. Lund: Studentlitteratur. Lund.

Vad är coaching? http://www.coachstjarnan.se/vad_ar_coaching.php

van Kessel, L. (2007). Coaching, a field for professional supervisors. Ljetopis socijalnog rada/Annual of Social Work, 14 (2), 387–431.

van Kessel, L./Fellermann, J. (2000). Supervision and Coaching in a European Perspective. Proceedings of the ANSE-Conference 2000, www.anse.eu, June 2013.

Vandamme, R. (2003). Handboek ontwikkelingsgericht coachen. Soest: Uitgeverij Nelissen.

Vizek Vidović, V., Vlahović Štetić, V. (2007). Modeli učenja odraslih i profesionalni razvoj/Models of adult learning and professional development. Ljetopis socijalnog rada/Annual of Social Work, 14 (2), 283– 310.

Watzlawick, P., Beavin, J., Jackson, D. (2011). Pragmatics of Human Communication: A Study of Interactional Patterns, Pathologies, and Paradoxes. W.W. Norton & Co.

Weigand, W. (2012). Beitrag der Zeitschriften zur Professionalisierung von Supervision – Felderkundungen, in: Forum Supervision, Heft 40, Oktober 2012.

Weigand, W. (2011). Organisation verstehen, in: Supervision, 01/2011.

Weigand, W. (2009). Methodenfetischismus und Angstabwehr, in: Harald Pühl (Hrsg), Handbuch der Supervision 3, Berlin 2009.

Weigand, W. (2006): Neue Herausforderungen an die Profession Supervision, in: Supervision 01/2006.

Wendel, B. http://keycoaching.net/coach/om-coaching/

Wikberg, E. (2010). Organisering av en ny Marknad- en studie av den Svenska coachningsmarknaden. Score; Stockholm: Stockholm centre for organisational research.

Wikipedia: "Supervision", http://de.wikipedia.org/wiki/Supervision, 30.05.2012

Wikipedia: "Coaching", http://de.wikipedia.org/wiki/Coaching, 30.05.2012

Tveiten, S. (2010). Yrkesmässig handledning – mer än ord. Lund: Studentlitteratur. Lund.

Van Kessel, L. (2007). Coaching, a field for professional supervisors. Ljetopis socijalnog rada/Annual of Social Work, 14 (2), 387–431.

Van Kessel, L., Fellermann, J. (2000). Supervision and Coaching in a European Perspective. Proceedings of the ANSE-Conference 2000, www.anse.eu, (Juni 2013).

Vandamme, R. (2003). Handboek ontwikkelingsgericht coachen. Soest: Uitgeverij Nelissen.

Vizek Vidović, V., Vlahović Štetić, V. (2007). Modeli učenja odraslih i profesionalni razvoj/Models of adult learning and professional development. Ljetopis socijalnog rada/Annual of Social Work, 14 (2), 283– 310.

Watzlawick, P., Beavin, J., Jackson, D. (2011). Pragmatics of Human Communication: A Study of Interactional Patterns, Pathologies, and Paradoxes. W.W. Norton & Co.

Weigand, W. (2012). Beitrag der Zeitschriften zur Professionalisierung von Supervision – Felderkundungen, in: Forum Supervision, Heft 40, Oktober 2012.

Weigand, W. (2011). Organisation verstehen, in: Supervision, 01/2011.

Weigand, W. (2009). Methodenfetischismus und Angstabwehr, in: Harald Pühl (Hrsg), Handbuch der Supervision 3, Berlin.

Weigand, W. (2006). Neue Herausforderungen an die Profession Supervision, in: Supervision 01/2006.

Wikberg, E. (2009). Organisering av en ny Marknad- en studie av den Svenska coachningsmarknaden. Score; Stockholm: Stockholm centre for organizational research.

Wimmer, R. (2004). Organisation und Beratung. Systemtheoretische Perspektiven für die Praxis. Heidelberg: Carl-Auer-Verlag.

Wirtberg, I. (2002). Att ge och ta emot handledledning. I Söderquist, M. (ed) (2002) Möjligheter handledning och konsultation i systemteoretiskt perspektiv. Stockholm: Mareld.

Wrangsjö, B. (ed). (2004). Utforska tillsammans. Handledande förhållningssätt. Stockholm: Mareld.

Žižak, A., Vizek Vidović, V., Ajduković, M. (2012). Interpersonalna komunikacija u profesionalnom kontekstu/Interpersonal communication in professional context. Zagreb: Edukacijsko-rehabilitacijski fakultet.

Žorga, S. (2009). Specifičnosti učenja u superviziji. In: Ajdukovic, M. (ed.) Refleksije o superviziji: Međunarodna perspektiva./Reflection about supervision: International perspective. Zagreb: Faculty of Law. Department of Social Work, 49–66.

Curricula

Curriculum Coaching, Chr. Rauen Coaching, http://www.rauen.de/ (Dez. 2012).

Curriculum Supervision & Coaching (2012), Katholische Stiftungsfachhochschule München, http://www.ksfh.de/studiengaenge (Dez. 2012).

Curriculum Supervision & Coaching Tops München-Berlin e.V., http://www.tops-ev.de/ (Feb. 2015).

Wimmer, R. (2004). Organisation und Beratung. SystemtheoretischePerspektiven für die Praxis. Heidelberg: Carl-Auer-Systeme.

Wirtberg, I. (2002). Att ge och ta emot handledledning. I Söderquist, M. (red) (2002) Möjligheter handledning och konsultation i systemteoretiskt perspektiv. Stockholm: Mareld.

Wrangsjö, B. (red). (2004). Utforska tillsammans. Handledande förhållningssätt. Stockholm: Mareld.

Wrangsjö, B. (red). (2004). Att utforska tillsammans. Handledande förhållningssätt. Stockholm: Mareld.

Žižak, A., Vizek Vidovi , V., Ajdukovi , M. (2012). Interpersonalna komunikacija u profesionalnom kontekstu/Interpersonal communication in professional context. Zagreb: Edukacijsko-rehabilitacijski fakultet.

Žorga, S. (2009). Specifičnosti učenja u superviziji. In: Ajdukovic, M. (ed.) Refleksije o superviziji: Međunarodna perspektiva./Reflection about supervision: International perspective. Zagreb: Faculty of Law. Department of Social Work, 49–66.

www.ageracoaching.se
www.anse.eu
www.assp.sk
www.bso.ch
www.coachfederation.org
www.coachfederation.org, May 14, 2013
www.dgsv.de
www.drustvozasupervizijo.si
www.hdsor.hr
www.hrcafe.eu/temakor/szupervizio, Febr 20, 2013
www.ispa-supervision.org
www.lfi.hu/coaching-vs-szupervizio.html, Febr 20, 2013
www.lvsc.eu
www.lvsc.eu Date of visit: 16th of May 2013
www.nobco.nl Date of visit: 16th of May 2013
www.nosco.no
www.oevs.or.at
www.sai.ir
www.supervision-coaching.it
www.supervizare.com
www.supervizija.lv
www.szupervizio.lap.hu, Febr 20, 2013
www.szupervizorok.hu, Febr 20, 2013
www.wikipedia.hu, Jan 21, 2013

Curriculum Supervision & Coaching, Universität Wien, http://www.postgraduatecenter. at/suco (Juni 2014).

Curriculum Supervision in Social Work, University of Zagreb, http://www.unizg.hr/ homepage/ (Mai 2015).

Curriculum, Systemische Supervision & Coaching (2014), Arbeitskreis für Systemische Sozialarbeit, Beratung und Supervision(ASYS), www.asys.ac.at (Juni 2014).

Curriculum Trainingsprogramma Coaching Alba Academie, https://www.alba-academie.nl/ (Feb. 2013).

Curriculum Trainingsprogramma Coaching Hanze Hogeschool Groningen, https:// www.hanze.nl/nld (Feb. 2013).

Curriculum Trainingsprogramma Supervisiekunde (2008), Hanze hogeschool Groningen, https://www.hanze.nl/nld (Feb. 2013).

http://www.coachingverband.org (Mai 2012)
http://coachszemle.hu/media/Lapszamok/MC_2013_1.pdf (März 2013)
http://www.dbvc.de (Mai 2012)
http://szupervizio.webs.com (Feb. 2013)
http://www.coachutbildning.se/Coachetik.html (Mai 2013)
http://www.coachstjarnan.se/vad_ar_coaching.php (Feb. 2013)
http://www.ecvet-info.at/de/node/2 (Juni 2015)
http://www.emccouncil.org/ (Mai 2013)
http://www.szupervizio.eoldal.hu (Feb. 2013)
https://www.be-twin2.eu/en/ (Nov. 2012)
https://nl.wikipedia.org/wiki/Coaching (Mai 2013)
www.ageracoaching.se (Mai 2013)
www.anse.eu (Mai 2013)
www.assp.sk (Mai 2013)
www.bso.ch (Mai 2013)
www.coachfederation.org (Mai 2013)
www.dgsf.de (Mai 2012)
www.dgsv.de (Mai 2012)
www.drustvozasupervizijo.si (Mai 2013)
www.hdsor.hr (Feb. 2013)
www.hrcafe.eu/temakor/szupervizio (Feb. 2013)
www.ispa-supervision.org (Feb. 2013)
http://keycoaching.net/coach/om-coaching/ (Jan. 2014)
www.lfi.hu/coaching-vs-szupervizio.html (Feb. 2013)
www.lvsc.eu (Feb. 2013)
www.lvsc.eu (Mai 2013)
www.nobco.nl (Mai 2013)
www.nosco.no (Feb. 2013)
www.oevs.or.at (Feb. 2013)
www.sai.ir (Feb. 2013)
www.supervision-coaching.it (Feb. 2013)
www.supervizare.com (Feb. 2013)
www.supervizija.lv (Feb. 2013)
www.szupervizio.lap.hu (Feb. 2013)
www.szupervizorok.hu (Feb. 2013)
https://www.wikipedia.org/

The Project Team – Biographies

Marina Ajduković, Zagreb, Croatia

Marina Ajduković (Department of Social Work, Faculty of Law, University of Zagreb) is a Ph.D. psychologist, university professor, family therapist and licensed supervisor. She is head of the Chair for social work and head of the Doctoral programme in social work and social policy. Her main teaching and research foci are critical social work, child abuse and neglection, intimate partner violence, group work and supervision.

Regarding Supervision, she significantly contributed to development and sustainability of supervision in Croatia. Marina Ajduković led the first education for supervisors from 2001 to 2004. She has developed the first 120 ECTS Postgraduate master programme in Supervision that has continually been carried out from 2006. Together with L. Cajvert, she is co-editor of the first university textbooks on supervision in Croatian and author of numerous articles on supervision. As an editor of the Croatian journal „Social Work Annual" she has prepared two thematic issues dealing with supervision (2007 and 2011). She has organised four national conferences on supervision with international participation (2004, 2006, 2008, and 2012).

Marina Ajduković was president of the Croatian Association for Supervision and Organisational Development from 2004 to 2012.

http://www.unizg.hr/homepage/

Lilja Cajvert, Gothenburg, Sweden

Lilja Cajvert (Department of Social Work at the University of Gothenburg) is a senior lecturer in social work, social worker, licensed psychotherapist, supervisor in psychosocial work and supervisor in family therapy. She is co-ordinator of the training course "Supervised Field Work", meta supervisor of the supervision training programme at the Department of Social Work, University of Gothenburg.

She initiated and led the first education for supervisors in Bosnia and Herze-govina (Tuzla and Sarajevo, 1998–2000). From 2001 to 2004 she was a

Projekt-Team – Biografien

Marina Ajduković, Zagreb, Kroatien

Fachbereich Soziale Arbeit, Rechtswissenschaftliche Fakultät, Universität Zagreb, Dr. phil., Psychologin, Universitätsprofessorin, Familientherapeutin und Supervisorin. Sie ist Inhaberin des Lehrstuhls für Sozialarbeit und Leiterin des Doktoratsstudiums Sozialarbeit und Sozialpolitik. Schwerpunkte ihrer Lehr- und Forschungstätigkeit sind kritische Sozialarbeit, Missbrauch und Vernachlässigung, Gewalt in der Familie, Gruppenarbeit und Supervision.

In Bezug auf Supervision trug sie wesentlich zur Entwicklung und Nachhaltigkeit der Supervision in Kroatien bei. Marina Ajduković leitete die erste Ausbildung für Supervision von 2001 bis 2004. Sie hat den ersten 120 ECTS umfassenden postgradualen Master-Studiengang Supervision entwickelt, der seit 2006 läuft. Sie ist mit L. Cajvert Mitherausgeberin der ersten Hochschullehrbücher für Supervision in kroatischer Sprache und Autorin zahlreicher Artikel über Supervision.

Als Redakteurin der kroatischen Zeitschrift „Soziale Arbeit" hat sie zwei Themenschwerpunkte zu Supervision (2007 und 2011) gestaltet. Sie hat vier nationale Konferenzen über Supervision mit internationaler Beteiligung (2004, 2006, 2008 und 2012) organisiert. Marina Ajduković war 2004–2012 Präsidentin der Kroatischen Gesellschaft für Supervision und Organisationsentwicklung.

http://www.unizg.hr/homepage/

Lilja Cajvert, Göteborg, Schweden

Dozentin für Sozialarbeit (Fachbereich Soziale Arbeit an der Universität Göteborg), lizenzierte Psychotherapeutin, Supervisorin in der psychosozialen Arbeit und Familientherapie. Sie ist Koordinatorin des Lehrgangs „Supervidierte Feldarbeit", sowie Lehrtrainerin und Lehrsupervisorin des Trainingsprogramms für Supervision am Institut für Soziale Arbeit, Univ. Göteborg.

Sie initiierte und leitete die erste Ausbildung für Supervision in Bosnien-Herzegowina (Tuzla und Sarajevo, 1998–2000). Von 2001 bis 2004 war sie

teacher, supervisor and consultant in the first education for supervisors "Introducing supervision in the social welfare system in Croatia". From 2005 to 2009 she was the project leader of two postgraduate master programmes in Bosnia and Herzegovina – "Supervision in Psychosocial Work" and "Management in Social Work".

Lilja Cajvert has developed her own model of supervision – working with unconscious processes in supervision – that she has described in articles and textbooks in Swedish, English, Croatian and Slovenian.

Lilja Cajvert was president of the Swedish Association for Supervisors for four years.

http://www.socwork.gu.se/kontaktaoss/Personlig_hemsida/Lilja_Cajvert/

Michaela Judy, Vienna, Austria

Michaela Judy studied literature, cultural management and educational management. Additionally, she is a trainer and instructor of group dynamics, supervisor (ÖVS) and coach.

For more than 20 years, she was the manager of an adult education center (Volkshochschule Ottakring, Vienna). At present, she is personnel developer and project manager at Die Wiener Volkshochschulen GmbH.

Additionally, she works as a freelance trainer, supervisor and coach with a focus on management in non-profit organisations, systemic approach and (managing) gender & diversity.

Lectureships at universities and adult education institutions.

Member of ASYS (Arbeitskreis für systemische Sozialarbeit, Beratung und Supervision), course director of the postgraduate course „Systemic Supervision" of ASYS.

Michaela Judy has edited two books and has published several articles.

http://members.aon.at/mjudy/judy.htm

Wolfgang Knopf, Vienna, Austria/EU

Studied social sciences at the University of Vienna and Innsbruck, finished 1983 with Ph.D. (Pedagogics/Psychology) Group Dynamics (1998–99), Sexual Therapy (1990–92), Supervision and Counselling (1992–95), Organisational Development (2001), Systemic Counselling (1999–2001).

Assistant Professor at University of Graz (1984–1994) at the Department for Further Education; Lector at University of Klagenfurt (1983–1984; 1998–2005), Institute for Interdisciplinary Studies at the Universities of Graz, Innsbruck, Klagenfurt and Vienna (1994–1998), University of Graz (1984–1993), University of Vienna (1993–1994; 2004; 2006–2011), University of Technology Vienna (1996–2001, 2006), University of Innsbruck (1998–

Lehrerin, Supervisorin und Beraterin in der ersten Ausbildung für SupervisorInnen „Einführung in die Supervision im Sozialsystem in Kroatien". Von 2005 bis 2009 war sie Projektleiterin der zwei Postgraduate Master-Studiengänge „Supervision in Psychosozialer Arbeit" und „Management in der Sozialen Arbeit" in Bosnien-Herzegowina.

Lilja Cajvert hat ihr eigenes Modell der Supervision entwickelt – die Arbeit mit unbewussten Prozessen in der Supervision – das sie in Artikeln und Lehrbüchern auf Schwedisch, Englisch, Kroatisch und Slowenisch beschrieben hat. Lilja Cajvert war vier Jahre lang Präsidentin der Schwedischen Vereinigung für Supervision.

http://www.socwork.gu.se/kontaktaoss/Personlig_hemsida/Lilja_Cajvert/

Michaela Judy, Wien, Österreich

Studierte Literaturwissenschaft, Kulturmanagement und Bildungsmanagement. Trainerin und Ausbildnerin in Gruppendynamik, Supervisorin (ÖVS) und Coach. Mehr als 20 Jahre war sie Managerin der Volkshochschule Ottakring in Wien. Derzeit ist sie Personalentwicklerin und Projektleiterin bei der VHS Wien. Darüber hinaus arbeitet sie als freiberufliche Trainerin, Supervisorin und Coach mit den Schwerpunkten Management in Non-Profit-Organisationen, systemisch Denken und Beraten, und (Managing) Gender & Diversity. Lehraufträge an Universitäten als auch an Einrichtungen der Erwachsenenbildung. Mitglied von ASYS (Arbeitskreis für systemische Sozialarbeit, Beratung und Supervision), Leiterin des Lehrgangs „Systemische Supervision & Coaching" von ASYS.

Michaela Judy hat zwei Bücher herausgegeben und mehrere Artikel veröffentlicht.

http://members.aon.at/mjudy/judy.htm

Wolfgang Knopf, Wien, Österreich/EU

Studium der Sozialwissenschaften an den Universitäten Wien und Innsbruck, abgeschlossen 1983 mit Dr. phil. (Pädagogik/Psychologie). Ausbildungen in Gruppendynamik, Sexualtherapie, Supervision und Beratung, Organisationsentwicklung, Systemischer Beratung.

Lektor an den Universitäten Graz, Klagenfurt, Linz, Innsbruck, Wien, der Technischen Universität Wien und Krems, an der Fachhochschule für Sozialarbeit und der Akademie für Sozialarbeit in Wien. Fächer: Pädagogik, Didaktik, Kommunikation, Gruppendynamik, Politische Bildung, Beratung usw.

Seit 1994 ist er freischaffender Supervisor, Coach und Management-Trainer. Verantwortlich für Design und Management-Kurse für TrainerInnen in den verschiedenen Arbeitsbereichen auf nationaler und internationaler Ebene

2003), University of Linz (2010–2011), University Krems (2006), College of Higher Education for Social Work Vienna (2001–2006) and Academy of Social Work Vienna (1994–2002) for subjects: pedagogy, didactics, communication, group dynamics, civic education, counselling etc.

Since 1994 he is a freelance supervisor, coach and management trainer.

Responsible for design and management courses for trainers in different work fields on national and international level and for supervisors and coaches.

Together with K. Steinhardt he is leading the postgraduate programme 'Supervision and Coaching' at the University of Vienna.

Wolfgang Knopf was President of the Austrian Association for Supervision (ÖVS) from 2004 to 2010 and President of the European Association for Supervision (ANSE) from 2006 to 2014.

www.systeam.at/personen/vknopf.htm

Hubert Kuhn, Munich, Germany

Born in 1963, Bavaria, Germany. Married, two children.

Independent organisational consultant, supervisor, management coach and -trainer both in national and international context, with main foci on team diversity, group dynamics and conflict solving, numerous publications since 2000. Associated with TOPS München-Berlin e.V. since 2000.

Qualifications:

- Diploma in Economics
- Trainer for group dynamics (DAGG), leading and consulting of groups, 6 years advanced training, DAGG, German Association of Group Psychotherapy and Group Dynamics,
- Coach/Supervisor, German Association of Coaching/Supervision; DGSv, since 2008 Senior Coach DGSv for three vocational training institutes for supervision,
- Systemic therapist and consultant, Institute for Systemic Therapy and Organisational Consulting,
- Organisational consulting, change management; mediation, nonviolent communication; transaction analysis and other methods.

www.hubertkuhn.de

Krisztina Madai, Budapest, Hungary

Krisztina Madai (self-employed) is ICF credentialed coach and licensed supervisor. Her first degrees are MBA in economic sciences and MA in applied psychology and gender studies. She is the co-founder and leader of the internationally accredited coach training programme 'CoachAkademia' in Hungary. She is a lecturer at the Supervision Training Program at Karoli

und für Supervision und Coaching. Zusammen mit K. Steinhardt leitet er das Aufbaustudium „Supervision und Coaching" an der Universität Wien. Wolfgang Knopf war 2004–2010 Präsident der Österreichischen Gesellschaft für Supervision (ÖVS) und 2006–2014 Präsident der Europäischen Vereinigung für Supervision (ANSE).
www.systeam.at/personen/vKnopf.htm

Hubert Kuhn, München, Deutschland

Geboren 1963 in Bayern, Deutschland. Verheiratet, zwei Kinder.
Freiberuflicher Organisationsberater, Supervisor, Management-Coach und -Trainer sowohl im nationalen als auch im internationalen Kontext, Schwerpunkte Team-Diversity, Gruppendynamik und Konfliktlösung seit 2000.
Zahlreiche Publikationen. Mit TOPS München-Berlin e.V. verbunden seit dem Jahr 2000.
Qualifikationen:
- Diplom-Volkswirt
- Trainer für Gruppendynamik (DAGG), Leiten und Beraten von Gruppen, 6 Jahre Weiterbildung, DAGG (Deutsche Arbeitsgemeinschaft für Gruppendynamik und Gruppenpsychotherapie)
- Coach/Supervisor gem. Bundesverband für Supervision und Coaching; DGSv, seit 2008 Lehrsupervisor DGSv in drei Supervisionsausbildungen.
- Systemischer Therapeut und Berater, Institut für Systemische Therapie und Organisationsberatung,
- Organisationsberatung, Change Management; Mediation, Gewaltfreie Kommunikation; Transaktionsanalyse und andere Methoden.
www.hubertkuhn.de

Krisztina Madai, Budapest, Ungarn

Krisztina Madai ist selbständig tätig als ICF akkredidierter Coach und lizenzierte Supervisorin. MBA in Wirtschaftswissenschaften und MA in angewandter Psychologie und Gender Studies. Sie ist Mitbegründerin und Leiterin des international akkreditierten Train-the-Trainer-Programms „Coach Akademia" in Ungarn. Sie ist Dozentin der Supervisionsausbildung an der Karoli-Universität Budapest und in mehreren anderen privaten Trainerausbildungen in Ungarn.
Die Schwerpunkte ihrer Lehr- und Forschungstätigkeit sind Kontrakt, Coach-Klient-Beziehung, organisatorische Kontexte von Coaching und Supervision und Gender-Fragen in Organisationen.
Krisztina Madai ist Co-Autorin des Buches „Methodisches Handbuch für Coaches II" und ihre Artikel über Coaching und Supervision erscheinen in

University and at several other private coach training programmes in Hungary. Her main teaching and research foci are contracting, coach-client relationship, organisational context in coaching and supervision and gender issues in organisations.

Krisztina Madai is co-author of the book 'Methodological handbook for coaches II' and her articles on coaching and supervision appear in the Hungarian online coaching journal 'Magyar Coachszemle'. Her mission is to work on the quality assurance of coaching in Hungary, first of all by introducing the importance of supervision for coaches and organising workshops with the leading of master coaches from around the world. She was co-organiser of the first Hungarian coaching conference in Hungary.

http://www.coachakademia.hu

Mieke Voogd, Eelde, Netherlands

Mieke Voogd (1965) is owner of Coachkwadraat, a network company for coaching, supervision and organisational development in the north of the Netherlands. This company was established in 2006.

Mieke is trained as an organisational psychologist and has worked as a consultant for nearly 20 years in various profit and non-profit organisations.

During that period she trained and registered as a supervisor. Mieke has a strong interest for research on coaching and supervision.

Since 2009 she is chairwoman of the scientific committee of the Dutch association of supervision and coaching (LVSC).

http://www.coachkwadraat.nl/

der ungarischen Online-Coaching Zeitschrift „Magyar Coachszemle".
Ihre Mission ist die Qualitätssicherung von Coaching in Ungarn, vor allem durch forcieren der Bedeutung der Supervision für TrainerInnen und die Organisation von Workshops unter der Leitung von Master Coaches aus der ganzen Welt. Sie war Co-Organisatorin der ersten Coaching-Konferenz in Ungarn.
http://www.coachakademia.hu

Mieke Voogd, Eelde, Niederlande

Mieke Voogd (1965) ist Inhaberin von Coachkwadraat, einem Netzwerkunternehmen für Coaching, Supervision und Organisationsentwicklung im Norden der Niederlande. Das Unternehmen wurde 2006 gegründet.
Mieke ist ausgebildete Organisationspsychologin und registrierte Supervisorin und Coach; sie ist als Beraterin seit fast 20 Jahren in verschiedenen Profit- und Non-Profit-Organisationen tätig.
Mieke hat ein starkes Interesse an Forschung zu Coaching und Supervision. Seit 2009 ist sie Vorsitzende des wissenschaftlichen Ausschusses der niederländischen Vereinigung für Supervision und Coaching (LVSC).
http://www.coachkwadraat.nl/

An Overview of Supervision and Coaching in Austria, Croatia, Germany, Hungary, Sweden, The Netherlands and Europe

Wolfgang Knopf

ANSE – History and Goals

From 1975, supervision became an increasingly professional means of process-oriented consulting with the founding of national associations for supervision in several European countries.

On November 21st 1997, the national professional organisations for supervision of Austria (ÖVS), Germany (DGSv), Hungary (MSZT), the Netherlands (LVSB) and Switzerland (BSO) established ANSE as a European umbrella association based in Vienna to meet the need for European cooperation and Europe-wide exchange of views among professionals.

ANSE takes care of professional interests on a supranational level. ANSE is in contact with professional organisations for supervision and coaching worldwide. ANSE defines standards for supervision and coaching and has adopted a code of ethics.

ANSE now represents more than 9,000 (2013) qualified supervisors and coaches in the field of consulting in over 80 training institutions in 22 European countries. In 2006, ANSE signed a mutual agreement on the recognition of accredited supervisors with ASSCANZ (Association for Supervision, Coaching and Consultancy in Australia and New Zealand).

In 2012 an agreement was signed in Brussels, regarding representation in the Social Dialogue by EUROCADRES (The Council of European Professional and Managerial Staff).

ANSE has professional links with/cooperates with EASC (European Association for Supervision and Coaching) and EMCC (European Mentoring and Coaching Council).

ANSE promotes
- sharing of information between/among national organisations and training institutes;
- exchange of experiences between/among experts in the field of counselling;
- expansion of supervision and coaching;
- quality assurance of supervision and coaching (standards).

and it supports
- the founding of national organisations for supervision and coaching;
- the development of their own culture of supervision and coaching;
- training initiatives in European countries;
- research and study initiatives to develop theories and methodologies for supervision and coaching.

ANSE promotes the importance of learning about cultural diversities and supports cooperation in Europe.

Supervision and Coaching in Austria

Wolfgang Knopf

Historic Highlights

As in other German-speaking countries, the start of an individual under-standing of supervision can be found in the late seventies of the last century, greatly influenced by psychoanalysis and group dynamics with strong foundations in social work. Practical instruction gradually became supervision. A supervisory stance and attitude entered school education through the Balint groups. It was not long before the first training programme was developed and offered (1981, University of Salzburg Institute of Psychology).

This was the start of a basic debate on the definition of the boundaries of the term supervision. At the same time a counselling scene with a supervisory identity was established. Using personal contacts, these content-based considerations were also discussed with German and Swiss colleagues. Thus, the insights gained in these countries could be taken into consideration. The debate took place primarily among teachers and those responsible for training programmes, including the first graduates (Supervision Discussion Group 1991 in Vienna).

In addition to the concept debate, a professional and political discussion also took place. The title of the first Austrian expert conference (of professional organisations), "Supervision in Conflict of Interests", depicted this subject clearly. All these activities led to the foundation of the ÖVS (Austrian Supervision Association) in 1994 through the then active educational institutions and alumnae societies.

Supervision as a Profession

From the outset, supervision was established within major social institutions, and therefore its position was self-evident in these areas. After initial difficulties supervision attained a critical mass of users in social work, schools and hospitals who served as multipliers in spreading the word.

Successful pilot projects in schools and hospitals contributed to its success on a structural level. This development received essential impulses through the theoretical work undertaken by Austrian colleagues which was reflected at conferences and in articles and books.

In spite of some constructive diversity, the differing theoretical approaches were and are still discussed in a cooperative and thus mutually beneficial way. Although the discussions initially met with opposition, later with reluctance, and finally with integration, this problem was able to be solved constructively by means of the "Phenomenon" coaching in the end.

With the establishment of ethical guidelines for the Austrian Supervision Association members in 2001, in which quality assurance was regulated in personal responsibility, a further foundation stone for the self-image of the profession was laid. Supervision – coaching partially included – is as a profession relatively undisputed in Austria today. The 'Community of Supervisors' has a recognised professional identity in Austria.

Legal Situation of the Profession

Austria is a 'state of chambers'. The majority of paid professions are regulated by trade law (in association with the Chamber of Commerce). In addition to these, there are so-called "freelance professions" (e.g. journalists). Supervision is also regarded as such.

This classification is frequently challenged by other competing professional groups (e.g. life coaches and social counsellors). For supervision and coaching, it is however significant not to be restricted to the confines of a chamber regulation, as the further development of the profession and the continuous assurance of quality standards can only be achieved effectively within an organisation and in cooperation with training institutions recognised by the Austrian Supervision Association.

Furthermore, only a minority of supervisors practise just supervision and coaching as a profession. Many offer these services alongside a main profession or within a wider range of freelance work. This is also an argument against regulation within commercial law.

The Market for Supervision and Coaching

Due to its historic roots, supervision has mainly been established within the social and non-profit sector. After the counselling "hype" in the nineties, today's market focuses more on efficiency, price and quality. Many large and important responsible organisations, especially in the healthcare sector, choose their supervisors according to the quality standards of the ASA. At the current time, small and medium-sized companies are still reluctant to recognise the supervision and coaching possibilities available.

In the so-called profit area, coaching rather than supervision is still in demand, although there is also a noticeable change here. In recent years acceptance has risen significantly and supervision is becoming increasingly required in these areas.

In general, it can be observed that there is a desire for counselling from one source only, "We have this problem, these difficulties – what shall we do?" It is therefore necessary for supervisors to expand their range of competences or to work in cooperations and networks. The latter is new and represents a specific challenge.

Current Issues/Trends

Three subjects are currently under discussion:
- The positioning of supervision and coaching within the scientific discourse around the concept of consulting science. This debate is predominantly taking place at universities and in training courses, whereby it is usually held in cooperation with colleagues from neighbouring countries, especially Germany. The main question is: Is supervision the practical and theoretical foundation for a consulting science in the context of work?
- Following supervision and coaching, management consultation of organisations is currently the counselling format under discussion.
- Quality assurance in supervision and coaching: as with colleagues in Switzerland and Germany, it has also become an important issue in Austria. It concerns the quality of both the counselling (efficiency, evaluation) and the counsellors.

A change in the self-organisation of counsellors is evident. Although these activities used to be carried out without any great organisational or structural background, company structuring has become increasingly noticeable

in the field of supervision. A new professionalism has established itself at this level.

Supervision has (again) become political. The demand for the provision of more supervision and coaching in the workplace and its financial compensation is supported by socio-political proposals and demands. Due to their counselling activities, supervisors and coaches acquire insight into many fields of work, where workers and employees are increasingly under pressure due to new economic and structural conditions. In order to support and promote change in society, counsellors should make public their knowledge concerning the stressful working conditions experienced by workers and employees today.

Supervision and Coaching in Croatia

Marina Ajdukovic

Supervision

History

There are five phases of development of supervision in Croatia to be recognised (Ajdukovic, 2005):

(1) Early ideas about the need for supervision originated in the early 1970s (Smolic-Krkovic, 1977). Supervision, however, did not become an integral part of psychosocial work practice due to the traditional approach to clients from the expert position and the lack of a life-long learning approach among the professionals.

(2) In the 1980s, professionals gathered first-hand experience in supervision as supervision became an integral part of training in various psychotherapeutic methods which were flourishing at that time.

(3) During the period of the Croatian War of Independence (1991–1995), supervision gained in importance and became professionally valued, because it was viewed as an important tool supporting professionals and paraprofessionals who were working with thousands of trauma victims, refugees, and the displaced.

(4) The turning point for the establishment of supervision was the first training for supervisors from 2001 to 2004 as part of the project entitled "Introducing supervision in the social welfare system in Croatia", organised by the Department of Social Work, Faculty of Law, at the University of Zagreb. The project was implemented in cooperation with the ministry responsible for social welfare, the Swedish International Development Agency (SIDA) and with strong educational support from the University of Göteborg and the University of Stockholm.

Ten trainers in supervision and 34 supervisors in psychosocial work were

trained according to the ANSE (Association of National Organisations for Supervision in Europe) standards for the education of supervisors.

As a consequence of this project, supervision was introduced into many social welfare organisations (Ajdukovic & Cajvert, 2003).

The training for supervisors within the educational system, entitled "Strengthening capacities for integrative supervisors in the Agency for Education" (from 2007 to 2009) was essential for the introduction and sustainability of supervision for teachers (Ambruš Kiš et al, 2009).

(5) The Department of Social Work at the University of Zagreb started the postgraduate specialisation study programme for supervision in psychosocial work, which was open to professionals from the social, humanistic, and pedagogical fields in 2006. It is the 120 ECTS post-master programme and organised according to ANSE standards for education in supervision. The current study programme has been continuously carried out with some inputs by faculty members of the Departments of Social Pedagogy and Psychology and other experienced supervisors, who have already had international licence as trainers in supervision. The last generation enrolled in 2012.

Recent Developments

In 2008, the Croatian Psychological Chamber introduced supervision as a means of achieving professional (re)licensing psychologists. From 2014 on, the recently established Croatian Chamber of Social Workers will recognise participation in supervision as a part of professional (re)licensing of social workers.

In 2011, Supervision was introduced into Social Welfare Law as the right and obligation of all professionals working in the field of social welfare (for social workers, psychologists, social pedagogues, and other helping professions).

The Main Approaches

The main approaches to supervision in Croatia are in line with the current ANSE definition of supervision. Consequently, three main approaches to supervision can be recognised:
- the concept of supervision as a format for professional development as developed in the Netherlands by Louis van Kessel and his predecessors (e.g., Van Kessel, 1999).

- the psychodynamic development-integrative approach to supervision as a creative space for practitioners developed by Lilja Cajvert (Cajvert, 2001; 2011).
- the integrative supervision concept based on the work of H.G. Petzold and his co-workers.

Fields of Work

Supervision is carried out in social work, education, in the mental health sector, civil society organisations and in the voluntary sector, pastoral work and organisational consultancy to promote the further development of professionals and assurance of of their quality of work.

University education and specialisation in helping professions (i.e. social work, psychology, and social pedagogy) use supervision as an integral part of learning during filed placement and internship at BA, MA and postgraduate education levels (Ajdukovic & Urbanc, 2010).

Organisation

The Croatian Association for Supervision and Organisational Development (Hrvatsko društvo za superviziju i organizacijski razvoj – HDSOR) was founded in 1998.

In 2004, the HDSOR became a member of the ANSE. By the end of 2013, the HDSOR had 76 members. In 2012, the system of (re)licensing supervisors was developed to ensure quality standards in supervision and was subsequently approved by all members of the HDSOR. In 2013, the HDSOR adopted its first strategic plan for the period 2014–2016 and a Code of Ethics for Supervision.

Coaching

History and Recent Developments

Although coaching is well developed in the European Union, in Croatia this professional work is still in its infancy. Almost anyone can call himself/herself a coach. No legal regulations or standards are defining coaching, and

specific qualifications, competence and responsibility are not defined or required.

Training for coaching is offered by various commercial and consulting companies that offer a variety of services in the field of organisational development. Typically, coaching training programmes are offered in collaboration with various European organisations or institutions; for example, in 2010, training in Systemic Gestalt Coaching in Croatia started in collaboration with a local commercial company for the "empowerment of personal, family and organisational potential" (www.dugan.hr; visited 27 December 2013) and the Institute for Gestalt Therapy of Würzburg in Germany (IGW). At the end of the 8-day programme (4 x 2 days), the IGW provides students with Certificates of Coaching.

A post-master level specialisation in supervision of psychosocial work at the Department of Social Work at the University of Zagreb offers the only elective ECTS course in the field of "Consultation and Coaching". Louis van Kessel (from the Netherlands), as co-creator of this course, prepared the most relevant text about coaching in Croatia to be published in both Croatian and English (van Kessel, 2007), with an extensive overview of different types, means of work, and outcomes of coaching.

Fields of Work

Multinational organisations, corporations and large companies are commonly using coaching for development of their top and middle management, and for specific areas of organisational development, such as efficient feedback, leading meetings, planning, and defining tasks.

Organisation

The key association in this field is the Croatian Association for Coaching (www.hr-coaching.hr) which was established in 2009. It has about thirty active members, and its aim and purpose are to promote coaching as a profession, to promote the Code of Ethics of the Association and a standard of excellence in the quality of coaching, the sharing of knowledge and experience and mutual cooperation among coaches. The Croatian Association for Coaching conducts training workshops through the Coaching Academy.

In June 2013, the Council for Mentoring & Coaching was established as part of the European Mentoring & Coaching Council (EMCC). This is another attempt to regulate coaching in Croatia. The immediate goal of the EMCC is to introduce standards for coaching, and the long-term objective is to set up a kind of Chamber of Coaching in Croatia.

References

Ajdukovic, M. & Cajvert, LJ. (2003) The development of social work supervision in countries in transition: Reflections from Croatia and Bosnia-Herzegovina. In: Social Work in Europe, 10 (2), 11–22.

Ajdukovic, M. (2005) Introducing supervision in the social welfare system in Croatia. In: Hessle, S., Zaviršek, D. (Hg): Sustainable development in social work – The case of a Regional Network in the Balkans. Stockholm: Stockholm University, Department of Social Work. International Projects, 113–141.

Ajdukovic, M. & Urbanc, K. (2010) Supervision as a safety net. In: Van Hess, G., Geissler-Pilitz, B. (eds.) Supervision meets education. Supervision in the Bachelor of Social Work in Europe. Maastricht: CERST Research Centre Social Integration, Faculty of Social Studies/Zuyd University of Applied Science, 114–133.

Ambruš-Kiš, R. et al. (2009) Integrativna supervizija u odgoju i obrazovanju./Integrative supervision in education, Zagreb: AZOO.

Cajvert, L. (2011) A model for dealing with parallel processes in supervision. In: Journal of Social Intervention: Theory and Practice, 20 (1) 41–56.

Cajvert, L. (2001) Kreativni prostor terapeuta: O superviziji/Creative space of the therapist: About supervision. Sarajevo: Svjetlost.

Smolic-Krkovic, N. (1977) Supervizija u socijalnom radu/Spervision in social work. Zagreb: Biblioteka socijalnog rada.

Van Kessel, L. (1999) Supervision – A necessary contribution to the quality of professional performance illustrated by the concept of the supervision used in the Netherlands/Supervizija – neophodan doprinos kvaliteti profesionalnog postupanja. Primjer nizozemskog modela supervizije. In: Annual of Social Work/Ljetopis socijalnog rada, 6 (1), 27–46.

Van Kessel, L. (2007) Coaching – A field for professional supervisors? In: Annual of Social Work/Ljetopis socijalnog rada, 14 (2) 387–432.

Supervision and Coaching in Germany

Hubert Kuhn

Supervision

History

Supervision originated at the beginning of the 20th century in the USA, in order to instruct, guide, control and motivate honorary assistants of social work by a superior. After the Second World War, North American emigrants introduced supervision, in particular as individual social casework, into German social work. Supervision was set up in education and the practice of social work in particular and was applied as a method to support social workers when working with an individual. In the 70s and 80s, the approach originally focused on individual faults, developed into emancipatory self-reflection which increasingly focused on the organisation, structures and institutional dynamics as a central theme. Supervision in the area of conflicting interests between person and institution has, to date, become an important issue. In German-speaking countries, supervision, control or purely professional questions as well as psychotherapy, mainly concerning personal problems, play a minor role.

Three phases of the institutionalisation of supervision can be distinguished in Germany:

- Supervision was set up in social and educational work by the free welfare associations from 1960–1989.
- The professionalisation of supervision began with the foundation of the "Deutsche Gesellschaft für Supervision"(DGSv) as a professional association in 1989. The association is available for therapeutically qualified supervisors and for other fields of work.
- Education/training by independent institutes is complemented by university courses; supervision is offered on the consultation market and focuses on the dilemma between "market and profession", different supervision-trainings are integrated into the DGSv.

Roots (main influences)

Supervision was significantly influenced by social work, psychoanalytic controlling analysis and the Balint groups.

Fields of work

After the original area of social work, supervision was also set up in other fields of non-governmental public welfare. Today, supervision is also accepted in many other fields of work, such as: health service, education, management, and church. In industry and small business enterprises, team and, above all, management consultation is mostly called coaching.

Organisation

The DGSv is a professional association with more than 3,700 members and 29 connected academies, universities and further education enterprises, and it is the most significant forum for supervision and professional life-related consultation in Germany. The DGSv sets demanding standards for the qualification of supervisors. Supervision training can be attained at universities and free institutes.

Further associations which also have supervisors as members are the German Society for System Therapy and Family Therapy (www.dgsf.de) and the professional association of German psychologists (www.bdp-verband.org).

References

Belardi, Nando, 2009: Supervision. Grundlagen, Techniken, Perspektiven, München: Beck, 9. Aufl., 15: Allgemeines Ziel: die Arbeit der Ratsuchenden zu verbessern.

DGSv Supervision ein Beitrag zur Qualifizierung beruflicher Arbeit, Grundlagenbroschüre, 8. Aufl., 2012.

Heltzel, Rudolf/Weigand, Wolfgang, 2012: Im Dickicht der Organisation. Komplexe Beratungsaufträge verändern die Beraterrolle, Göttingen: Vandenhoeck& Ruprecht.

Möller, Heidi, 2001: Was ist gute Supervision? Grundlagen-Merkmale-Methoden, Stuttgart: Klett-Cotta.

Pühl, Harald, 2009: Handbuch Supervision und Organisationsentwicklung, Hrsg., Wiesbaden: Verlag für Sozialwissenschaften, 3. Aufl.

Coaching

History

Coaching originated in Germany in the middle of the 1980s as „consultation for executives" with a focus on actual challenges in everyday working life. It was preceded by sporadic single consultations as a side product of executive trainings that were performed by psychologically skilled trainers. The positive image of coaching top sportsmen made its acceptance easier for executives of profit companies.

The rapid establishment of coaching in the FRG is shown by the amount of publications: until 1990, there were very few experts for coaching, the number of annual publications was below 20; from 2000, this figure rose steadily; from 2006, there were more than 100 per year, and since 2010 there have been more than 160 publications per year. At the end of October 2013, amazon.de showed more than 4,500 entries for Coaching (in comparison to 2,200 for supervision).

Roots (main influences)

Coaching was applied in England and in the USA in sports, starting as early as 1885. The North American tennis teacher Timothy Gallwey had a big influence with his book "The Inner Game of Tennis" which first appeared in 1974.

In Germany, coaching was introduced into sports in the 1960s.

Fields of work

Coaching is used in profit enterprises predominantly for executives in the context of leadership, change, stress, burnout, and cultural development. Mostly, it is carried out as a single consultation, however, group or team-coaching is also possible. "Executive Coaching" refers explicitly to the coaching of (higher) executives, "Business Coaching" designates in particular the subjects and fields of coaching as opposed to other fields, for example, „Life-, Health-, Education-Coaching". Increasingly, the word coaching is also used for the consultation of management staff in social and state organisations.

Organisation

The German coaching market is not regulated and very confusing. Only about ten of at least 20 coaching associations in Germany, Austria and Switzerland have more than 100 members.

Furthermore, there are no given standard certification directives for coaching education. It is estimated that about 4000 new coaches finish their training each year. Most training courses offered by scientific institutes, clubs and associations and continuing education institutes last between 150 and 300 hours.

According to the Magazine for Organisational Development, Nr.3/2013, about 11,000 coaches work in Germany currently, 8,000 of which call themselves business coaches and 5,200 executive coaches (with presumably multiple entries in the survey index). In Germany, there are statistically 769 executives per coach as opposed to the ratio of 154 to one in Austria.

In 2007, only 1.5% of the executives were coached, whereas in 2012, there were already 5.6% showing an upward trend.

References

Draht, Karsten, 2012: Coaching und seine Wurzeln. Erfolgreiche Interventionen und ihre Ursprünge, Haufe: Freiburg.

Fatzer, Gerhard, 2012: Supervision, Coaching und Organisationsentwicklung – ein Überblick, in: Eberle, Thomas S./Spoun, Sascha (Hg.), 2012: Durch Coaching Führungsqualität entwickeln. Kernkompetenzen erkennen und fördern, Versus: Zürich, 31–50.

Greif, Siegfried, 2008: Coaching und ergebnisorientierte Selbstreflexion, Hogrefe: Göttingen u.a.

König, Eckard/Volmer, Gerda, 2009: Handbuch Systemisches Coaching. Für Führungskräfte, Berater und Trainer, Beltz: Weinheim und Basel.

Loos, Wolfgang, 2006: Unter vier Augen. Coaching für Manager, EHP: Bergisch Gladbach.

Perspektiven: Change-spezifisches Coaching. Einblick in empirische Forschungsergebnisse 2013, in: Organisationsentwicklung. Zeitschrift für Unternehmensentwicklung und Change Management, Nr. 3/13, 99–103.

Winkler, Brigitte/Lotzkat, Gesche/Welpe, Isabell M., 2013: Wie funktioniert Führungskräfte-Coaching? Orientierungshilfe für ein unübersichtliches Beratungsfeld, in: Organisationsentwicklung. Zeitschrift für Unternehmensentwicklung und Change Management, Nr. 3/13, 23–33.

Supervision and Coaching in Hungary

Krisztina Madai

Supervision

In Hungary, supervision first appeared within the psychoanalytic movement at the beginning of the 20th century primarily focusing on professional socialisation. After 1940 the organisational structure of psychology and social work was eliminated, hence supervision also disappeared. The rebirth of helping professions began from the 1960s, in which the professionals of previous psychoanalytical schools, e.g. Mérei and his students, played a key role.

The first social workers with professional training and experience who could provide supervision entered the scene from the mid 1990s. The Professional Association of Social Work (Szociális Szakmai Szövetség) determined the accreditation criteria for supervisors of social work, which are still the basis for the current regulation, in 1996. Based on the supervision model of the association, the supervisor is an independent party and not a member of the organisation who needs supervision.

From the 1990s, several therapeutic techniques entered the field of supervision, bringing their own method-specific supervision system with them (e.g. family therapy, Gordon, video training).

Already at the beginning of the 1990s the 'Supervisio Hungarica' work group had been launched. The main objectives of the work group were acting for the European concept of supervision, acknowledging supervision as an independent profession and launching training for supervisors.

In 1996, the 'Association of Hungarian Supervisors' (Magyar Szupervizorok Társasága) was founded by 19 members to implement the European concept of supervision.

Among the founders there were the members of the Supervision Hungarica work group and 12 supervisors who were trained at the Katholische Hochschule in Berlin.

In 1993, two professionals from Dutch and German Supervision Training Programmes had started to qualify the Hungarian trainers in a specific supervision training. After that, the postgraduate training programme on supervision was launched in 1998 at Haynal Imre University. Later, this training programme was taken over by Károli University where it is still offered today. In 1997, some professionals of the previous work group founded a new supervisor training programme in organisational development at the International Business School (continuing until 2008). The third training programme on supervision ran from 2005 until 2008 at ELTE University. The profile of this programme was based on the recognition that, besides the European supervision concept, a more traditional American concept was required to meet the needs of the newly founded social and child care institutes, where professional training, monitoring and evaluation of the work was needed.

In 2013, a team of international coaches and therapists started their own supervision training programme accredited by the ICF.

References

Bányai, E; Nemes, É; Wiesner, E (2014): Szupervízió védőnőknek, módszertani leírás, being currently published.

Bányai, Emöke (2006): A szociális munka szupervíziója történeti megközelítésben. Esély, 4. szám, 86–100.oldal, http://www.esely.org/kiadvanyok/2006_4/BANYAI. pdf date of last access: 18th of November 2013.

Wiesner, Erzsébet (1996): Szupervízió a gyermekvédelemben. Család, Gyermek, Ifjúság, 4. szám, http://www.csagyi.hu/home/item/93, date of last access: 4th February, 2013.

Wiesner, Erzsébet (2011): Gondolatok a szupervízió történetéről; Szupervízió & Coaching, A Magyar Szupervizorok és Szupervizor-Coachok Társaságának lapja IX.évfolyam, 2011/1 szám.

Coaching

Coaching as a form of dialogue between the coach and the client first appeared in the Hungarian for-profit organisational context at the end of the 1990s, after Hungary had opened its borders to the West and multinational companies appeared on the market introducing a completely new organisational culture.

The first small group of counsellors who called themselves coaches were consultants on organisational development, supervisors or professionals of various psychotherapeutic schools. The first coaches who were trained in coaching (mostly in Anglo-Saxon schools) entered the market around the millennium. The main objective of coaching was considered to be the opportunity for leaders and managers of organisations to learn, change, and regenerate.

The first official coaching training courses held in Hungary were mainly influenced by psychology: the solution-focused brief coaching training by Peter Szabo, a Gestalt coaching training by Flow Coaching School (lead by Tünde Horváth and Ilona Erős), psychodrama-oriented coaching training led by Gabriella Szabó, TA-based coaching represented by Zsuzsa F. Várkonyi and Saari van Polje. Various supervision-based coaching schools led by Erzsébet Wiesner, Zsuzsa Bán and György Sárvári were also influential.

The real boom of coaching began between 2005–2010. The word coaching became familiar within and outside of the organisational context and has been considered as one of the most efficient tools in personal development. As demand for coaching grew, dozens of new coach training programmes of various lengths and backgrounds were launched. Coaching for leaders in the social field and outside the organisational context appeared and spread out to nearly every sphere of life. Consequently, variations in quality and approach of coaching services were observed.

As a parallel tendency, the first professional associations were founded. Some of these started as alumni of coaching schools, others as the Hungarian chapters of significant international associations. The biggest and most influential among them has become the Hungarian chapter of the International Coach Federation (ICF).

In 2011, six coaching associations – representing the majority of qualified coaches in Hungary – signed the code of conduct for coaches (ICF Hungarian Chapter, European Coaching Association, Hungarian Coach Association, Association of Business Coaches, CoachOK Professional Association, Association of Coaches, Developers and Organisations with Solution Focus/Approach). This collaboration was unique in the coaching business at that time. The code of conduct was based on the joint code of conduct of ICF and EMCC, accepted by the EU shortly before. On this basis the coaching profession was added to the self-regulatory professions in the EU database.

The code of conduct aims to create self-regulation based on professional and ethical standards and guidelines, which ensure that coaches act professionally and ethically while practising their profession. The code of conduct does not only state the competences and professional training requirements

necessary to provide coaching services, but also the need for continuous professional development and the ethical standards of the profession. However, one of the most important tasks was to still ensure that the wider public sees coaching as an effective method in professional and personal development.

In 2012, the first professional e-journal on coaching (CoachSzemle) appeared on the market. The 'Coaching Without Borders' training programme with international experts on coaching was launched, providing the opportunity for further ongoing international influence.

With the growing demand for coaching (accelerated by the financial and economic crisis), the quality assurance of the profession became a significant challenge. In 2013, the six associations, which had signed the code of conduct earlier, officially launched 'The Association of Hungarian Coach Organisations'. This association represents a consistent self-regulatory body aiming to set transparent and accountable professional standards and norms. Besides the previously mentioned Professional Codex, the members also signed the Ethical Codex for Coaches. Further intentions of the association include the creation of an integrated coach database which is based on a comprehensive quality assurance system.

Coaching plays an important role in enhancing employees' well-being and efficiency today. Almost two thirds of Hungarian companies have already hired a coach, and coaching is regarded as an effective tool in organisational development, even within small and middle-sized companies. Additionally to one-to-one coaching, team coaching is used increasingly in organisations.

The work involved in building up a comprehensive quality assurance system is still in progress and presents a big challenge for the credibility of the coaching profession in Hungary.

References

Horváth, T. (2004): Helyzetkép a magyarországi coachingról. In: Pszichoterápia, 08/2004, uploaded from http://www.anima-racio.hu/pdf/coaching_Mo.pdf, last access 11/11/2013

Hungarian Chapter of ICF (2011): Hungarian coaching associations allied for self-regulation, press release, 23/11/2011

MCSz (2013): Példaértékű szakmai összefogás: zászlót bontott a Magyarországi Coach-Szervezetek Szövetsége, press release 28/05/2013

Personal interviews with Tünde Horváth MCC, Dr. Vince Székely, Dóra Hegedűs and Edit Wiesner.

Supervision and Coaching in the Netherlands

Mieke Voogd

Supervision

History & recent developments

After the Second World War social casework was introduced as a method of social welfare in the Netherlands. Supervision became known as a method for professional development of expertise in this field of work. The first Dutch articles and books on supervision were published around 1960. Since then, supervision has developed towards an important method of education for developing competences in people-oriented occupations. The first training programmes for supervisors were established in the 1960s.

In the Netherlands, three concepts of supervision can be found: the Dutch supervision concept, the psychotherapeutic supervision concept, and the integrative supervision concept. The Dutch supervision concept, which is mainly a didactical method for implementing personal and group learning processes in communication and interaction in professional work, has been dominant for many years. Since the psychotherapeutic concept has become more generic, both concepts are being taught in most training programmes for supervision. Lately, more tentative forms of supervision have been developing. A recent development places supervision within the broader field of organisational development; for example, the journal that has been published by the LVSC since 2012 is entitled Journal of 'Begeleidingskunde'. This subject is characterised as an approach with a combined focus on the development of individual professionals and on the development of teams and the organisation in which they function. Several methods are used, e.g. supervision, coaching, training, conferences, and action research.

Fields of Work

Supervision is carried out in social work, the health sector, education, pastoral work, human resources, management, and organisational consultancy. Higher education uses supervision for traineeships. In addition, supervision is being used for further development of experienced professionals.

Organisation

In 1980, a forerunner of the Dutch Association for Supervision was formed. The aim of that organisation was quality assurance and professionalisation of supervision. In 1989, the national association of supervision and other forms of professional guidance (LVSB) were established. Subsequently, the organisation initiated the registration of supervisors and training programmes for supervisors. The LVSB maintains a generic concept of supervision, meaning that the method of supervision is not bound to one specific profession, working method or function.

In 1997, the LVSB became a member of the Association for National Organisations for Supervision in Europe (ANSE). After that, in 2010, the LVSB changed its name to LVSC (National Association of Supervision and Coaching).

Later, in July 2013, the LVSC had 2,300 members and hosted 17 accredited training programmes for coaching and 12 accredited programmes for supervision. There are also three master training programmes for supervision and coaching.

References

www.lvsc.eu (29-10-2013)

LVSB registratie reglement 2005 (herziene versie).

Siegers, F. en D. Haan, Handboek Supervisie, Samsom, Alphen aan de Rijn/Brussel, 1988 (1983).

Praag-Van Asperen, H van & Ph. H. van Praag (red), Handboek supervisie en intervisie in de psychotherapie, Academische uitgeverij, Amersfoort, 1993.

Praag-Van Asperen, H van & Ph. H. van Praag (red), Handboek supervisie en intervisie, De Tijdstroom, Leusden, 2000.

Coenen, B., Een onderzoek naar de ontwikkeling van supervisie in Nederland, Soest, Uitgeverij Nelissen, 2003.

Coaching

History & Recent Developments

Socrates is seen as the 'godfather' of coaching because of the way he practised the art of not-knowing and his mastery of dialogue and asking questions. In the 20th century, there are the roots of thinking that have contributed to the coaching profession: psychoanalysis, behaviourism, humanistic psychology, Gestalt approach, organisational theory, positive psychology, and change theory. Gallway (The Inner Game of Tennis, 1974) and Whitmore (1992) transferred coaching from the world of sports to the organisational world.

In the Netherlands, the demand for coaching began to rise in profit and non-profit organisations in the 1990s. Interventions aimed at a better performance and overcoming difficulties at work. At that time there were 2 training programmes for coaches and the first Dutch books on coaching were published. A few influential pioneers were trained as supervisors. The number of coaches grew rapidly. Estimates for the total number of coaches vary between 20,000 and 35,000. This large group includes coaches with and without professional training working in a wide variety of contexts.

Nowadays, coaching in the context of work/employment has a broad focus on personal development. Coaching is seen as an instrument in Human Relations Management (HRM) to increase the employability of personnel and to stimulate organisational learning. Coaching is more and more used in combination with training and management development programmes.

Field of Work

Professional coaches work in all sectors of Dutch society, in their capacity as personal coach, career coach, business coach, executive coach, mental coach, E-coach, intervision coach, coach the coach, and also supervisor or trainer. Coaching is provided for individuals, teams and larger organisational units and can be carried out face to face, by telephone, e-mail, Skype and other forms of social media on the Internet.

Organisation

In 2003, Alex Engel founded the Dutch Organisation of Professional Coaches (NOBCO). The NOBCO currently has 2,100 members. It cooperates with the

EMCC (European Mentoring and Coaching Council) for the accreditation of coaches and coach training programmes. In 2003, the Dutch Journal of Coaching appeared for the first time.

Coaches can register with the NOBCO (Nederlandse Orde voor Beroeps-coaches), the STIR (Stichting Registratie), an organisation for certification of coaches) and with the LVSC (Landelijke Vereniging voor Supervisie en Coaching).

They can also choose between an international certification with ICF-NL or EMCC. Career coaches can register with the NOLOC (Nederlandse Organisatie voor Loopbaancoaches), an association for coaches dealing with career management. Roughly estimated, nowadays there are around 10,000 registered professional coaches/supervisors in the Netherlands.

As for training programmes for coaching, there are 17 accredited training programmes with the LVSC. Additionally, there are three master training programmes for supervision and coaching and one academic training programme for executive coaching (VU Amsterdam). The NOBCO provides EQA certification of training programmes together with EMCC representing four levels. The scheme below shows the number of accredited training programmes on each level.

EQA Level	Number of accredited training programmes in the Netherlands (29-10-2013)
Foundation	12
Practitioner	14
Senior Practitioner	2
Master Practitioner	2

References

www.nobco.nl (29-10-2013)

www.emccouncil.org (29-10-2013)

Pol, I.G.M. van der, Coachen als professie. Den Haag, Boom Lemma uitgevers, 2012.

Tros, A., Coaches en Coaching in Nederland en daarbuiten. In: De Coachapproach, organisaties veranderen door een coachende benadering.

Stammes, N. & B. van Baarsen, A. Kooij, H. de Koning. Deventer, Gellingen Van Hoog, 2006.

Supervision and Coaching in Sweden

Lilja Cajvert

Supervision

In Sweden the word "handledning" is used rather than the English expression "supervision" or the French "controle". In spite of the different connotations, this text will use "supervision". The roots of the current view of supervision may be traced to the old tradition of master – apprentice, whereas the psychotherapist/social worker of today uses his/her own personality as the most important professional tool.

Modern supervision methods/techniques both originated in the US and British trainings of social workers in the early 20th century and also in the trainings of European psychoanalysts in the 1920s focusing on case work and individual supervision. After World War II, group therapy sessions for prior prisoners of war were established at British military hospitals, supplementing individual treatment and introducing a therapeutic community. In Sweden, these ideas were further developed by Gustaf Johnsson at Barnbyn Skå. During the 1950s and 1960s, attention to the group, group dynamics, the organisation and the relation to the community geared these developments. The importance of continued training and group supervision was increasingly recognised in a number of fields (cf. Katz o Kahn, 1966, quoted in Sundin, 1971, SOU 1978:5 pp. 96–7).

Training

In Sweden, fairly early on, there was interest to establish continued training of teachers and supervisors in psychotherapy, and the first national training in supervision started in 1974. Supervision was considered as one of the most important ways for an experienced psychotherapist to further develop

his/her therapeutic work. Newly employed social workers within child psychiatry/psychiatry and family counsellors were offered individual supervision by an experienced colleague already in the late 1940s. Within social services, supervision of the employees was introduced in the 1970s.

Swedish social workers in the 1980s requested supervision that developed and strengthened the professional role. Group supervision was seen as a means of diminishing the power and authority of the supervisor; there is theoretical support for that view in system, organisation and role theories. Self-awareness, a must in social work, can better be developed in a group where you often have to focus on how to use your abilities in relation to others and the need to reflect on your own attitudes and prejudices.

In 1982, the first education of supervisors in psychosocial work started at the department of social work at the Göteborg University by Lisbeth Johnsson, Gunnar Bernler, Barbro Lennéer Axelson, Sven Hessle and Göran Sandell. In their thesis, Bernler & Johnsson (1985) defined supervision and presented a theory for supervision in psychosocial work.

They suggested today still valid criteria that supervision in psychosocial work should meet:
- continuity (usually at least for one year),
- a global aim (the supervisee should be able to integrate all aspects of psychosocial work),
- process direction (focusing on the attitudes of the supervisee, use of one's self as a tool and reflection on one's own reactions in psychosocial work),
- non-linear organisational relationship (there should preferably be at least one external supervisor),
- process responsibility (the supervisor(s) is (are) responsible for the process of supervision but neither for direct work nor for the client),
- facultative obligation (everyone ought to have supervision), and
- expertise (in psychosocial work, supervisory techniques and cultural competence).

According to Petitt (2002), a unique tradition of supervision was developed in Sweden; supervision should be an expected part of the regular process of work and offered by an external supervisor twice a month. Supervision will also support the development of group culture in a working group.

In the 1990s, supervision was widely introduced in higher education of teachers by building on the concept of humanistic psychology by Franke (1990). According to Grönquist (2004), nursing staff working in the health and social care sector have left the apprenticeship model for a kind of process supervision.

Education of supervisors is now part of the University curricula across Sweden, but there are also a few private institutes that are approved of delivering training of supervisors.

Fields of work

Supervision has a long history in the professional practice of social workers and psychologists. Since the 1970s, supervision has been requested within the *health care* sector (for physicians, midwifes, nurses etc.), at *schools* (for teachers, special pedagogues, pupil assistants etc.) and in the *social care* sector (for habilitation assistants, nurse aids, after school teachers, preschool teachers etc.), with *new groups within other institutions* (e.g., churches, charities) and in *businesses* of humanitarian nature. Today, there is also an increasing demand for supervision of leaders and managers at all levels of occupational groups.

Today, most social workers in Sweden (78 %) are supervised in their work, mainly as group supervision by an external supervisor, Höjer, S. & Beijer, E. & Wissö, T. (2007). Each therapeutic tradition requires a specific structure and content matter to provide for increased knowledge and to strengthen the therapist's/social worker's specific professionalism. Therefore, there is a need for different types of supervision within psychosocial work and the caring professions, such as cognitive – or behavioural therapeutic -, systemic -, psychodynamic -, or family therapeutic supervision.

Organisation – Professional Association

The Swedish Association for supervisors in psychosocial work was formed in 1984 by students who had undergone the first education at the department for social work in Gothenburg, aiming at being a forum for collegial support and professional development for university-trained supervisors in psychosocial work. Presently, the function of the society has changed due to new laws and regulations. Most supervisors have their own private enterprises which offer external supervision. According to a new act on public procurement, each municipality should procure university-trained supervisors for different activities, stating specific criteria for each procurement. Those procured are listed and can be contacted e.g. by project/department managers for interviews and potential employment.

Thus, the present aims of the Society are to advance the development of supervision of psychosocial work within:

- administrative supervision (method supervision, work supervision),
- educational supervision (during higher education and student practice),
- supervision for professionals (case work and process supervision), and
- super-supervision (i.e. supervision on supervision) as a quality assurance of the supervisor's contribution.

References

Bernler, G. & Johnsson, L. (1985). Handledning i psykosocialt arbete. Natur och Kultur, Stockholm.

Boalt Boëthius, S. och Ögren, M-L. (2012). Möjligheter och utmaningar i grupphandledning. Teori och verklighet. Studentlitteratur. Lund.

Boalt Boëthius, S. & Ögren, M-L. (2000). Grupphandledning. Den lilla gruppen som forum för lärande. Mareld och Erikastiftelsen, Stockholm.

Cajvert, L. (2013). Handledning – behandlarens kreativa rum. Studentlitteratur. Lund.

Gordan, K. (1992). Psykoterapihandledning inom utbildning, i kliniskt arbete och på institution. Natur och Kultur, Stockholm.

Grönquist, G. (2004). Handledning inom vård och omsorg ur ett psykosocialt perspektiv. Gothia. Stockholm.

Hessle, S. & Höjer, K. (1979). Handledning och psykosocialt arbete. Ska-rapport 47. Metodbyrå 1. Stockholms Socialförvaltning. Stockholm.

Höjer, S. & Beijer, E. & Wissö, T. (2007). Varför handledning? Handledning som professionellt projekt och organisatoriskt verktyg inom handikappomsorg och individ och familjeomsorg. FoU i Väst/GR. Göteborg.

Lundsbye, M. & Sandell, G. (1981). Handledning i psykosocialt arbete. Särtryck ur Socialmedicinsk tidskrift nr 10 (p 569–578). Stockholm.

Näslund, J. (1994). Insyn i grupphandledning. Ett bidrag till förståelsen av ett av de människobehandlande yrkenas hjälpredskap. Filosofiska fakulteten. Linköpings Universitet Linköping.

Petitt, B. (2002). Reflektioner. i Söderquist, M, (2002). Möjligheter. Handledning och konsultation i systemteoretiskt perspektiv. Mareld. Stockholm.

Sundin, B. (1970). Individ institution ideologi – anstaltens socialpsykologi. Bonniers. Stockholm.

www.handledarforeningen.com [last accessed 23 January 2014]

Coaching

In Sweden, coaching has been a new phenomenon since the millennium with roots that may be traced back to ice hockey and other athletic games. Later development here was inspired by international trends, particularly from the United Kingdom where coaches were brought into private enterprises during the 1970s.

Coaching has increasingly spread in the public and private sectors and lately also in university education by satisfying the needs of renewed leadership in a society shifting from being industry-based to knowledge-based. Traditional institutions (e.g., the church and trade unions) are on the decline, and each individual is left to find one's meaning and sense in life. Coaching offers methods, supported by the present government, to let people take on more responsibility for their own lives – in line with the current policies in Sweden.

Training

Sweden still lacks a unified education in coaching. Only very recently some universities and colleges have started to offer basic programmes specifically aimed at coaching.

Certification is offered almost exclusively by private enterprises and not standardised in Sweden but usually refers to some affiliation with international organisations that certify coaches, such as the International Coach Federation (ICF), the European Mentoring and Coaching Council, and the International Coaching Community (ICC).

The methods applied in coaching are not new. It uses methods and techniques that are well established and commonly used, such as supportive dialogues/conversations in ambulatory psychotherapy. However, coaching is always directed at healthy persons and usually related to personal development in the areas of work or health. In this case, coaching is often defined as the art of asking questions.

Berg (2012) describes the core of coaching as a way for people to develop, a method to carry out that process and to define who is responsible for success. There are many types of coaching, such as coaching conversations, career coaching, life coaching, weight coaching and stop smoking coaching, executive coaching, business coaching etc.

Gjerde (2002, 2012) describes how the first generation of coaches developed in the USA and UK during the 1980s. In her opinion, supervision has a

strong position within educational institutions, and there are people who ask if coaching is just a new name for supervision. According to her, coaching has now reached a certain maturity as can be seen in scientific articles that report varying results of coaching. There is a tendency to move from leadership coaching to a second generation of coaching, realising the importance of building a theoretical basis and by studying essential elements of coaching. A clear theory and practice of coaching has begun to be created by experienced psychologists, psychotherapists, and university lecturers. Therefore, coaching as a method is slowly entering the universities. Finally, coaching is gradually approaching supervision as indicated before by new concepts expressed in book titles, such as Coaching supervision, Kellheim, A & Weide, B. (2013) and Coaching and supervision in groups within university programmes, Anderson, G. & Persson, A. (2002, 2011).

Fields of work

During the last decade the term "coaching" was used within a number of different fields ranging from technology, health care, psychology, management to business and social work – and opened up for a fragmentary view of what was indeed meant by coaching.

Wikberg (2010) discusses coaching from an economical market perspective and considers the "Swedish coaching market" to be a new market.

He provides an outline of the Swedish domestic market for coaching products and services and holds the opinion that the Swedish coaching market is characterised by the uncertainty of what a coach is, and what services and products he or she may provide. According to Wikberg, the growing need for coaching in Sweden was closely linked to the deregulation of Arbetsförmedlingen (corresponding to the British Labour Exchange or job centre), previously a governmental monopoly.

Furthermore, the National Labour Exchange was commissioned by the government in 2009 to procure coaching services from external/private enterprises for 2.9 billion SEK in the course of three years. A total of 952 submissions were granted. The aim was to support unemployed people with a personal coach to facilitate their entry into the labour market. The expected increase of the labour force has, however, not yet been fulfilled.

Wikberg considers the government as the main and most important factor to explain the recent spectacular growth of a Swedish coaching market. The heavy governmental involvement in coaching has been criticised by claims such as: the government is at fault by procuring such services; coaches tend

to become self-proclaimed experts or else express a pretentious narcissism; coaching may cover up structural problems of society.

Furthermore, such training offered by private enterprises may assume a kind of legitimacy usually only obtained by recognised universities in the field, and may be marketed to persons that lack qualifications for applying to higher education (p.36).

Academic Coaches in Sweden

There is no national association of coaches in Sweden today. The ICF, formed in the USA in 1995, established the ICF Nordic that was in charge of Sweden in 1999. It was replaced by the ICF Sweden, which is linked to one of the major coaching companies in the country (cf. Wikberg 2010). Students and alumni from the Psychological Coach Program at Högskolan i Skövde form the new association of Academic Coaches in Sweden, and it is the first association of coaches with a university affiliation in the country.

References

Anderson, G. & Persson, A. (2002, 2011). Coaching och handledning av grupper – inom universitets- och högskoleutbildning. Studentlitteratur. Lund.

Berg, M. E. (2007, 2012). Coaching – att hjälpa ledare och medarbetare att lyckas. Studentlitteratur. Lund.

Gjerde. S. (2004, 2012). Coaching. Vad – Varför – Hur. Studentlitteraturen. Lund.

Hilmarsson, H.T. (2012). Coachingtrappan – en handbok i att coacha och motivera till resultat. Studentlitteratur. Lund.

Kellheim, A & Weide, B. (2013). Coachande handledning – en metodbok för ledarutveckling och professionellt klientarbete. Liber. Stockholm.

Moltke. H. V. & Molly. Asbjorn. (red.). (2011). Systemisk coaching. En grundbok. Studentlitteratur. Lund.

Wikberg, E. (2010). Organisering av en ny marknad. En studie av den svenska coachingsmarknaden. Scores rapportserie 2010:6.Stockholms centrum för forskning om offentlig sektor. Stockholm.

http://www.psykologiguiden.se/www/pages/?ID=234&Psykologilexikon [last accessed 21 January 2014]

http;//www.coachfederation.org [last accessed 21 January 2014]

http://www.akademiskacoacher.se/[last accessed 21 January 2014]